CHILDREN, SEXUALITY, AND THE LAW

FAMILIES, LAW, AND SOCIETY SERIES
General Editor: Nancy E. Dowd

Justice for Kids: Keeping Kids Out of the Juvenile Justice System
Edited by Nancy E. Dowd

Masculinities and the Law: A Multidimensional Approach
Edited by Frank Rudy Cooper and Ann C. McGinley

The New Kinship: Constructing Donor-Conceived Families
Naomi Cahn

What Is Parenthood? Contemporary Debates about the Family
Edited by Linda C. McClain and Daniel Cere

In Our Hands: The Struggle for U.S. Child Care Policy
Elizabeth Palley and Corey S. Shdaimah

The Marriage Buyout: The Troubled Trajectory of U.S. Alimony Law
Cynthia Lee Starnes

Children, Sexuality, and the Law
Edited by Sacha M. Coupet and Ellen Marrus

Children, Sexuality, and the Law

Edited by Sacha M. Coupet and Ellen Marrus

NEW YORK UNIVERSITY PRESS
New York and London

NEW YORK UNIVERSITY PRESS
New York and London
www.nyupress.org

© 2015 by New York University
All rights reserved

References to Internet websites (URLs) were accurate at the time of writing. Neither the author nor New York University Press is responsible for URLs that may have expired or changed since the manuscript was prepared.

Library of Congress Cataloging-in-Publication Data
Children, sexuality, and the law / edited by Sacha M. Coupet and Ellen Marrus.
pages cm — (Families, law, and society series)
Also available as an ebook.
Includes bibliographical references and index.
ISBN 978-0-8147-2385-2
1. Children—Legal status, laws, etc.—United States. 2. Children and sex—United States. 3. Children's rights—United States. 4. Sexual rights—United States. 5. Child sex offenders—United States. 6. Sexual minority youth—Legal status, laws, etc.—United States. 7. Juvenile justice, Administration of—United States. I. Coupet, Sacha M., editor. II. Marrus, Ellen, editor. III. Series: Families, law, and society series.
KF479.C465 2015
345.7302'530835—dc23   2014045529

New York University Press books are printed on acid-free paper, and their binding materials are chosen for strength and durability. We strive to use environmentally responsible suppliers and materials to the greatest extent possible in publishing our books.

Manufactured in the United States of America

10 9 8 7 6 5 4 3 2 1

Also available as an ebook

To Lee and Alex. You are my light and my love.—Sacha Coupet

To M. M. and R. S. S. Thank you for your patience, encouragement, and support.—Ellen Marrus

CONTENTS

Acknowledgments	ix
Introduction *Sacha M. Coupet and Ellen Marrus*	1
1. Smells Like Teen Spirit: The Conundrum of Kids, Sex, and the Law *Paul R. Abramson and Annaka Abramson*	6
2. Consent, Teenagers, and (un)Civil(ized) Consequences *Jennifer Ann Drobac*	30
3. The Wages of Ignorance *Franklin E. Zimring*	72
4. Sugar and Spice and Everything Nice: Definitely Not the Girls in the Juvenile Justice System *Ellen Marrus*	87
5. Sexual Media and American Youth *Piotr Bobkowski and Autumn Shafer*	108
6. Sex, Laws, and Videophones: The Problem of Juvenile Sexting Prosecutions *Seth F. Kreimer*	133
7. The Right to Comprehensive Sex Education *Hazel G. Beh*	163
8. Policing Gender on the Playground: Interests, Needs, and Rights of Transgender and Gender Non-conforming Youth *Sacha M. Coupet*	186

9. Gender at the Crossroads: LGBT Youth in the
   Child Welfare and Juvenile Justice Systems   224
      Barbara Fedders

About the Contributors   255

Index   259

ACKNOWLEDGMENTS

SACHA M. COUPET AND ELLEN MARRUS

This book would not have come to fruition were it not for the creative (and provocative) decision that Professor Odeana R. Neal made as chair of the then newly formed Association of American Law Schools (AALS) Section on Children and the Law to assemble a small panel of experts to present on the topic of kids, sex, and the law. Our hope at the 2009 annual meeting of the AALS was to attract a wide cross section of conference attendees from sections that would not otherwise have reserved time in their schedules to attend a panel focusing on children's issues. Odeana's bold decision paid off, and the panel presentation and the discussion that followed were meaningfully enriched by the input of many legal scholars from not only child and family law but also criminal law, torts, and law and psychology, among others. The panel's focus went beyond the traditional exploration of children as victims of adult sexuality, and it is this facet, we believe, that made this gathering unique. We thank Odeana and the other members of the AALS Section on Children and the Law Executive Committee who supported the section's early efforts to shift the discourse around children and sex toward one that acknowledged children as agents and rights holders. We also thank the panelists, Shannon Price Minter, Jennifer Drobac and the late Dr. Ted Shaw, for their valuable contributions. The 2009 AALS panel became the launchpad for this book, and we feel fortunate to have been given the opportunity to broaden the conversation even further here. Our contributors deserve a special thanks for accepting the invitation to participate in a new dialogue about a traditionally taboo subject and for their patience with us as we worked to weave together their various perspectives on the topic of children and sex.

We thank Deborah Gershenowitz for initiating the conversation that transformed the panel presentation into this book and for her enthusiastic, insightful, and creative feedback and support in the initial stages. We offer much thanks to Nancy Dowd for generously making room for this book under the umbrella of her Families, Law, and Society series and for her critical feedback and are honored that this book will sit alongside other innovative texts within this series that are prompting new conversations about provocative changes within the modern family. We are grateful to Clara Platter, editor at NYU Press, for her careful shepherding of this book, and to Constance Grady, editorial assistant at NYU Press, for her tireless work in moving this book to final production.

We relied heavily on the assistance of students and staff at the University of Houston Law Center, who spent countless hours reviewing chapters and assisting with all aspects of formatting. A special note of gratitude is due to all of the Irene Merker Rosenberg Child Advocacy Scholars of the Center for Children, Law and Policy at the University of Houston Law Center, in particular Katherine Quinn, Chloe Walker, and Patricia Zesut, whose editorial assistance was absolutely invaluable. In addition, we would like to thank research assistant Patrick N. McMillin, UHLC '14, who put in endless hours to help with the editing process. Ellen wishes to thank the University of Houston Law Center for a generous research leave that allowed her to devote time and attention to the completion of this book and for support in convening the 2009 Children, Sex, and the Law symposium, at which some of the contributors shared working drafts of their chapters. In addition, Sacha wishes to thank her home institution, Loyola University Chicago School of Law, for a summer research grant that supported a portion of this project.

Introduction

SACHA M. COUPET AND ELLEN MARRUS

When we were first approached about editing a book on children, sex, and the law, we were hesitant. First, the topic evokes a powerful taboo—so powerful, in fact, that our initial electronic conversations about the book itself were stymied by e-mail filters designed to catch the prohibited combination of the terms "children" and "sex." Second, neither of us had written in this area, although both of us publish, teach, and present on various topics related to children and the law. Nonetheless, hesitancy gave way to curiosity as we reflected on the myriad ways in which the discourse could and *should* be shifted beyond the limited traditional focus on child victims *of* adult sexuality. What we quickly came to realize in our search for authors who could contribute to a book that explored the topic of children and sex from a novel perspective was that, where the law and legal scholars tended to address the topic of "children and sex," it had historically done so in the context of protecting children *from* adult sexuality. This traditional approach, which frames children as victims, has led to the development of broad, valuable, and robust protections across many domains (criminalizing such things as child pornography, sexual contact with minors, etc.). All of these efforts, however, are aimed at reifying a normative assumption that children—or, rather, childhood itself—is, and should remain, void of any trace of sex and sexuality—an assumption we are now called to examine more deeply. It is within the context of this normative assumption that we see volumes of texts exploring the topic of adult sexuality as it affects children but few approaching the topic with a different framework in mind. Our curiosity grew to excitement as we discovered the few scholars tackling these touchy issues, all of whom accepted the invitation to contribute to the first single text presenting as rich a variety and range of perspectives on children, sex, and the law as the present one.

This book attempts to move the discourse farther along by broaching a novel framing of the topic of children and sex, one in which we position children not only as objects of protection but also with *agency* in the context of sex and sexuality and as *rights holders* within a broader discussion about sex, sexuality, and related aspects of gender. While recognizing the value of protecting children from sexual predation, we are compelled to broaden our focus in response to the increasing frequency with which we are confronted with examples that hint at the erosion of long-standing normative assumptions about children and sex. Children are not only exposed *to* sexual environments, they are engaging *in* sexual conduct and *with* sexual media in ways that we have never before contemplated. Whether and how we acknowledge this new reality is the challenge.

This book aims to set the stage for a more enlightened dialogue on the topic of children and sex—one that invites new legal responses reflective of both children's agency and rights.

This collection of essays reflects some of the unique challenges that accompany placing children in the broader context of sex, exploring from diverse perspectives where children emerge in sexually related dimensions of law and contemporary life. The book examines emerging issues in which children are positioned as both agents and rights holders in the realm of sex. It is the first academic or commercial text to present these issues in one comprehensive collection and from such a variety of perspectives. As our approach to the topic of children, sex, and the law frames the discussion as one primarily concerning agency and rights, this anthology unfolds in the same manner.

Within the scope of agency, the text explores the ways in which the law conceives of children's capacity for choice in the context of sex as well as their actual conduct. Paul Abramson and Annaka Abramson open the dialogue in Chapter 1 by presenting psychological theory and research pertaining to children as sexual beings. A full appreciation of both children's agency and rights within the scope of sex and sexuality rests on our baseline understanding of children's sexuality and how these understandings are present and absent within law. The research presented raises thorny questions about children as agents and, arguably, as rights holders of sexual information, conduct, and expression. Borrowing from numerous contemporary examples, Paul Abramson and

Annaka Abramson ask provocative questions regarding sexual risks and sexual rights that lay the groundwork for subsequent chapters in the text.

Jennifer Drobac's chapter combines her expertise in both sexual harassment legal theory and juvenile law to address the inconsistent legal treatment of adolescent consent. By highlighting the influence of adolescent cognitive capacities in understanding adolescent sexual contact with adults, her chapter exposes gaps in current tort, criminal, and employment law and the challenges presented in aligning these areas of law with current knowledge about adolescent cognitive and emotional development.

Frank Zimring contributes to this collection a sharp critique of the law's treatment of juvenile sex offenders, a population typically lumped together with adult sexual offenders for the purposes of punishment and treatment. His chapter examines existing tensions in the development of appropriate responses to juvenile sex offending based on social science research. It explores the degree to which our conceptualizations about children are transformed when regarding children as sexual actors rather than merely victims of adult sexual transgressions and the dangers of overreaching when ascribing agency to minor sexual conduct. He warns against the dangers of misidentification of juvenile sex offenders in our broader attempt to "protect" children from sexual contact.

Whereas Frank Zimring's focus is primarily on boys, Ellen Marrus shifts attention to the specific challenges faced by girls within the juvenile justice system—challenges that stem from their gendered identities and perceptions about female sexuality. She traces discrepancies from the point of girls' entry into the system to the ways in which girls are treated differently once in the system. This chapter sheds light on the ways in which girls' sexual agency is criminalized, in contrast to that of boys, rendering girls' sexual conduct non-normative or deviant. Her chapter also addresses issues concerning the appropriateness or efficacy of "treatment" for girls in a system that was designed to "protect" them from their own immoral behavior.

Much like Paul Abramson and Annaka Abramson's introductory chapter, Piotr Bobkowski and Autumn Shafer's chapter is intended to set the stage for the second half of our text by presenting data about children's agency that may naturally raise questions about a corresponding scope of rights. The authors provide meaningful research in the field of communications that can be used to support the premise of children's right to sexual information. They focus on the ways in which children are not merely passively witnessing or being exposed to, but, rather, actively engaging with, sexual imagery in the media. This chapter serves as a critical bridge between our two frames of agency and rights by raising important questions, for example, about the ways in which children's active engagement with and exposure to sexual information shape how we conceive of children's First Amendment rights in this area.

The text then shifts in focus to a discussion framed more so along the dimension of rights—exploring whether and when children have a right to expression as understood within the First Amendment, a right to access information about sex and sexuality, a right to expression of gender identity, and rights of protection or special treatment based on sexual orientation.

In Chapter 6, First Amendment scholar Seth Kreimer explores children's right to sexual expression, focusing primarily on the phenomenon of "sexting," the electronic transmission of sexually suggestive text messages and images, and the constitutional tensions implicit in the regulation of children's speech. Utilizing an emblematic Pennsylvania case that captures the key issues arising in juvenile sexting prosecutions, his chapter explores whether legal responses to sexting are impermissibly restrictive of children's First Amendment rights.

Hazel G. Beh then lends her expertise to a chapter addressing children's right to sexual education and sexual information, which includes a rich analysis of the conflicting interests of children, parents, and the state. This chapter addresses children's right to sexual information, including affirmative sexual education in schools, sexual health services, and contraception. It is intended to present in a broad fashion the many areas in which children are either provided opportunities for or denied access to information pertaining to their sexual lives.

Sacha Coupet approaches the topic of sexual rights from the perspective of gender identity and gender expression in transgendered and gender non-conforming children. She provides a context for understanding the phenomenon of transgenderism and gender non-conformity in minors and the ways in which gender expression is subject to regulation within the public schools. Gender identity "rights" are also examined as they relate to dependent and delinquent children in custody of the state.

And finally, in the last chapter of the text, Barbara Fedders addresses the distinct legal rights of lesbian, gay, bisexual, and transgender (LGBT) children who are in state custody. This chapter explores misconceptions about LGBT youth identity development and the influence of stereotypes regarding LGBT youth on interactions with personnel and policies in the juvenile justice system.

We acknowledge that this book falls short of addressing *all* of the issues that may arise when discussing children as sexual agents and right holders, rather than victims. We are, however, hopeful that the essays within will lead to meaningful discussions, better informed policy making, and a richer debate regarding the legal regulation of children's sexual lives and identities.

1

Smells Like Teen Spirit

The Conundrum of Kids, Sex, and the Law

PAUL R. ABRAMSON AND ANNAKA ABRAMSON

Do kids have agency in the arena of sex? Are they rights holders as well? Does the pursuit of happiness entitle minors to sexual liberties? If so, whose liberties prevail when rights collide, parents or children? Can children be protected from sexual harm without usurping potential sexual rights? These questions and more are discussed herein, serving as an introduction for the chapters that follow.

Mainly, however, this chapter is a primer on childhood sexuality, particularly as it relates to the pleasures of sex, which form the centerpiece throughout.

Childhood Sexuality

Childhood sexuality encompasses many issues; self-exploration, biological development, evolutionary psychology, the cultural processes through which kids learn about sex, the cognitions that determine how kids operate sexually, and so forth. The unifying theme throughout this discussion, however, is the recognition of sexual pleasure, as the primary reason that humans of all ages engage in some form of sex.[1]

It starts right after birth. Male infants are capable of erections, whereas female infants are capable of vaginal lubrication.[2] Masturbation, in the form of a pleasure-seeking, rhythmic manipulation of the genitals, is not far behind, at one to three years of age.[3] Sexual curiosity is evident by nine, with kids being interested in nudity, sexual talk, hugging and kissing, sexual feelings, and reproduction.[4] As puberty unfolds, goal-seeking sexual activity begins (e.g., kissing, touching, etc.), ultimately culminating around sixteen years of age in penetrative or orgasmic sex.[5]

These are the general parameters of childhood sexual development,[6] but they are markedly imprecise. The data, unfortunately, are sparse and rudimentary, and kids vary enormously between genders and across cultures. Methodological limitations also characterize the field (e.g., reliance on self-report), and gaining university human subjects approval for research on childhood sexuality is another matter entirely.

Recalled by adults, childhood sexuality is undoubtedly distorted, too, and the questions we ask are heterosexually biased.[7] But, among the few things that we do know, it appears that sexual exploration with other children, and exposure to routine parental nudity and behavior, are unrelated to adverse psychological aftereffects.[8] Educated moms are also more likely to have sexually exploratory kids (reflecting a more permissive parental attitude about sex),[9] but gay and lesbian children are more likely to suffer cultural condemnation when compared to their heterosexual counterparts.[10]

Childhood sexual rights, however, are something else again. Though we protect kids from sexual harm, we don't want to straightjacket them, either. The real question, then, is whether the capacity for intense sexual pleasure serves as an entitlement to rudimentary sexual rights for kids. If sex (starting with masturbation) feels great and is void of tangible harm, should kids have discretionary choices on how to express their burgeoning sexuality? Are kids sexual agents, or is childhood sexuality subsumed under parental control, irrespective of its psychological value to kids?

These are among the factors that arise when wrestling with the conundrum of children, sex, and the law, but they all build upon our understanding of the significance of the pleasurability of sex in childhood.[11]

Sexual Pleasure

Sexual pleasure encompasses a loosely defined collection of physiological and psychological responses. Physiologically, it appears that the capacity for sexual pleasure is hard-wired in the sense that, as noted previously, it constitutes an innate and universal aspect of human sexual anatomy. Like any intrinsic characteristic, however, sexual pleasure is moderated by and unfolds within a particular physical and cultural milieu, all of which is also shaped by how children perceive the etiquette of sex as assimilated through societal norms and influences (e.g., television, movies, Facebook, Google, YouTube, iPhones, etc.). These cultural vagaries undoubtedly also influence both the overt expression and subjective experience of sexual pleasure.

Even if the capacity for sexual pleasure is innate and in some sense basic for the human species, one might argue that pleasure is secondary to procreation. This is certainly true for the lower orders of mammals, which, if they experience pleasure at all, are nonetheless restricted sexually to the reproductively fertile estrous periods of the female. With primates, however, one begins to see a bifurcation in the functional meaning of sex. Although the reproductive cycle of many nonhuman primates remains at least partially bound to hormones, sexuality is no longer entirely restricted to the female estrous cycle.[12]

In humans, the divergence of reproductive and non-reproductive sex is even more striking. Essentially free of the hormonal regulation of sexual desire, women can—and do—engage in sex at any time in their menstrual cycle, irrespective of fertility status. Sexual pleasure is thus not dependent upon fecundity. Postmenopausal women and prepubescent children of both sexes (as noted above) also experience sexual pleasure, but neither is capable of reproducing.

Human sexual anatomy is likewise specialized for pleasure no less than procreation. The sole function of the clitoris, for example, is the generation of sexual pleasure. Though male orgasm is a reproductive function, female orgasm is not, being superfluous to conception. Pleasure, not reproduction, also provides the most parsimonious explanation of non-obvious erogenous zones (e.g., kissing.)

The wide variation in sexual practices observed across historical epochs and cultures, and even within cultures, is largely inexplicable within a reproductively oriented explanatory framework as well. Marriage and monogamy, for example, have vast cross-cultural differences, as does sexual orientation, too.[13]

Sexual pleasure also provides the foundation for ancillary psychological functions, such as emotional bonding; it is the superglue of humanity.[14] The overall evidence thus suggests that the pleasurable and procreative aspects of human sexuality are interrelated but also conceptually, anatomically, and psychologically distinct.[15]

Where the evolutionary function of sexual pleasure is concerned, the most obvious explanation is that it serves to encourage humans to engage in penile-vaginal intercourse and, thereby, to propagate their genes. That explanation notwithstanding, most people have sex because it is feels good, not because they desire offspring. The mechanism of sexual pleasure is thus an evolutionary adaptation that solves the motivational problem of ensuring that sex takes place despite obstacles or drawbacks.[16]

If sex could be dangerous for ancient protohumans, sexual pleasure would have made it worthwhile. Pleasure would offset the potential sizable costs of time and energy expenditures, vulnerability to attack, the hazards of pregnancy and childbirth, and so on. Natural selection thereafter would favor those who experienced greater pleasure in sex because they would invest more time into the pursuit of sex. They would have more kids, too, who in turn would inherit copies of the enhanced pleasure-seeking genes.[17]

Freedom from a fixed hormonal schedule is thus the primary advantage of sexual pleasure. Sexual pleasure can be pursued any time of the day, any time of the year, any time over the course of the menstrual cycle, and ultimately, anytime that humans are relatively healthy. Yet, curiously, sexual pleasure is *not* limited to penile-vaginal intercourse. Non-procreative sex (from masturbation to oral sex to intercourse with contraception, etc.) is highly pleasurable, too. How then can sexual pleasure ensure the survival of the species if the non-procreative alternatives are equally gratifying?

The answer is that the non-procreative alternatives (masturbation, kissing, touching, oral or anal sex, etc.) are simply an unanticipated concomitant of the evolution of sexual pleasure. Though the alternatives feel exceptionally good as well, enough humans enjoy penile-vaginal intercourse that the species survives—overpopulates, in fact. Since non-procreative sexual activities do not interfere with the reproductive inclinations of most people, they have not been eliminated through the callous machinations of natural selection.

The theory, in a nutshell, is as follows. Sexual pleasure evolved through natural selection to expand the opportunities for protohumans to engage in reproductive behaviors, despite the sometimes substantial risks that these behaviors entailed. The underlying neurophysiology, however, did not restrict the pleasurability of sex to purely reproductive acts or reproductively mature adults. A wide range of sexual behaviors were thus enjoyed at all ages.[18] Since sexual diversity did not interfere with the propagation of genes or the regeneration of the species, the pleasures of sex are now integral to the breadth of all forms of human sexual expression.[19]

If sexual pleasure is an evolved adaptation in humans, when does it manifest itself? The answer, as noted previously, is in infancy and early childhood. Like smiling and laughing, interest in genital stimulation begins early and, for most people, never fades. Childhood sexual feelings, interests, and motivations are also naturally heterogeneous (i.e., open to many sexual possibilities) because childhood is a time for exploring the world, including the proximal world of the flesh.

As puberty unfolds, however, the drive for sexual pleasure is intensified; the aim of sex also shifts from purely self-pleasuring to the consummation of reproductive-like activities and a generalized sensitivity to all things sexual. Though evident in both genders, the shift is especially noticeable in postpubertal males, with the increasing emphasis on orgasm and ejaculation.

Though heterogeneous sexual pleasure is overtly manifested in prepubertal childhood, too, the freedom of exploration is circumscribed by the absence of procreative pressures and constraints. As childhood melts into the postpubertal teenage years—with its attendant sexual opportunities and risks—sexual exploration is thereby amplified.[20] The fundamental question herein is whether this age group has legal rights to act upon it.

The Data Dilemma

Though we have provided a useful prototype of childhood sexuality built upon the edifice of sexual pleasure, we have largely refrained from quoting data. As noted previously, there are enormous hurdles to obtaining information about children and sex in particular. Institutional review boards, acquiring parental consent, adverse consequences for honest disclosure, and so forth, add further caution to the findings.

Also complicating this picture is the fact that childhood sexuality is largely interpreted through the perceptions and nomenclature of adults. Even if we could assess contemporaneous sexual experiences from children, children are often ill equipped to report upon their internal states (e.g., sexual arousal), let alone their reluctance to discuss such matters entirely. When an adult recalls his or her own childhood sexual experiences, other problems arise, not only distorted memories but also the need to reshape the past to create more confluence with the present.[21]

Nevertheless, there are some meticulous studies on childhood sexuality, the recent survey on teenagers being a case in point.[22] The problem with this study, however, is relevance. Being a teenager is not synonymous with being a minor. Though based upon a large sample (4,662 teenagers) and a rigorous methodology, the Martinez *et al.* research conflated minors and adults by focusing upon teenagers between the ages of fifteen and nineteen. Though this age distribution has psychological value (a relevant cohort for studying dating, for example), the legal implications are confounded. Subjects eighteen or older are obviously adults with broad sexual privileges; below eighteen years of age they are minors. State residency also complicates the picture because the age of consent varies by state.[23] A sixteen-year-old from Connecticut can legally consent to sex, whereas a sixteen-year-old from California cannot. Even the conditions for participating in this study varied by age. Subjects eighteen and older were asked to sign a consent form but were not required to do so (adding credence to anonymous participation.) Subjects *below* eighteen years of age were required to have signed parental (or guardian) consent and were also required to sign an assent form as well. If a minor refused to sign the assent form, the minor was not allowed to participate in the survey.

Though these findings distort the boundaries between minors and adults, the results of this 2011 study are nonetheless worth noting as an estimate of teenage sexuality. Forty-three percent of never-married female teenagers, for example, and about 42% of never-married male teenagers have had sexual intercourse at least once. These data are comparable to those obtained in 2002. When sexual intercourse occurred, 78% of females and 85% of males used some form of contraception, the condom in particular—a finding that has also not changed since 2002.

Though these data are undoubtedly more robust than those from most sex surveys, they are nonetheless highly circumscribed as well. The focus was heterosexuality, and the survey failed to assess the diversity of sexual expression among couples (e.g., oral sex), the frequency of sexual self-exploration (e.g., masturbation), the reliance on high-tech alternatives to sex (e.g., sexting [sending sexual text messages], phonication [exchanging nude photographs on cell phones]), and so on. Even more noteworthy, as detailed above, the findings are not specific to minors.

What, then, is the take-home message from these data? Teenagers are undoubtedly preoccupied with sex and often act upon those preoccupations, but the data are frustratingly imprecise. We also know from previous research that kids masturbate and eventually engage in a wide range of sexual activities before the age of eighteen. The question before us now is whether they have a legal right to do so.

The Role of Consent

Though the topic of consent is discussed in detail in Jennifer Drobac's subsequent chapter ("Consent, Teenagers, and (un)Civil(ized) Consequences"), we briefly introduce it here as well. It is hard to discuss childhood sexuality without reference to consent, and many of the psychological issues underlying consent are also fundamental to sexual expression. For these reasons alone we now begin a discussion of consent, leaving fuller exposition to Professor Drobac.

If a bank is robbed, children generally know that convicted robbers go to jail. If a teenager has sex with another teenager, however, the legal consequences are less assured.[24] A teenager might reasonably ask, Why is it a crime if the sex is voluntary and consensual? Or why is it a crime in one state, but not another?[25] A teenager might also note that there is no agreement in the definition of sex.[26] A president of the United States once claimed that oral sex was not sex.

Though many other nuances come to mind as well, we introduce this topic here to highlight the fact that a teenager (eighteen years old or older) can be convicted of statutory rape (i.e., sex between an adult and minor) without fully understanding the circumstances or facts that made his or her sexual conduct illegal.[27] Though the general rule of thumb is that someone is criminally liable if he or she has a "vicious will" and has engaged in an "unlawful act," statutory rape is one of the exceptions. In statutory rape, the mental state of the defendant has been deemed irrelevant, purportedly to eliminate a specious defense that relies upon statements like "She looked eighteen" or "She said she was eighteen," and so forth. The intent of this strategy is obviously to protect kids from defendants who actively seek sex with minors.

But what if, instead, an eighteen-year-old is enjoying a sexual relationship with his sixteen-year-old boyfriend or girlfriend? Should we, in this case, exclude a defense that relies upon a psychological explanation of the relationship itself? Unlike adults who prey upon minors, teenage romances incorporate sex for many reasons, including the conveyance of love, the desire for physical intimacy, and so forth—not to mention the ever-present sexual machinery (e.g., postpubertal sexual development, the biological drive for sexual pleasure, etc.).[28] Might a high school student truly believe that he or she had a right to a consensual sexual relationship by virtue of the fact that relationships are sustained by psychologically and physically intimate exchanges?[29]

Should the law prohibit a sexual relationship between an eighteen-year-old and sixteen-year-old in the first place? The age of consent, in some states, would confirm as much, but that rationale is usually framed around the implications of sexual intercourse—that is, the sizable risks (e.g., pregnancy and sexually transmitted infections) and responsibilities (e.g., parenting).[30] But to high school students, sex is so much more than intercourse. What if a high school couple decided to limit themselves to mutual masturbation—and were capable of honoring that limit? Is the age of consent still relevant? If not, why—and what is the dividing line?

If our culture accepts that romantic relationships in high school are inevitable, does it also imply tacit acceptance of sex—at least in some form—as a foreseeable outcome in those associations? The data would suggest that this is a logical prediction,[31] raising the question of whether it is hypocritical to permit the former (romance) while criminalizing the latter (sex).

Romance obviously offers many emotional benefits (e.g., affection, support, etc.) independent of sex. But what if sex and romance are inseparable? Is it sensible to expect high school romances to be chaste? Prohibiting romance to preclude sex seems an excessively intrusive alternative. Perhaps, instead, it is more reasonable to assume that sex is an inevitable consequence of romance and then provide the rights and education that would sustain sex-safe alternatives.

What if a high school student also knew that intimate relationships between sixteen-year-olds and eighteen-year-olds are legal in Connecticut? Is it reasonable for high school students to expect that the laws would be equivalent across states? Would it be logical to a high school student to also conclude that the Connecticut law provides a potential justification for a sexual relationship in California? Deducing that, the need for an equitable solution to the role of consent might serve as a rational defense.

The complicating problem, of course, is that statutory rape was historically considered a crime of moral turpitude—that is, that it is patently immoral. This is no doubt true for pedophilic defendants, where the need to protect vulnerable children is paramount, but it is a vastly inappropriate characterization for teenagers in love or lust. If the strict liability standard for statutory rape also presumes knowledge of age-relevant laws, prosecutors would want to know, at the very least, if such knowledge is indeed possessed by minors themselves.

What, for example, do the data say? Do high school students in California, for example, truly understand the legal implications that the age of consent is eighteen within their state? If not, are high school students acting recklessly when engaging in sex without consulting the law? Are they also negligent? Or have we failed to give them the right incentives to learn the law, or, as an alternative, have we failed to teach it in school? Would that help students understand how consent might apply to the full range of sexual activities—from kissing to oral sex to sexting (or phonication, as the case may be)?

The media, in contrast, is replete with examples of teenagers in lust, enjoying it fully without legal constraint—perhaps further confusing teenagers in America. Take the episode titled "Hot Child in the City" from the extraordinarily popular television show *Sex and the City*. It has a very young actress who claims that she has been giving blowjobs since the age of twelve. What are teenagers supposed to think? Are blowjobs legal at twelve, or are some kids more outrageous than others?

Consider the subplot of the movie *Crazy, Stupid, Love*. A thirteen-year-old boy (Robbie) is infatuated with a seventeen-year-old girl (Jessica), who also happens to be infatuated with his father (Cal). Various twists and turns transpire, but by the end of the movie, Jessica takes pity on Robbie and gives him a gift of nude photographs of herself to spark his masturbation. It is the warm and fuzzy finale of the PG-13-rated movie.

What are teenagers supposed to make of Jessica and Robbie? Is she distributing child pornography? She is only seventeen, and the photographs were designed for sexual provocation. What about sexually corrupting a minor? Robbie is only thirteen. In the movie, giving the nude photographs is purportedly an act of compassion: an older girl taking pity on the crush of a young boy.

Why then, some kids may wonder, is it a crime for teenagers to exchange nude photographs on their iPhones in the real world? What role does consent play in phonication cases? Do kids know that this conduct may be regarded as child pornography? It was innocent in this movie, empathetic, too. Answers to these questions would be a startlingly complex departure from the aforementioned warm and fuzzy ending of *Crazy, Stupid, Love.*

There are countless other media-based examples (TV, movies, etc.) that perhaps could persuade a conscientious teenager that the law does *not* prohibit their sexual conduct or, for that matter, maintain that their sexual conduct is inherently morally wrong. Their biological drive for sexual pleasure is innate and self-confirming; the media examples may simply add credence to this motivation. The intent among many teenagers may not be to circumvent the law but to express a biologically compelling desire for sexual pleasure with a consensual partner in a socially accepted format, for example, with an age-appropriate relationship.

Consent, nonetheless, is still a very thorny a problem, regardless of the age of the participants. Obtaining consent that relies, for example, on interpreting a head nod, observed by a partner and never documented in any form, is a case in point. If disagreement ensues, the contesting parties are reduced to arguing about the proverbial "he said/she said," when in fact nobody said anything. Credibility of the witnesses, collateral evidence, physical findings, police reports, and so forth, would have to serve as substitutes for resolving the conveyance of consent.[32]

The manner in which we intuitively categorize our psychological experiences may also play a part in sexual consent as well—especially with teenagers. Can sex, for example, be ordered like a Guttman Scale,[33] a unidimensional hierarchy from French kissing to penetrative intercourse? If so, does consent to one step automatically insure consent to others below it? Or even above it? If someone has consented to touching genitals over clothing, for example, does that imply consent to French kissing? Does it also imply consent to oral sex as well? If not, why? Other examples readily come to mind (e.g., phonication, sending erotic pictures over the iPhones, etc.), but the ultimate question for a teenager is whether consent is necessary for every step. If so, what exactly are the steps, and what ages—or age discrepancies—should be tolerated or prohibited?

Sex is a complex negotiation for an admittedly ephemeral act. Obtaining consent in a forthright and timely manner is a cumbersome hurdle—particularly for awkward teenagers, worse even if drugs and alcohol are involved. Though most adults navigate these waters with success, the same may not be true for the teenagers. This, too, must be considered as well, particularly in regard to age-staggered sexual rights for kids that simultaneously protect them from sexual harm.

Finally, there is the issue of informed consent prior to the commencement of sexual activity. Adults not only need to show a willingness to participate in sex, but they must also demonstrate that they understand the nature and consequences of their sexual actions. The same, obviously, must be required of teenagers; the risks of unwanted pregnancy and sexually transmitted infections would demand as much. The question, however, is how to insure informed consent with a teenage sexually active population? Sexual literacy is obviously one strategy,[34] but perhaps additional tactics are needed as well, ones that might also evolve out of comprehensive sex education.[35]

In re Gault: A Cautionary Tale

Before turning to sex education, however, we want to consider one last issue; the possibility that we have overstated the problems associated with consent and that our rhetoric is unduly alarmist. Insightful parents, informed teachers, benign prosecutors, and benevolent judges could render all of our concerns moot.

History, then again, would suggest otherwise.

For all the power of *In re Gault*[36] to establish legal rights for kids, it is important to remind the reader that this was ultimately a case about sex: a phony phone call gone awry.[37]

The backdrop was regrettable: a punitive juvenile system that justified sending kids to an isolated desert prison in Arizona (Fort Grant) that was notorious for abuse (physical and sexual). Rather than clog the juvenile system with lawyers, appeals, and chronic litigation, Arizona reasoned that a benevolent judge could make an enlightened decision in the best of interest of wayward kids.

The problem, of course, was that the judges were often less than benevolent, the children had no rights or advocates, the sentences were indeterminate, and Fort Grant was extraordinarily punitive.

Gerald Gault had come into contact with the Arizona juvenile system twice before; the infractions then were obscure, and probation was the result. The third time, however, was different. On June 15, 1964, The fifteen-year-old Gault was sent to Fort Grant to serve an indeterminate sentence.

What was his crime? He was accused of either making or listening to (the details were never resolved) an obscene phony phone call to a Ms. Ora Cook. Obscene phone calls are admittedly disturbing and certainly warrant efforts to eliminate them. There is a deliberate intrusion upon an unwilling listener in the home, where the recipient often fears that he or she has been personally targeted. In *In re Gault*, however, there was no record of the call or a transcript, either. The presiding judge simply ruled that the purported phone call was obscene and that Gerald was "habitually dangerous."

Was the phone call obscene? Was Gerald dangerous? Or was it retribution for being a teenager unencumbered by excessive moral constraints?

Though Gerald admitted making "silly" phone calls in the past, he asserted that he never made the call to Ms. Cook. It was his friend Ronnie Lewis who made the call from Gerald's home. In either case, the conversation went something like this: "Are your cherries ripe? Do you have big bombers? Do you give any away? Do you have a big long prick?"

Two things are immediately apparent: First, there was no profanity; double entendres were used instead. Second, it was also no doubt an annoying phone call, but the real question is whether it was obscene (ca. 1964). Gault had no legal representation, no expert witnesses, was unable to confront his accuser (even to ask if she could recognize the voice of the caller—which was in dispute), and so on.[38] If Gerald Gault had been an adult found guilty of making an obscene phone call, the maximum sentence would have been sixty days in jail and a $50 fine.

Although the Supreme Court ultimately resolved Gault's Fourteenth Amendment rights, it might still be useful now to consider whether the comments were obscene to begin with. J. D. Salinger's *Catcher in the Rye* (1951) is another case in point. Though repeatedly censored because of the use of double entendre language (e.g., "screw up"), it was never ruled obscene. Nor, for that matter, was James Joyce's *Ulysses*, when the case against it was heard in 1933. Even John Cleland's *Memoirs of a Woman of Pleasure* (popularly known as *Fanny Hill*), a sexually explicit book with a long history of censorship, was given constitutional protection two years after *In re Gault*.

More telling, perhaps, is the history of rock and roll. Big Joe Turner's infamous song "Shake, Rattle & Roll," originally released in 1954, and made famous by Bill Haley & His Comets (also in 1954), included the following line: "I'm a one-eyed cat peepin' in a seafood store," a double entendre meant to signify a penis and a vagina. Equally infamous, but for very different reasons, is the song "Louie, Louie," released by The Kingsmen in 1963. A sailor's lament was misinterpreted as a song about sex—largely by a fanatical mom who complained to Attorney General Robert Kennedy. The Federal Bureau of Investigation conducted an obscenity investigation, but it was ultimately dropped. "Louie, Louie" never had any sexual content to begin with, explicit or otherwise.

Though teenage sexuality is often viewed with benign tolerance, that is by no means universal or a sufficient guarantee for protecting teenagers in love or lust. *In re* Gault, and "Louie, Louie," for that matter, are alarming precedents, suggesting that any system that rests upon cultural benevolence may be risking calamity. How many children sexting or phonicating, one now wonders, will face obscenity trials in the future? Where are the Jessicas from *Crazy, Stupid, Love*? And how many teenage couples will face statutory rape prosecutions? At the very least, this book hopes to resolve some of the dilemmas that put kids at risk from draconian accusations and consequences.

Sexual Literacy and Sex Education

Returning now to sex education, some introductory comments will serve this topic as well. Professor Hazel G. Beh, in turn, will devote substantially more depth to this theme in a subsequent chapter.

If the First Amendment protects access to sex education for kids, should it be limited to reproductive knowledge or instead include the vast array of behaviors that are unified through sexual pleasure? The data on human sexuality would suggest the latter.[39] Sex education thus needs to be constructed on the edifice of sexual pleasure, not merely, as confirmed by Professor Beh, as preparation for reproduction. Prepubertal childhood sexuality alone dictates as much; pleasure heralds reproductive fruition by at least a decade.

Though there are good books about reproduction for kids (Babette Cole's *Mummy Laid an Egg*,[40] readily comes to mind), the same is not true for sexual pleasure; the concept is largely illusory in educational materials, which is ironic. Humans spend more time enjoying the pleasures of sex than procreating. Sexual pleasure is a lifetime pursuit, whereas procreation is highly circumscribed. The most populous country in the world, China, for example, limits married couples to one child. Tailoring sex education for kids to reproduction is shortsighted at best.

This is not to say that the biology of reproduction, or reproductive strategies writ large, are ill suited to sex education; quite the contrary. The prospect of unwanted pregnancy alone demands it. Evolutionary psychology is also built upon a foundation of reproduction.[41] This, too, is fundamental to our understanding of sex, but it encompasses so much more than the mechanics of conception.

The ultimate goal, therefore, of sex education for kids, and the corresponding legal rationale underlying it, is to facilitate intelligent decision making.[42] The sexual landscape is exceedingly complex, with advanced technology (e.g., iPhones, YouTube, Facebook, Google, computers, etc.) making it even more so. Sex education for kids is thus a necessary requirement for physical and psychological health, and the law, as Professor Beh fully notes, might now be a useful tool to substantiate that.

What then is the modicum of knowledge that kids would need as a prerequisite to making responsible and well-informed choices about sex?[43] What would make them sexually literate?[44] And should that be a societal priority?

Building sex education on an edifice of risk inevitably gives precedence to education about sexual harm, unwanted pregnancy, and sexually transmitted infections. All are certainly perils of childhood sexuality, and all are essential to the education of children.[45] Nevertheless, sex in childhood is largely about kids having fun. Their rights to comprehensive education must be inclusive enough to also make informed, developmentally relevant decisions about engaging in the pleasurable aspects of sex (e.g., masturbation, kissing, etc.).

Kids must additionally know the basic biological facts, such as sexual anatomy and physiology. Medically relevant information is important, too (e.g., sexually transmitted infections, the debate about circumcision, etc.). Perhaps even more imperative, especially to kids, is the psychological side of sex, including how people develop sexual identities, sexual orientation, sexual feelings (e.g., pleasure, desire, etc.), sexual emotions (e.g., guilt, jealousy), and sexual choices (e.g., when and where to masturbate, etc.). This is especially true because sex can be very difficult to navigate psychologically. Even bodily changes, for instance, can provoke challenges. Undergoing early puberty comes to mind, and the opposite—the effects of delayed puberty—too.

Sexual orientation can be especially problematic. Kids are generally socialized to a heterosexual norm. Boyfriends, girlfriends, and marriage are portrayed as a heterosexual privilege. Lesbian, gay, bisexual, and transgender (LGBT) kids are thus inevitably confused and risk further condemnation for acknowledging their sexual feelings.[46]

Alternatively, if children are routinely taught to understand the wide variation of human sexual expression, it allows them to situate themselves within a broader societal context. It also helps them better comprehend the complexities of sex. Sex is an extraordinarily powerful emotion, and our culture reacts to it in an astonishingly powerful way. Enhanced sexual literacy is thus an essential tool for psychological growth and understanding.

Besides providing a rationale for more comprehensive sex education, First Amendment rights might conceivably also provide a foundation for permitting kids to comment upon sex as well. Freedom of speech obviously protects both listeners and speakers. That, too, could also justify what is now called *sexting*, that is, the sexual commentary that is texted on cell phones. If kids are entitled to sex education, they are also, one might argue, entitled to discuss and debate sex as well (provided, of course, that the commentary is not obscene, defamatory, fighting words, or other constraints on the freedom of speech; see Chapter 6 for a broad discussion of these topics).

The more complicated issue, however, is *phonication*, the sending of nude photographs on a cell phone. That is another matter entirely. Though sexually explicit photographs also have First Amendment protection (provided that they are not obscene via *Miller v. California*),[47] sexually explicit photographs of minors do not, *Crazy, Stupid, Love* notwithstanding.

Perhaps as an alternative, sex education should also strive to counsel teenagers about the risks of sending digital nude photographs of minors—even if they have a right to do so. Urging prosecutors not press charges against teenagers who exchange nude photos of each other might be a wise move as well.

There is also the question of acquiring contraception. If, as noted previously, children have participated in qualified sex education and are now sexually literate, the probability of responsible sex becomes more pronounced—meaning that the acquisition of contraception needs to become a primary focus of sex education, too.

Though the age of consent may be eighteen, contraceptives (such as condoms) are made available to thirteen-year-olds at health clinics. How, one might reasonably ask, is this justified? Do the relevant agencies conveniently ignore the patient's age? Or is there an exception for condoms, a more benign corollary to sex than an unwanted pregnancy or a sexually transmitted infection?

In either case, kids are given contraceptives well in advance of the age of consent. This could perhaps reassure teenagers that the sexual act is legal, that they can thereby defy the law without consequence. This may also have relevance to the question of notice. How can teenagers be held to statutory rape standards if they also know that a formidable agency, such as Planned Parenthood, will give contraceptives to thirteen-year-olds?

Perhaps condoms should come with warning labels: "appropriate for eighteen-year-olds and older"? Or similarly, perhaps Planned Parenthood (and other health clinics) should stop distributing condoms to minors? The problem, however, is that if the age-of-consent requirement reduces condom compliance among teenagers, the result would be disastrous for everyone: unwanted pregnancies and sexually transmitted infections.

Last, sexual literacy also demands awareness of social, cultural, and political practices and expectations. Kids need to know what sexual behavior is legal and when (above and beyond consent and statutory rape), how each culture perceives sexual expression, how peer groups influence sexual mores, how the definition of obscenity differs from the concept of pornography, and so on. Knowing that these issues can have an enormous impact on how kids perceive and act upon their sexuality is indispensable to constructing sex education, too.[48]

Finland, as an example, has had a long history of promoting sexual health in schools.[49] Openness to sexuality is a venerable Finnish tradition; the sauna culture has normalized nudity as well. Progressive sex education has thus been mandatory in the schools since the 1960s, whereby topics like sexual enjoyment have shared the bill with topics like unwanted pregnancy, sexually transmitted infections, and sexual harm. But sex education in Finnish schools was largely disbanded for economic reasons in the 1990s. Sex took a back seat to reading, writing, and arithmetic.

If religious education can flourish without public school support, then sex education must also eventually do the same. Having access to sex education, whether publically subsidized or not, will increase the probabilities of children actually obtaining it.

What are the general guiding principles for sex education? Though thoroughly discussed in Professor Beh's chapter, we'd like to briefly note that the first order of business is teaching children how to protect themselves from sexual harm. That would be a monumental change in public health policy. Kids simultaneously also need to be given the freedom to celebrate sex, to fully appreciate this wonderful gift to humanity. To maximize that effect, however, kids also need to know the precautions for sex, ranging from contraception to the selection of a loving romantic partner. Empowering children psychologically will insure this goal as well. Kids need to be further encouraged to dialogue about sex with friends, teachers, parents, doctors, and the community at large. The best way to formalize sexual agency is to advocate for sexual rights—including the voice of kids. Finally, kids also need to understand that sex has many faces and practices and that discrimination is destructive. They must understand (in age-appropriate language) that people are entitled to make consensual sexual choices that are void of tangible harm.[50]

There are, of course, obvious limits to sex education; teaching does not guarantee practice. Another obstacle is the absence of sexual rights. If we acknowledge the pleasures of sex but simultaneously punish kids for safe-sexual conduct, then we have failed miserably, or, worse yet, we have perpetuated a Kafkaesque "bait and switch." What may be needed instead is a model for safe-sexual rights for kids that places a premium on happiness.

Happiness

We protect kids from sexual harm to eliminate excessive trauma, an essential priority for any culture. What, then, is the corresponding rationale for sexual rights? Why does it matter?

So what if kids don't have sexual rights? Sex is a trivial thing, one could maintain; it is marriage and reproduction that counts, and kids are not entitled to either. Religious texts allegedly confirm as much as well. Why, then, bother with sexual rights for kids, since it will do more harm than good?

There are many people who believe as much, but that alone is hardly persuasive. Slavery had many advocates in high places; proponents of discrimination have had even more. There is also nothing like sex to bring on societal restraints. Sex has been denied, in one form or another, to women (except as necessary receptacles for men), to masturbators ("the sin against oneself"), to those seeking birth control, to those who enjoy sexually explicit materials (e.g., the Comstock and anti-obscenity movements), interracial couples (e.g., marriage), statistical minorities (LGBT), the developmentally disabled (out of fears of pregnancy),[51] the severely mentally ill,[52] and so on.[53] Why should kids be any different?

The answer is that they are not. They deserve the pleasure and happiness that sex provides just as much as woman, masturbators, family planners, and others do. Why not let kids cherish the idyllic joys that blossom in the absence of adult pressures and responsibilities, including the thrill of safe sexual exploration? To protect that privilege, however, it must be elevated to a right, the right to the pursuit of happiness, in particular.

Happiness is an obvious choice because there is a long-standing philosophical tradition that has informed governments, including the United States. John Locke's *Second Treatise* is a case in point. At the heart of Locke's argument is the premise that a "social compact" is created between the people and their government. Though some individual rights are necessarily relinquished for the collective good, the people nonetheless retain their inviolable natural rights, the pursuit of happiness being fundamental among them.

Locke equated happiness with sensible pleasure. He graded it from an "utmost pleasure" to a pleasure "without which anyone cannot be content." For Locke, "the pursuit of happiness" was the ultimate determiner of people's actions. Actions were undertaken, or not, as they tended to increase or decrease a person's overall happiness.[54] Though Locke never listed the ultimate pleasures, sex could easily fit in this conceptualization as both a pleasure enhancer and an "utmost pleasure."

Thomas Jefferson formalized the Lockean perspective in the Declaration of Independence. The pursuit of happiness, he believed, is a self-evident truth. James Wilson, a Constitutional Convention delegate, went a step further by stating that happiness "is the first law of government."[55]

If happiness is equated with pleasure, and if pleasure is fundamental to sex, then happiness and sex are inexorably linked as well. If governments have a duty to respect the pleasures of their citizens, sexual freedom must be one of them. Since the Constitution safeguards liberty and facilitates the pursuit of happiness, it may be reasonable to ask whether the Constitution should be the natural place to seek a foundation for sexual freedoms.[56]

The big leap, however, is to extend this logic to kids. Adults have a broad range of sexual liberties, but by what justification should this be expanded to children?

Kids deserve pleasure as much anyone—perhaps even more so. The real question is, What are the risks? Is sex, for example, analogous to drugs and alcohol, pleasures that include sizable costs to individuals and societies (e.g., unwanted pregnancy, sexually transmitted infections, emotional upheaval, etc.)? If so, do we need to set comparable limits on childhood sexuality as a matter of protection?

Or is sex like sports: something that is pleasurable to kids, that also involves risks? If the latter is true, we note that parental consent is often needed for children to participate in sports. Would the same logic be necessary for childhood sexuality? Would parental consent be necessary, too?

Neither, we believe, is an ideal metaphor for childhood sexual rights. The pleasures of sex are biologically intrinsic; drugs and alcohol are not. And though sex and play may share many similarities, parental consent is only necessary for the latter, where organized sports are concerned. Playing at the beach, the backyard, the local park, or wherever is not accompanied by parental consent. Kids are destined to play and find ways to implement it.

The same may be true of childhood sexuality. It brings much joy and happiness, and children find a way to express it. Though it, too, involves real risks, the burden, we believe, is similar to play. We must teach children how to avoid or minimize those risks, not prohibit the activity entirely.

Which brings us back to sexual pleasure. If sexual pleasure starts at birth, and masturbation is evident by three-years-old, the clock is ticking well in advance of puberty. Sexual rights for children must therefore be commensurate with the onset, and psychological significance, of pleasure. Pleasure is essential to the pursuit of happiness, regardless of the age of the person.[57]

Conclusion

There is, admittedly, nothing conclusive about this chapter. The underlying problems are complex, and the remedies are unclear. We have, instead, striven to raise questions and propose suggestions rather than to offer definitive policy. Laying the groundwork for serious discussion (elaborated upon in future chapters) has been the generic objective, and shifting dialogue from reproduction to sexual pleasure has been the specific goal. We believe the latter is a more theoretically defendable rationale for constructing a foundation for the sexual rights of kids, particularly within the context of pursuing happiness.

Acknowledgments

We wish to thank the following individuals for comments on drafts of this chapter: Michael Boucai, Terri Conley, David Lick, Steve Pinkerton, and Eugene Volokh.

NOTES

1. P.R. Abramson & S. D. Pinkerton, *With Pleasure: Thoughts on the Nature of Human Sexuality* (Oxford Univ. Press 2002).
2. W.H. Masters, V. Johnson, & R.C. Kolodny, *Human Sexuality* (Little, Brown 1982).
3. J.D. DeLamater & W.N. Friedrich, *Human Sexual Development*, 39 J. Sex Res. 10 (2002); E. Galenson, *Observation of Early Infantile Sexual and Erotic Development*, in 7 *Handbook of Sexology* (M.E. Perry ed. 1990); W.N. Friedrich et al., *Normative Sexual Behavior in Children: A Contemporary Sample*, 88 Pediatrics 456 (1998); F.M. Martinson, *The Sexual Life of Children* (Bergin & Garvey 1994); F. Mercer & P.R. Abramson, *Masturbation*, in *The Child* (R.A. Shweder ed. 2009).
4. H. de Graaf & J. Rademakers, *The Psychological Measurement of Childhood Sexual Development in Western Societies: Methodological Challenges*, 48 J. Sex Res. 118 (2011); B. Schuhrke, *Young Children's Curiosity about Other People's Genitals*, 12 J. Psychol. & Hum. Sexuality 27 (2000).
5. *Sexual Nature/Sexual Culture* (P.R. Abramson & S.D. Pinkerton eds., Univ. Chi. Press 1995); de Graaf & Rademakers, *The Psychological Measurement of Childhood Sexual Development in Western Societies*, supra note 4; I. Larsson & C.G. Svedin, *Sexual Experiences in Childhood: Young Adults' Recollections*, 31 Archives Sexual Behav. 263 (2002); E. O. Laumann et al., *The Social Organization of Sexuality* (Univ. Chi. Press 1994); L.F. O'Sullivan & H.F.L. Meyer-Bahlburg, *African American and Latina Inner-City Girls' Report of Romantic and Sexual Development*, 20 J. Soc. & Pers. Relationships 221 (2003).
6. *Sexual Development in Childhood* (J. Bancroft ed., Ind. Univ. Press 2003); J. Bancroft, *Human Sexuality and Its Problems* (Elsevier 2009); J. Bancroft et al., *Masturbation as a Marker of Sexual Development*, in *Sexual Development in Childhood* (J. Bancroft ed.), supra; DeLamater & Friedrich, *Human Sexual Development*, supra note 3; L. Diamond, *Sexual Fluidity* (Harv. Univ. Press 2008); Friedrich et al., *Normative Sexual Behavior in Children*, supra note 3; de Graaf & Rademakers, *The Psychological Measurement of Childhood Sexual Development in Western Societies*, supra note 4; Martinson, *The Sexual Life of Children*, supra note 3; Masters et al., *Human Sexuality*, supra note 2; P. Okami et al., *Sexual Experiences in Early Childhood: 18-Year Longitudinal Data from the UCLA Family Lifestyles Project*, 34 J. Sex Res. 339 (1997); P. Okami et al., *Early Childhood Exposure to Parental Nudity and Scenes of Parental Sexuality ("Primal Scenes"): An 18-Year Longitudinal Study of Outcome*, 27 Archives Sexual Behav. 361 (1998); R.A. Posner, *Sex and Reason* (Harv. Univ. Press 1992); M.A. Reynolds et al., *The Nature of Childhood Sexual*

Experiences: Two Studies 50 Years Apart, in *Sexual Development in Childhood* (J. Bancroft ed.), *supra*.

7. P.R. Abramson, *Sex, Lies and Ethnography*, in *The Times of Aids: Theory, Method and Practice* (G. Herdt & S. Lindenbaum eds., Sage 1992); P.R. Abramson et al., *Experimenter Effects on Responses to Sexually Explicit Stimuli*, 9 J. Res. Personality 133 (1975); R. Berk et al., *Sexual Activities as Told in Surveys*, in *Sexual Nature/Sexual Culture* (Abramson & Pinkerton eds.), *supra* note 5; de Graaf & Rademakers, *The Psychological Measurement of Childhood Sexual Development in Western Societies*, *supra* note 4; G. Herdt & A. Boxer, *Children of Horizon* (Beacon Press, 1996).

8. Okami et al., *Sexual Experiences in Early Childhood*, *supra* note 6; Okami et al., *Early Childhood Exposure to Parental Nudity and Scenes of Parental Sexuality ("Primal Scenes")*, *supra* note 6.

9. Friedrich et al., *Normative Sexual Behavior in Children*, *supra* note 3.

10. Herdt & Boxer, *Children of Horizon*, *supra* note 7.

11. P.R. Abramson, *Sex Appeal: Six Ethical Principles for the 21st Century* (Oxford Univ. Press 2010); *Sexual Nature/Sexual Culture* (Abramson & Pinkerton, eds.), *supra* note 5; *Abramson & Pinkerton, With Pleasure*, *supra* note 1; P.R. Abramson et al., *Sexual Rights in America: The Ninth Amendment and the Pursuit of Happiness* (NYU Press 2003); H.F.L. Meyer-Bahlburg, *Psychneuroendocrinology and Sexual Behavior*, in *Sexual Nature/Sexual Culture* (Abramson & Pinkerton, eds.), *supra* note 5.

12. F.B.M. de Waal, *Peacemaking among Primates* (Harv. Univ. Press 1989); F.B.M. de Waal, *The Ape and the Sushi Maker* (Basic Books 2001); F.B.M. de Waal, *Our Inner Ape* (Penguin 2005); D. Symons, *The Evolution of Human Sexuality* (Oxford Univ. Press 1979).

13. *Sexual Nature/Sexual Culture* (Abramson & Pinkerton, eds.), *supra* note 5; Diamond, *Sexual Fluidity*, *supra* note 6; M. Foucault, *The History of Sexuality* (Random House 1978); M. Foucault, *The Use of Pleasure* (Random House 1985); M. Foucault, *The Care of the Self* (Random House 1986); R. Godbeer, *Sexual Revolution in Early America* (Johns Hopkins Univ. Press 2002); G. Herdt, *Guardians of the Flute* (McGraw-Hill 1981); G. Herdt, *The Sambia: Ritual, Sexuality, and Change in Papua New Guinea* (Wadsworth 2006); P. Robinson, *Queer Wars* (Univ. Chi. Press 2005); E. K. Sedgwick, *Epistemology of the Closet* (Univ. Cal. Press 1990); M. Stein, *Sexual Injustice* (Univ. N.C. Press 2010); J. Weeks, *Sexuality and Its Discontents* (Routledge 1985); B. Werth, *The Scarlet Professor: Newton Arvin: A Literary Life Shattered in Scandal* (Anchor 2001).

14. Abramson, *Sex Appeal*, *supra* note 11.

15. *Sexual Nature/Sexual Culture* (Abramson & Pinkerton, eds.), *supra* note 5; *Abramson & Pinkerton, With Pleasure*, *supra* note 1; T.D. Conley, *Perceived Proposer Personality Characteristics and Gender Differences in Acceptance of Casual Sex Offers*, 100 J. Personality & Soc. Psychol. 309 (2011).

16. *Sexual Nature/Sexual Culture* (Abramson & Pinkerton, eds.), *supra* note 5; *Abramson & Pinkerton, With Pleasure*, *supra* note 1.

17. *Sexual Nature/Sexual Culture* (Abramson & Pinkerton, eds.), *supra* note 5; *Abramson & Pinkerton, With Pleasure*, *supra* note 1.

18. De Waal, *Peacemaking among Primates*, supra note 12; de Waal, *The Ape and the Sushi Maker*, supra note 12.

19. *Sexual Nature/Sexual Culture* (Abramson & Pinkerton, eds.), supra note 5; Abramson & Pinkerton, *With Pleasure*, supra note 1.

20. *Sexual Nature/Sexual Culture* (Abramson & Pinkerton, eds.), supra note 5; Abramson & Pinkerton, *With Pleasure*, supra note 1.

21. J. H. Gagnon & W. Simon, *Sexual Conduct* (Aldine 1973).

22. G. Martinez et al., *Teenagers in the United States: Sexual Activity, Contraceptive Use, and Childbearing, 2006–2010 National Survey of Family Growth*, 23 U.S. Dep't of Health & Human Servs. 31 (2011).

23. R.A. Posner & K.B. Silbaugh, *A Guide to America's Sex Laws* (Univ. Chi. Press 1996).

24. P.R. Abramson, *Sarah: A Sexual Biography* (SUNY Press 1984); Abramson, *Sex Appeal*, supra note 11; Abramson & Pinkerton, *With Pleasure*, supra note 1; P.R. Abramson et al., *Sexual Rights in America*, supra note 11; P.R. Abramson et al., *Consenting to Sex and Severe Mental Illness: Terra Incognita and a Priest with AIDS*, 30 Sexuality & Disability 357–366 (2012); A. C. Michaels, *Constitutional Innocence*, 112 Harv. L. Rev. 828 (1999); E. Nevins-Saunders, *Incomprehensible Crimes: Defendants with Mental Retardation Charged with Statutory Rape*, 85 N.Y.U. L. Rev. 1067 (2010); Posner, *Sex and Reason*, supra note 6; Posner & Silbaugh, *A Guide to America's Sex Laws*, supra note 23; M. Waites, *The Age of Consent: Young People, Sexuality and Citizenship* (Macmillan 2005).

25. Posner & Silbaugh, *A Guide to America's Sex Laws*, supra note 23.

26. *Sexual Nature/Sexual Culture* (Abramson & Pinkerton, eds.), supra note 5; Foucault, *The History of Sexuality*, supra note 13; Foucault, *The Use of Pleasure*, supra note 13; Foucault, *The Care of the Self*, supra note 13; Herdt, *The Sambia*, supra note 13; Posner, *Sex and Reason*, supra note 6; Weeks, *Sexuality and Its Discontents*, supra note 13.

27. E.g., Garnett v. State, 632 A.2d 797 (1993).

28. *Sexual Nature/Sexual Culture* (Abramson & Pinkerton, eds.), supra note 5; Abramson & Pinkerton, *With Pleasure*, supra note 1.

29. Abramson, *Sex Appeal*, supra note 11.

30. Abramson et al., *Sexual Rights in America*, supra note 11.

31. E.g., Martinez et al., *Teenagers in the United States*, supra note 22.

32. Abramson et al., *Consenting to Sex and Severe Mental Illness*, supra note 24; E. Saks, *Competency to Refuse Treatment*, 69 N.C. L. Rev. 946 (1990–91); E. Saks, *Refusing Care: Forced Treatment and the Rights of the Mentally Ill* (Univ. Chi. Press 2002).

33. L. Guttman, *The Basis for Scalogram Analysis*, in *Measurement and Prediction*, 4 S.A. Stouffer et al., *The American Soldier* (Wiley 1950).

34. Abramson et al., *Sexual Rights in America*, supra note 11; P.R. Abramson & S.D. Pinkerton, *Sexual Illiteracy*, 3 Am. Sexuality, no. 4 (2005).

35. *Abramson, Sex Appeal, supra* note 11; *Sexual Nature/Sexual Culture* (Abramson & Pinkerton, eds.), *supra* note 5; Abramson et al., *Consenting to Sex and Severe Mental Illness, supra* note 24.

36. In re Gault, 387 U.S. 1 (1967).

37. D.S. Tannenhaus, *The Constitutional Rights of Children*: In re Gault *and Juvenile Justice* (Univ. Press Kan. 2011).

38. R. Green, *Sexual Science and the Law* (Harv. Univ. Press 1992); Tannenhaus, *The Constitutional Rights of Children, supra* note 37.

39. *Sexual Nature/Sexual Culture* (Abramson & Pinkerton, eds.), *supra* note 5; *Abramson & Pinkerton, With Pleasure, supra* note 1.

40. B. Cole, *Mummy Laid an Egg* (Red Fox Picture Books 1994).

41. *Symons, The Evolution of Human Sexuality, supra* note 12.

42. *Abramson, Sex Appeal, supra* note 11; Abramson & Pinkerton, *Sexual Illiteracy, supra* note 34; Abramson et al., *Sexual Rights in America, supra* note 11.

43. *Abramson, Sex Appeal, supra* note 11.

44. Abramson & Pinkerton, *Sexual Illiteracy, supra* note 34; Abramson et al., *Sexual Rights in America, supra* note 11.

45. *Abramson, Sarah, supra* note 24; *Abramson, Sex Appeal, supra* note 11.

46. D.J. Lick et al., *The Rainbow Families Scale (RFS): A Measure of Experiences among Individuals with Lesbian and Gay Parents*, 12 *J. Applied Measurement* 222 (2011).

47. Miller v. California, 413 U.S. 15 (1973).

48. Abramson & Pinkerton, *Sexual Illiteracy, supra* note 34; Abramson et al., *Sexual Rights in America, supra* note 11.

49. R. Cacciatore, *Sexual Health in Children*, in *New Views on Sexual Health: The Case of Finland* (I. Lottes & O. Kontula eds., Population Research Institute 2000); E. Kosunen, *Adolescent Sexual Health*, in *New Views on Sexual Health* (Lottes & Kontula eds.), *supra*.

50. *Abramson, Sex Appeal, supra* note 11; *Stein, Sexual Injustice, supra* note 13.

51. P.R. Abramson et al., *Sexual Expression of Mentally Retarded People: Educational and Legal Implications*, 93 *Am. J. Mental Retardation* 328 (1988).

52. Abramson et al., *Consenting to Sex and Severe Mental Illness, supra* note 24.

53. *Abramson & Pinkerton, With Pleasure, supra* note 1.

54. J. Locke, *Second Treatise of Government* (Hackett 1980) (1690).

55. G. Wills, *Inventing America* (Vintage 1978).

56. P.R. Abramson, *Romance in the Ivory Tower: The Rights and Liberty of Conscience* (MIT Press 2007); Abramson et al., *Sexual Rights in America, supra* note 11.

57. *Sexual Nature/Sexual Culture* (Abramson & Pinkerton, eds.), *supra* note 5; *Abramson & Pinkerton, With Pleasure, supra* note 1.

2

Consent, Teenagers, and (un)Civil(ized) Consequences

JENNIFER ANN DROBAC

American criminal and civil laws treat adolescents and their "consent"[1] very differently, even within the same context. Take, for example, the California case of *Doe v. Starbucks*,[2] a 2009 civil sexual harassment case. Timothy Horton, the Starbucks supervisor who seduced his sixteen-year-old barista, ultimately pled guilty to criminal unlawful sexual intercourse with a minor under *Cal. Penal Code* § 261.5(a).[3] In that associated criminal case, Doe's "consent" to sex failed to provide Horton with a legal defense. In the civil sexual harassment case, however, the federal court left open the possibility that Doe's "consent" might serve to insulate Starbucks and Horton from civil liability. Other civil cases similar to this Starbucks sexual harassment case exist across the nation. How is it logical that Doe's "consent" fails to earn legal significance under criminal law but may operate to bar civil liability? Does Doe even have capacity under the law to consent to sexual intercourse with an adult? Isn't eighteen the "age of consent" in California?

This chapter highlights the inconsistent legal treatment of adolescent "consent," particularly in sexual harassment cases, in order to recommend civil law reform based on the science of adolescent neurological and psychosocial development. Part I defines key terms, such as *consent* and *capacity*, to give those legal concepts more precise meaning with respect to juveniles. Parts II and III explore whether the law, such as that applied in *Starbucks*, is consistent in its treatment of adolescent "consent." Part III also explores whether the law applied to teenagers produces logical and just outcomes. It raises the question of whether the law should treat teenagers as adults, as it sometimes does. Part IV reviews the new science of adolescent cognitive, neurological, and psychosocial development and demonstrates that the scientific evidence does not support many legal presumptions regarding juveniles and their legal capacity. Further, it questions whether state "age of consent" laws should set somewhat arbitrary but predictable points for attributing legal capacity to teenagers. If not, should presumptions give way to case-by-case evaluations of teenage maturity?

Part V incorporates the science of adolescent development for an evaluation of whether the law pertaining to juvenile "consent" is even logical. The conclusion that it is not prompts Part VI's discussion of responsive strategies. In particular, Part VI proffers a new legal approach to adolescent "consent." Based on the science of juvenile neurological and psychosocial development, this approach also incorporates sociolegal theory and public policy. It offers the concept of *legal assent*, a voidable "consent" that carries no presumption of legal capacity. Whether or not adolescents have legal capacity, the neuroscience and psychosocial evidence confirms that teenagers are developmentally less mature than adults, suggesting that adolescents may need maturing experiences in order to develop. This new legal approach—legal assent—resembles voidable juvenile consent under contract law because it affords teenagers decision-making power while protecting them under the law when they inevitably make unwise choices. Legal assent mandates placing the burden on mature adults to moderate their behavior involving teenagers in light of adolescent "developing capacity."[4] Part VII concludes the chapter.

I. Distinguishing Lay Terms and Legal Concepts

Before examining the case law and the factors that guide legal reform concerning civil law's treatment of adolescent "consent," it is necessary to explore the definitions of some key terms.

Consent, Assent, and Acquiescence

Consent means "to permit, approve, or agree."[5] Slightly different from consent, *assent* means "to agree or concur."[6] By this definition, *assent* denotes cooperation or secondary status. Both terms arguably include two prerequisites: knowledge regarding the choice, and volition. In the first aspect, consent and assent must be informed and must match the activity they justify. Ignorant cooperation does not indicate consent or assent. Additionally, any misrepresentation taints associated consent or assent. The individual must also possess the cognitive ability to reason about a choice. In the second aspect, consent and assent must indicate freedom of choice and volition. The individual must be able to guide her own responsive choices. *Acquiesce* means "to assent tacitly; submit or comply silently or without protest"[7] and indicates neither full consent nor assent.

In distinguishing acquiescence, a third requirement is added to consent and assent: a measure of power and autonomy. For example, if someone has no opportunity or authority to dissent, can we value that person's consent? Consent and assent must be free of coercion and duress. Arguably, they assume a level of equality and mutuality between those persons making the bargain or coming to an agreement. Consent carries with it a presumption of intellectual, emotional, and developmental capacity. These characteristics are what undergird legal capacity.

Legal Consent and Capacity

This elucidation of consent is consistent with an interpretation of consent found in the *Restatement (Second) of Torts* § 892A. Subsection (2)(a) specifies that in order to extinguish tort liability, consent must be "by one who has the capacity to consent."[8] A comment to this subsection provides:

> If, however, the one who consents is not capable of *appreciating the nature, extent or probable consequences of the conduct*, the consent is not effective to bar liability unless the parent, guardian, or other person empowered to consent for the incompetent has given consent, in which case the consent of the authorized person will be effective even though the incompetent does not consent.[9]

This passage clarifies that one who consents must understand what he or she is doing and be able to anticipate results. Such appreciation requires counterfactual thinking, or "what if" reasoning. This explanation focuses on the cognitive aspects of consent.

Contract law has also examined the notions of legal consent and capacity. Contract law has long held that minors lack the capacity to consent.[10] This conclusion results, in part, from the fear that adults may take legal advantage of minors who make contractual agreements. Contract law, therefore, makes contracts voidable by the minor.[11]

Contract law also distinguishes between cognitive and volitional incapacity, especially in the context of mental disabilities. The *Restatement (Second) of Contracts* § 15(1) states:

> A person incurs only voidable contractual duties by entering into a transaction if by reason of mental illness or defect
> (a) he is unable to understand in a reasonable manner the nature and consequences of the transaction, or
> (b) he is unable to act in a reasonable manner in relation to the transaction and the other party has reason to know of his condition.

Part (a) mirrors the torts guidance. However, (b) relates to volitional incapacity or the inability to regulate one's responses in a social context. Some incapacitated individuals may understand the nature of a transaction or conduct but not be able to reasonably control their responsive behavior.

Comment b. to § 15 explains:

> Even though understanding is complete, *he may lack the ability to control his acts in the way that the normal individual can and does control them*; in such cases the inability makes the contract voidable only if the other party has reason to know of his condition. Where a person has some understanding of a particular transaction which is affected by mental illness or defect, the controlling consideration is whether the transaction in its result is one which a reasonably competent person might have made.[12]

This passage naturally prompts the question whether some teenagers suffer from a similar volitional incapacity that shares the same features as a "defect." One might argue that a teenager "may lack the ability to control his acts in a way that the normal individual [adult] can and does control them." For example, she may understand the facts regarding sexual activity but not control her conduct the way an adult would.

Different disciplines employ a variety of terms to express the notion of adolescent behavior as markedly different from adult behavior. Psychologists refer to this phenomenon as *psychosocial immaturity*.[13] Legal scholars sometimes refer to this difference as *diminished capacity*.[14] I find the term *diminished capacity* inappropriate because the word *diminished* carries a negative connotation. Additionally, it suggests that full capacity should exist or may once have existed. Most teenagers suffer not from impairment but from immaturity–a blameless stage of life and a natural phase of growth. I prefer the term *developing capacity* because of a teenager's transitional status from childhood to adulthood and his or her developing maturity. Semantics aside, the question remains whether the contracts' guidance on incapacity accurately describes many adolescents, at one point or another.

Medical Assent

This discussion of key terms has highlighted the similarities between consent and assent. Government regulation of human subject medical research brings nuanced meaning to assent as it applies to children in that context. The *Code of Federal Rules* mandates that institutional review boards (IRBs) may approve research on children if "adequate provisions are made for soliciting the assent of the children and the permission of their parents or guardians."[15] An IRB decides whether a child is even "capable of providing assent" by considering the child's age, maturity, and psychological state.[16] No additional guidance suggests how IRBs should weigh these factors. The boards may waive parent permission only under special circumstances.[17] Thus medical assent does not equate with legal consent since parental permission—consent—typically bolsters the child's assent. Similarly, capacity for medical assent does not equate with legal capacity since the decisions contemplated are so narrowly defined and well informed. The responsibility for any decision to conduct medical research on a minor is typically shared by the researchers, the IRB, the parents, and—lastly—by the juvenile.

Juvenile "Consent" and Capacity

People considering juvenile legal autonomy might agree that teenagers are capable of assent and acquiescence. Similarly, while even a six-year-old may "know" or recognize Barack Obama and Mitt Romney and may "voluntarily" pick one or the other for president, we do not allow that child to cast a political vote, however. Additionally, we might agree that many juveniles understand the concept of sexual intercourse.[18] Their understanding of sexual activity does not necessarily qualify them, however, as competent decision makers or as ready to engage in the behavior. Many adults, judges, and courts disagree. For them, relative cognitive maturity, or even apparent physical maturity, equates with adult capacity. They ignore or are ignorant of the level of psychosocial maturity required for competent decision making.

II. "Consent" or Consent: Criminal Law and Civil Law

In *Starbucks*, a California federal district court analyzed whether a minor could bring a sexual harassment case against her supervisor and employer when she "consented" to some or most of the alleged offensive conduct.[19] The question of the legal significance of the "consent" was pivotal in this case. In *Faragher v. City of Boca Raton*, the U.S. Supreme Court emphasized that, in a sexual harassment case under Title VII of the Civil Rights Act of 1964 (Title VII),[20] the "objectionable environment must be both objectively and subjectively offensive, one that a reasonable person would find hostile or abusive and one that the victim in fact did perceive to be so."[21] One might refer to the objective component as the "reasonableness" standard and to the subjective element as the "unwelcomeness" requirement. Every state's fair employment practice statute that similarly prohibits sexual harassment also makes "unwelcomeness" an element of the prima facie case.[22] Thus, if Doe's "consent" garners legal significance, she loses her sexual harassment case because the conduct is not subjectively "unwelcome."

The complicating factor for employers defending sexual harassment cases and the jurists evaluating those cases, as discussed above, arises from state sex crime statutes that specifically prohibit sexual conduct with minors. Typically, "consent" provides no defense for the criminally accused adult. So what happens when criminal and civil claims stem from the same conduct? Is the minor's "consent" treated consistently? Perhaps not. A review of several recent cases superbly showcases the conflicts that can lead to bizarre results.

Doe v. Starbucks, Inc.: The Facts

Starbucks hired Jane Doe in July 2005 when she was then sixteen years old. She worked closely with her supervisor, Timothy Horton, who was then twenty-four years old. After her hire, Horton allegedly asked Doe out on dates repeatedly, and she initially rebuffed his advances.[23] In pleadings, Doe declared that Horton made "perhaps hundreds" of sexually explicit or profane statements to her at work in front of coworkers concerning his sexual interest in her.[24] Later, she "finally said 'yes,' hoping it would make him stop."[25] They ultimately engaged in sexual activity in November or December 2005.[26] Doe declared, "'[Horton] demanded that I perform oral sex on him, which I did. I felt like I had to—that I had no choice.... I felt that, because he had given me marijuana and I had smoked it with him, I had to do what he said, because he was my Supervisor and I didn't want to lose my job.'"[27] Horton told Doe not to tell anyone about their relationship.

In February 2006, however, Doe told her mother that she was having sex with Horton. Doe's mother requested an investigation and that Starbucks take steps to protect her daughter. The store manager, Lina Nobel, did not ask Horton about a sexual relationship "because she thought it was not her place to do so."[28] Nobel informed Doe's mother that Horton had "'denied any wrongdoing with [Plaintiff], ... and if she fired him or terminated him, she was afraid that she was going to have a wrongful termination claim on her hands.'"[29] Thereafter, Doe requested a transfer to a different Starbucks store "because she 'felt like she had to.'"[30] Finally, in 2006, Doe left her job and "enrolled in a treatment facility out of state to address mental and emotional problems."[31] Horton ultimately pled guilty to criminal unlawful sexual intercourse with a minor.

The Starbucks Summary Judgment Opinion

In the civil sexual harassment case later filed on behalf of Doe, the federal court left open the possibility that Doe's "consent" might serve to insulate Starbucks and Horton from civil liability. First, the court evaluated *Cal. Penal Code* § 261.5, "Unlawful sexual intercourse with person under 18," to which Horton had pled guilty. Doe argued that §

261.5 confirmed her lack of capacity to consent to sexual contact. Section 261.5(a) states, "Unlawful sexual intercourse is an act of sexual intercourse accomplished with a person who is not the spouse of the perpetrator, if the person is a minor. . . . [A] "minor" is a person under the age of 18 years." The *Starbucks* court rejected Doe's reasoning that she lacked capacity to consent, relying on *People v. Tobias*.[32] In doing so, the court effectively denied Doe's sexual harassment claim.

People v. Tobias

Starbucks relied on dictum from a 2001 California Supreme Court criminal case, *People v. Tobias*, which evaluated a defense to a *Penal Code* § 285 incest charge. The *Tobias* perpetrator alleged that the "consenting" minor was an accomplice, not a victim. The *Tobias* court found against the accused but in dictum said:

In 1970, the Legislature created the crime of unlawful sexual intercourse with a minor (§ 261.5) and amended the rape statute (§ 261) so that it no longer included sex with a minor in the definition of rape. As a result, the circumstances surrounding sexual intercourse with a minor became highly relevant, because this conduct might in some cases be a distinct and less serious crime than rape, particularly where the minor engages in the sexual act *knowingly and voluntarily*. (*Compare* § 261.5, subds. (b), (c), (d) [offense classification and punishment for unlawful sexual intercourse with a minor] with § 264, subd. (a) [punishment for rape]).[33]

Oddly, neither § 261.5 nor § 261 refers to a minor acting "knowingly and voluntarily." The court continued:

> In making this change, the Legislature implicitly acknowledged that, *in some cases at least, a minor may be capable of giving legal consent to sexual relations*. If that were not so, then every violation of § 261.5 would also constitute rape under § 261, subdivision (a)(1). (*Cf.* Michael M. v. Superior Court (1979) 159 Cal.Rptr. 340). Of course, a minor might still be found incapable of giving legal consent to sexual intercourse in a particular case, but [the legislature] abrogate[ed] the rule that a girl under 18 is in all cases incapable of giving such legal consent.[34]

Whether or not the California court accurately interpreted the legislature's statutory reforms is beyond the scope of this chapter. This passage, quoted in *Doe v. Starbucks*, however, announces a new determination that unequivocally contradicts hundreds of years of court precedent finding that girls[35] under a specified age are unable to give consent as a matter of law, regardless of their actual "consent."[36] Essentially, it makes minors civil law accomplices in their own sexual victimization, as determined by § 261.5. The *Starbucks* court failed to explain why, if some minors are capable of giving legal consent, § 261.5 is a strict liability offense. The court acknowledged that *Tobias* was a criminal case but held that *Donaldson v. Department of Real Estate* had extended its rule to civil cases.[37]

Donaldson v. Department of Real Estate

In *Donaldson*, the court considered whether the California Department of Real Estate had wrongfully revoked the real estate license of a twenty-four-year-old licensee who had seduced his sixteen-year-old sister-in-law. Robert Donaldson had pled no contest to charges brought under *Penal Code* § 261.5. When the California Real Estate Commissioner revoked his license, she interpreted his actions to be "[s]exually related conduct causing physical harm or emotional distress to a . . . non-consenting participant in the conduct."[38] The California civil appellate court reversed her revocation, relying on *Tobias*. Summarizing its holding, the *Donaldson* court stated:

> The Commissioner thus relied upon a presumption which in an earlier time was judicially inferred from the legislative creation of the offense of "statutory rape." That crime, however, was abolished 35 years ago [and replaced with § 261.5 "Unlawful sexual intercourse with person under 18"], and the California Supreme Court has authoritatively declared the concomitant presumption of nonconsent to have been likewise abrogated. Accordingly, a minor victim of a sex offense cannot be declared a "non-consenting participant" based solely upon her age.[39]

In this professional discipline case, the *Tobias* dictum made its way into California civil law precedent to protect the respondent, adult licensee.

When reviewing the case against Donaldson, the appellate court reviewed the legislature's passage of § 261.5. The court reasoned that § 261.5 effectively restored rape "to its traditional outlines."[40] It explained that "the Legislature abolished the crime of statutory rape and, with it, the presumption of juvenile non-consent. The latter effect was not explicit, but neither was the presumption itself. Instead it appears to have been developed by courts as a gloss on, or rationalization for, the crime of statutory rape."[41] The *Donaldson* court recommended referring to conduct prohibited under § 261.5 as "criminal intercourse" to avoid confusion.[42] It offered no support other than the *Tobias* dictum for its interpretation of the 1970 legislative amendments to § 261 and the passage of § 261.5.

The court also considered the "age of legal consent." The court explained that "this phrase, like 'statutory rape,' has passed into lay usage and been incorporated into folk law."[43] Folk law? The court did not explain this term or distinguish it from common law. However, the court explored to what age and activity the phrase "age of consent" referred. In a detailed discussion, citing to both civil code sections and case law, the court concluded that the phrase was used primarily in the context of consent to marriage—even with respect to the former "*tort* of 'seduction of a person under the age of legal consent.'"[44] It meant the age at which consent to marriage would garner legal authority. Acknowledging, however, that many courts have used the phrase in reference to sexual relations, the *Donaldson* court held, "Just as there is no longer any "statutory rape" in this state, so there is no "age of consent" as concerns sexual relations, and references to such a concept can only muddy the analytical waters."[45]

There is no "age of consent" in California? This may come as grim news to California parents. Apparently, neither court—neither *Donaldson* nor *Tobias*—believed that the California legislature intended merely to simplify the forcible rape statute (§ 261) and to classify more precisely criminal (but perhaps not resisted) sex with a minor (§ 261.5). Such reorganization arguably allowed the legislature to confirm what had been implied in the so-called statutory rape provisions of the former penal code: that minors are *legally incapable* of consenting.[46] Why else simultaneously enact a statute that prohibits all sexual intercourse with a minor female? The suggestion that the legislature intended to target teenage pregnancy[47] suffers from the fact that the statute applied to pre-menarcheal girls and now includes both minor females and males.

Meritor Savings Bank v. Vinson

Given this evolution of California law, one must consider whether the *Tobias* court (or the 1970 California legislature) confused or conflated acquiescence and legal consent. Confusion concerning these similar but distinct concepts is common. In *Meritor Savings Bank v. Vinson*,[48] the first U.S. Supreme Court Title VII case to recognize workplace sexual harassment, the Court examined adult volition in its discussion of unwelcomeness:

> While the question whether particular conduct was indeed unwelcome presents difficult problems of proof and turns largely on credibility determinations committed to the trier of fact, the District Court in this case erroneously focused on the "voluntariness" of respondent's participation in the claimed sexual episodes. The correct inquiry is whether [the adult] respondent by her conduct indicated that the alleged sexual advances were unwelcome, not whether her actual participation in sexual intercourse was voluntary.[49]

Here, we understand from the Supreme Court that acquiescence is not legal consent. If adult knowing and voluntary participation does not necessarily equate with consent, then surely juvenile acquiescence and "consent" deserve special regard.

Doe v. Oberweis Dairy

Starbucks Doe also cited *Doe v. Oberweis Dairy*[50] in support of her contention that minors lack the capacity to consent to sex with adults. The court found that *Oberweis* had "little persuasive effect" since it was a Seventh Circuit, Illinois, case that contradicted *Tobias* and did not consider California law. A closer look at *Oberweis*, however, may lead others to believe that it had more to offer in the *Starbucks* sexual harassment case than the *Starbucks* California federal district court determined.

Like *Starbucks*, *Oberweis* was a sexual harassment case involving a sixteen-year-old teenager and her twenty-four-year-old supervisor.[51] Like California, Illinois prohibits sex between minors (under seventeen) and adults.[52] The Illinois *Oberweis* federal district court found that the "unwelcomeness" requirement applies in employment cases involving minors and that the conduct about which Doe complained was not "unwelcome."[53] The court stated:

> It is undisputed that Plaintiff voluntarily visited Nayman's [the supervisor's] apartment alone the day of the encounter. It is also undisputed that Plaintiff asked Nayman to put a condom on [which he did not][54] before they had sex. It is further undisputed that after the sexual encounter, Plaintiff voluntarily interacted with Nayman in social situations outside of the workplace. As such, no genuine issue of material fact exists as to whether the sexual harassment was not unwelcome either in fact or law.[55]

The district court clearly equated voluntariness or acquiescence with legal consent. Because Doe did not resist or otherwise indicate that the conduct was unwelcome, the court dismissed her sexual harassment case against Oberweis Dairy. This result was wrong for a variety of reasons, in addition to the problematic treatment of voluntariness, later recognized on appeal.

The appellate court reversed.[56] It found that while Nayman had not committed forcible rape, he had committed "statutory rape,"[57] "which is made a crime because of a belief that below a certain age a person cannot (more realistically, is unlikely to be able to) make a responsible decision about whether to have sex."[58] The *Oberweis* federal appellate court emphasized the age disparity between Nayman and Doe. It explained, "In Illinois as elsewhere the crime is considered more serious the greater the disparity in ages between the parties. The theory is that a young girl (or boy) is likely to have particular difficulty resisting the blandishments of a much older man."[59] Note how this recognition of juvenile limitation resembles the incapacity defense contemplated in the *Restatement (Second) of Contracts* § 15 discussed above.

Because of the belief that minors may not make responsible decisions about sex, the *Oberweis* appellate court devised a plan for dealing with adolescent "consent" to sex under Title VII. The court held that litigants should look to the "age of consent" set under state law to determine whether the plaintiff's "consent" will have legal significance under Title VII.[60] The court explained:

> To avoid undermining valid state policy by reclassifying sex that the state deems nonconsensual as consensual . . . and to avoid intractable inquiries into maturity that legislatures invariably pretermit by basing entitlements to public benefits (right to vote, right to drive, right to drink, right to own a gun, etc.) on specified ages rather than on a standard of "maturity," federal courts, rather than deciding whether a particular Title VII minor plaintiff was capable of "welcoming" the sexual advances of an older man, should defer to the judgment of average maturity in sexual matters that is reflected in the age of consent in the state in which the plaintiff is employed. That age of consent should thus be the rule of decision in Title VII cases.[61]

In this passage, the *Oberweis* appellate court also referred to the need to avoid maturity evaluations. A serious problem with this plan becomes obvious immediately, though. For states, such as California, with no "age of consent," adolescent "consent" garners legal significance, whether or not the minor has legal capacity in the criminal context.

The *Oberweis* appellate court acknowledged that its approach would necessarily mean that "the protection that Title VII gives teenage employees will not be uniform throughout the country, since the age of consent is different in different states, though within a fairly narrow band."[62] This federal appellate court clearly did not know in 2006, however, that only a few months earlier in California, the *Donaldson* state district court had declared the end of the "age of consent" in California civil cases.

Thus, the Seventh Circuit court offered the nation a logical, if imperfect, formula for responding to adolescent "consent" in sexual harassment and sexual abuse cases. Conceivably, this standard produces different results in the case of the seduction of a sixteen-year-old Starbucks barista (or, for example, a Burger King cashier) depending on where she lives. In Indiana, where the age of consent is sixteen, she loses her Title VII sexual harassment case.[63] In Illinois and Wisconsin, where the ages of consent are seventeen and eighteen, respectively,[64] she may get beyond the summary judgment phase. Within the Seventh Circuit, McDonald's and other employers of teenagers navigate three different ages of consent. A random age demarcation alone does not make logical or legal sense. Moreover, this Seventh Circuit formula provides no clear guidance in states where criminal and civil law conflict in the way they treat adolescent non-resistance or "consent."

III. National Treatment of Adolescent "Consent"

As noted earlier, the controversy involving the legal significance of adolescent "consent" exists across the nation. California and Illinois serve as just two examples of how different courts within those respective states treat adolescent non-resistance or acquiescence to sex. In 2004, I reviewed the conflicting laws across the United States and evaluated what chance a sixteen-year-old, such as *Starbucks*'s Doe, might have in pursuing a sexual harassment or other related tort case. At that time, I concluded that the answer depended on where she consented and filed suit. The claims she brought would also influence the outcome. In the then twenty-four states that set the age of consent at sixteen or lower, she had almost no chance for success under antidiscrimination law or tort law. That number increased to thirty-five if certain courts rejected or ignored the alleged special aggravating facts of her case.[65] Those states would treat her as an adult, and her consent would bar most claims. Even a successful statutory rape prosecution against the perpetrator might not assist her in states like Wisconsin, Tennessee, Louisiana, and California, where civil legal precedent muddied the proverbial legal waters.[66]

My 2004 analysis and this summary review of developments in California and Illinois highlight the inconsistencies and problems for "consenting" minors across the United States. Now that California has rejected the proffered *Oberweis* plan in favor of the *Tobias* dictum, one can anticipate that more courts will grant summary judgment for employers like Starbucks against acquiescing or cooperative teenagers.

So where does this discussion of legislative intent and case law interpretation leave us? Are the inconsistencies problematic and why do they persist? What can we say about the current state of the law in California and the prospects for the nation?

Inconsistent Results

Inconsistent treatments do not always result in illogical results. For example, we can understand that a criminal jury might acquit O. J. Simpson of the murder of his wife and that a civil jury might find him liable. Those outcomes are inconsistent, but they are not illogical. The burden of proof for criminal conviction, proof "beyond a reasonable doubt," is much more rigorous than that for civil liability, proof by "a preponderance of the evidence."[67] The O. J. criminal trial jury apparently did not have enough evidence to convict on the higher standard. If the burdens are stricter in a criminal case, however, the adult respondent who engages in sexual intercourse with a teenager should more likely face liability in civil court. Since 2001, that outcome does not necessarily follow in California if the teenager "consented." Now California's criminal laws function much more restrictively than do the civil laws regarding the same episode. One wonders whether there is any other area of law in which civil liability attaches much less readily than criminal guilt. And, if not, one wonders why.

Conflicts Stemming from Misguided Confusion

One might suggest that this problem is a simple one of misguided interpretation and confusion. *Starbucks* relied on dictum from the *Tobias* California Supreme Court case that was arguably internally inconsistent in its treatment of sex crimes against minors. The *Tobias* court was not reviewing *Penal Code* § 261.5 or a civil sexual harassment claim. When it announced that minors might consent to sexual intercourse in 2001, the *Tobias* majority set California civil and criminal law completely at odds. Either the California legislature or the California Supreme Court can respond and ameliorate this resulting situation. However, more than ten years later, neither has moved to do so. As the body of legal precedent grows, scholars will find it less plausible to attribute the resulting conflicts between civil and criminal law to continuing confusion or misunderstanding.[68] One possible explanation for the apparent conflict rests with bias against sexually active teenagers, especially teenage girls and boys who have sex with men.

Teenagers on "Trial"

The *Starbucks* case settled shortly before trial.[69] However, had it not settled, Doe would have faced a trial of her maturity and "consent" under the "unwelcomeness" standard of the California fair employment practice statute. As a minor plaintiff, *she* would have gone "on trial" despite the fact that her adult consort was prosecuted under the applicable state sex crime law. How can one predict such a dire outcome? Compare *Doe by Roe v. Orangeburg County School District*.[70] In that case, a sixteen-year-old mentally handicapped student allegedly raped a fourteen-year-old girl after the coach left them alone in the school gym. The plaintiff, through her parents—since juveniles do not have capacity to sue in court—sued the school district and the coach.[71] The *Orangeburg* court relied on *Barnes v. Barnes*,[72] a challenge to the Indiana Rape Shield Statute.[73] *Orangeburg* ruled to admit evidence of Doe's "consent" at the damages phase of trial, if not at the liability phase.

Quoting *Barnes*, the *Orangeburg* court reasoned:

> Unlike the victim in a criminal case, the plaintiff in a civil damage action is 'on trial' in the sense that he or she is an actual party seeking affirmative relief from another party. Such plaintiff is a voluntary participant, with strong financial incentive to shape the evidence that determines the outcome. It is antithetical to principles of fair trial that one party may seek recovery from another based on evidence it selects while precluding opposing relevant evidence on grounds of prejudice.[74]

This passage highlights the court's focus on fairness. The court ignored, however, that prejudice regularly justifies the exclusion of probative evidence.[75] Additionally, the court missed the point of exclusion. The main reason for excluding the consent was not the prejudice potentially created but, rather, the minor's incapacity that rendered the consent legally invalid. Moreover, it was not the minor who sued in this case but her adult guardian. This court did not even hesitate to put the consenting minor "on trial," at least during the damages phase. Did anyone question the motivations of the suing parents?

No matter what might have resulted had the *Starbucks* case gone to trial, other teenagers (and their prosecuting parents) should anticipate that defense lawyers will find the *Starbucks* summary judgment opinion and use it to defeat sexual harassment and other civil rights and tort cases across the nation.

Judges are already using this recent precedent outside of the employment context. For example, a new California Title IX case foreshadows future issues for teenagers across the nation. Title IX of the Education Amendments of 1972 prohibits discrimination in educational institutions.[76] In *Doe v. Willits Unified School District*,[77] the magistrate judge ruled on a defense motion regarding discovery of the fifteen-year-old student's sexual history, sexual conduct with her thirty-eight-year-old teacher, and her "consent." Following a sexual liaison with her teacher, Clint Smith, Doe had alleged a Title IX claim and various tort claims against him, the school district, and her principal. During Doe's deposition, suspended because of discovery conflicts, defense counsel pursued questions concerning Doe's sexual history and other topics. The court denied discovery regarding Doe's sexual history[78] but granted limited discovery regarding whether she "welcomed" or "consented" to Smith's sexual overtures.

In making its ruling, the *Willits* court acknowledged that other circuits had explored whether the "unwelcomeness requirement" is appropriately part of a prima facie case involving the sexual harassment of a minor at school. The court relied particularly on two cases. In *Mary M. v. North Lawrence Community Sch. Corp.*, the Indiana federal court agreed that a thirteen-year-old student could not "welcome" the sexual advances of a twenty-one-year-old school employee. The Seventh Circuit court found that, if "children cannot be said to consent to sex in a criminal context, they similarly cannot be said to welcome it in a civil context. To find otherwise would be incongruous."[79] In *Chancellor v. Pottsgrove Sch. Dist.*, the Pennsylvania district court held that despite a high school senior's voluntary and willing participation in sexual relations with a teacher, the student could not "welcome" the teacher's sexual advances. The court reasoned, "Plaintiff did not have the legal capacity to welcome Oakes' sexual advances."[80] Finding that consent has not been relevant in jurisdictions outside the Ninth Circuit, the *Willits* court explained, "The common theme of *Mary M.* and *Chancellor* is that consent or welcomeness should not be conflated with capacity to consent, and that where capacity is absent, any evidence of consent or welcomeness is irrelevant as a matter of law." [81]

This analysis confirms that the *Willits* court well understood the complexity of the issue. *Willits* explicitly distinguishes "voluntary and willing participation" noted in *Chancellor* and capacity to consent that can produce true, legally significant consent. In *Willits*, the court seemed inclined to adopt the reasoning of sister courts regarding capacity to consent and adolescent "consent" to sex with an adult teacher.

In footnote 4 following this analysis, however, the *Willits* court explained that "California case law is unsettled on this point [regarding the relevance of 'consent']." The court cited both *Tobias* and *Donaldson*. The court then ruled on the discovery of *Willits* Doe's "consent:"

> To the extent that cases squarely have addressed the question of whether "consent" or "welcomeness" is an element of a Title IX claim, the answer has been a resolute "no." However, because the law in this circuit is unsettled, and because this Court does not wish to prematurely define the elements of the causes of action in this case (a question more properly addressed by the trial judge), this Court will allow limited questions on the issue of whether plaintiff welcomed or consented to her sexual encounters with Smith.[82]

This compromise and the footnote acknowledgment of the *Tobias* dictum, later adopted in *Donaldson*, virtually guaranteed that *Willits* Doe would face humiliating and perhaps traumatizing questions by defense counsel at her deposition's resumption. Defense counsel would have focused on whether *Doe* set limits with her thirty-eight-year-old teacher and thus would have cast Doe as the "responsible" actor. Ignoring the impact on *Willits* Doe, one can anticipate the chilling effects of this case on other teenagers who might report inappropriate sexual advances by teachers and on their parents who might consider prosecuting such cases on behalf of their teenagers.

With the exception of *Oberweis*, these decisions arguably assume that the teenaged plaintiffs are fully "capable of appreciating the nature, extent or probable consequences of the conduct" *and* conforming their behavior in an adult-like fashion to meet the demands of the particular situation. They beg the question, however, of whether teenagers *really do* think and function like adults. An understanding of adolescent development informs any evaluation of whether teenagers are capable of making wise choices concerning sexual activity. Simply put, do teenagers have the capacity to opt for and handle sex with a work supervisor such as Tim Horton, a teacher such as Clint Smith, or a brother-in-law such as Robert Donaldson?

IV. Adolescent Neurological, Cognitive, and Psychosocial Development

When children reach eight to fourteen years of age, they enter puberty.[83] Adolescents experience physical, cognitive, sexual, and psychosocial development during this long maturation phase.[84] The survey of changes discussed below indicates that transitional adolescent functioning differs significantly from adult behavior.

Neurological Development

Evidence released in 1999 by the National Institute of Mental Health (and, thus, available to courts since then) suggests that the adolescent brain undergoes dramatic changes.[85] Dr. Jay Giedd, a neuroscientist at the National Institute of Mental Health, examined adolescent brains using advanced imaging technology.[86] He discovered nearly a doubling of gray matter in some brain sectors within a year.[87] The gray matter consists of cells and neuron connections—synapses—that enable high cognitive functioning.[88] Depending upon the brain sector, non-linear increases in gray matter peak between ages eleven and sixteen for girls and about a year later, respectively, for boys. Following the growth period, the body purges connections not used and reorganizes the functioning of the brain. Previously, scientists had known that such growth and reorganization phases occur during gestation and the first eighteen months after birth. They did not know about this second wave of overproduction and winnowing that occurs throughout puberty.[89]

The dramatic changes that occur during puberty may also influence adolescent reasoning and the ability to formulate consent because of the functions of the particular areas of the brain involved.[90] Neuroscientist

Dr. Elizabeth Sowell and her colleagues explain that "[n]europsychological studies show that the frontal lobes are essential for such functions as response inhibition, emotional regulation, planning and organization. Many of these aptitudes continue to develop between adolescence and young adulthood."[91] The more mature the frontal cortex, "the area of sober second thought," the better teenagers can reason, control their impulses, and make considered judgments. "Thus, there is fairly widespread agreement that adolescents take more risks at least partly because they have an immature frontal cortex, because this is the area of the brain that takes a second look at something and reasons about a particular behavior."[92]

Other areas of the brain also influence teen judgment and behavior. Similar to the frontal cortex, the cerebellum matures well into adolescence.[93] Giedd believes that the cerebellum enhances functioning in all forms of higher thought, from mathematics, to decision making, to social skill.[94] The corpus callosum connects the two hemispheres of the brain and appears to influence creativity and problem solving.[95] A primitive area of the brain, the amygdala, likely governs emotional and "gut" responses during adolescence. While adults rely primarily on the frontal cortex when interpreting emotional information, adolescents tend to use the amygdala.[96] Scientists hypothesize that the use of the amygdala rather than the frontal cortex explains why teenagers experience trouble regulating their emotional responses.[97]

The pruning and organization of the new neural connections in the brain continue throughout the teen years. Giedd asserts that "[m]aturation does not stop at age 10, but continues into the teen years and even the 20s."[98] One might think that more gray matter means higher functioning. Not so, says Giedd. "Bigger isn't necessarily better, or else the peak in brain function would occur at age 11 or 12. . . . The advances come from actually taking away and pruning down of certain connections themselves."[99] Drawing conclusions from the research, some scientists suggest that the pruning occurs on a "'use it or lose it' principle," such that used connections survive.[100] Unused connections "wither and die."[101] "If a teen is doing music or sports or academics, those are the cells and connections that will be hardwired. If they're lying on the couch or playing videogames or MTV, those are the cells and connections that are going to survive."[102]

During the gray matter pruning phase, white matter increases. The white matter supports neural connections in the brain.[103] "A layer of insulation called myelin progressively envelops these nerve fibers, making them more efficient, just like insulation on electric wires improves their conductivity."[104] According to Dr. Francine Benes, myelination levels increase into the early twenties. "During child development, myelination correlates with maturing patterns of behavior."[105]

This new research confirms that adolescent brain development extends into the twenties, beyond "the age of consent" set in every state. Thus critical abilities—including impulse control, emotional regulation, planning, decision making, and organization—may not fully mature until the third decade of life. Additionally, behaviors and experiences may determine the winnowing and reorganization of gray matter during adolescence. It is possible that teenagers subtly hard-wire experiences, such as algebra homework or sex in the Starbucks parking lot, into their brains.

Cognitive Development

In association with the physical changes in the brain, adolescents mature cognitively. Cognitive changes include the development of advanced reasoning and thinking skills.[106] Adolescents also develop *meta-cognition*, the ability to understand why they think and feel the way they do.[107] Dr. Kurt Fischer explains that adolescent cognitive and emotional capabilities continue to transition into early adulthood:

> At 9 to 10 years children become able to construct flexible abstract concepts, such as conformity, responsibility, and the operation of multiplication; but when they try to relate two abstractions to each other, they muddle them together. At about age 15 they can build flexible relations between a pair of abstractions and thus stop muddling them so badly. At age 19 or 20 they can build complex relations among multiple abstractions, and at 25 they can connect systems of abstractions to understand principles underlying them. Each of these developments involves the capacity to build a new kind of understanding, but that capacity is evident only in areas where young people work to construct their understanding—the new abilities do not appear in all skills but only in those where the individual demonstrates optimal performance.[108]

This passage leads to the conclusion that adolescents practice and learn cognition, at least in part, once they become developmentally capable. This information, combined with the research on hard-wiring, suggests that we should not shelter teens from experimentation and gradual learning regarding sexuality, workplace relationships, and other concrete skills and abstract issues. Instead, we should facilitate their learning and maturation under circumstances that safeguard their developmental vulnerabilities. Thus, attributing full capacity to minors may not safeguard them, just as insulating them from all experimentation could stunt their development.

Research from the 1980s suggested that adolescent cognitive development enabled youth to make hypothetical decisions comparable to adults.[109] The recent increase in the number of adolescents tried in criminal court as adults prompted researchers to revisit the issue of adolescent competence. The MacArthur Juvenile Adjudicative Competence Study investigated whether adolescents are competent, intellectually and emotionally, to stand trial in adult criminal court.[110] Dr. Laurence Steinberg reported, "Our findings indicate that significant numbers of juveniles who are 15 and younger are probably not competent to stand trial as adults."[111] "[Y]ounger individuals were less likely to recognize the risks inherent in different choices and less likely to think about the long-term consequences of their choices."[112] This last finding supports the neuroscience evidence regarding maturity in those brain sectors responsible for inhibition and decision making. The performance of sixteen- and seventeen-year-olds did not differ from the adults.[113]

In 2009, however, Fischer and his colleagues emphasized that adolescent cognitive development does not cease at sixteen. They argued that "[m]ore complex skills such as reflective judgment, logical reasoning, and even working memory for sophisticated concepts . . . do not plateau in the teenage years."[114] Additionally, these skills vary dynamically across contexts. Factors such as stress, novelty, and self-organization drive variations. Fischer explained, for example, that

> [r]easoning about abortion, where a doctor or health-care worker can support the teen's thinking over a length of time, is very different from acting violently in the heat of the moment. Teenagers' capabilities are tied to contexts and emotional states. Teenagers are not simply cognitively

mature and psychosocially immature. Context is radically implicated in the nature of capabilities. . . . Depending on context and support, the same individual can function in drastically different ways, and there is not one condition that represents the true capacity.[115]

This passage highlights, as psychologists have determined, that emotional states and other factors influence cognitive capability. Moreover, cognitive ability is not the only trait useful for effective function and decision making. Other traits come into play.

Psychosocial Development

Evidence of psychosocial maturation supports the notion that adolescents experience significant changes not only during their teenaged years but also into their early twenties and beyond. Adolescents explore at least five psychosocial avenues during their maturation: individual identity, autonomy, interpersonal intimacy, sexuality, and personal achievement.[116] They may not work on these issues consciously. Over time, they adopt the attitudes, values, and behaviors of others as they identify what feels comfortable for them.[117]

Characteristics common in teenagers identify the transition to adulthood. We know, for example, that adolescents take more and greater risks than do adults.[118] Neither a lack of information nor cognitive capacity explains their risk-taking tendency. Studies have demonstrated that increasing knowledge does not necessarily lead people to make better decisions.[119] Other studies suggest that adolescents hold different priorities than do adults. First, teens "view long-term consequences as less important than short-term consequences."[120] Second, they demonstrate a preference for sensation seeking. Third, they are preoccupied with their own social status.[121] Given these priorities, one can see how sex with an adult coworker might seem like a good idea. De-emphasizing the long-term career, reputation, and health risks, a teen might choose an exciting sexual relationship and the concomitant status increase with an older, more "sophisticated" man offering such a prize.

In theorizing about traits other than cognition that operate in mature decision making, Dr. Elizabeth Cauffman and Dr. Laurence Steinberg explained what they called *maturity of judgment*. They proposed that mature judgment comprises three core features:

(1) responsibility, which includes healthy autonomy, self-reliance, and clarity of identity;
(2) perspective, or the ability to acknowledge the complexity of a situation and see it as part of a broader context; and
(3) temperance, which refers to the ability to limit impulsive and emotional decision-making, to evaluate situations thoroughly before acting (which may involve seeking the advice of others when appropriate), and to avoid decision-making extremes.[122]

These three core components deserve greater discussion since they may influence a decision to "consent." Cauffman and Steinberg caution that "[a]dolescents who demonstrate that they meet the criteria for informed [medical] consent may nevertheless lack the psychosocial maturity required to make consistently mature judgments."[123]

Responsibility

With respect to the development of responsibility, Cauffman and Steinberg described three foci: autonomy, identity differentiation, and ego development. They noted that adolescents are most susceptible to peer influence at about age fourteen, after which that influence declines. Studies, however, indicate that a coherent sense of identity does not emerge until about age eighteen. Ego development or individuation, according to some studies, increases throughout adolescent years.

As teens individuate, other people exert influences that affect various aspects of adolescent life. For example, parents influence adolescents in matters of religion and career choice, whereas peers sway choices regarding daily concerns such as clothing and music preferences.[124] Cauffman and Steinberg suggested that "adolescents' display of independence—and hence, maturity of judgment—may be highly situation-specific, with youngsters being influenced more on some topics than others, and by different sources of influence to differing degrees, depending on the decision in question."[125]

Because little research has been done correlating responsibility development, various specific ages, and maturity of judgment, psychologists hesitate to draw any conclusions for the practical application of what they do know.[126] This new information, however, raises several important questions for our purposes. For example, who influences an adolescent's decision to have sex with her supervisor? A parent? Her peers? Only the boss? Moreover, if she has not formed a coherent, independent identity, should we consider her "consent" to sex with an adult coworker legally significant?

Temperance

Several factors contribute to personal temperance. Preliminary studies of childhood impulsivity suggest that it remains relatively stable until age sixteen, when it increases, and then again stabilizes at age nineteen. Impulsivity declines during adulthood. More investigation is needed regarding the relation between impulsivity, sensation seeking, and judgmental maturity. Stress and mood state also influence temperate decision making. Studies indicate that older teenagers exhibit greater mood volatility than do adults.[127] Again, more investigation is needed to correlate these factors with maturity of judgment. If we can, however, say that adolescents are more impulsive and moody, we can anticipate another issue. Do adolescent impulsivity and moodiness combine with stress (on-the-job pressure for sex) to influence a teen's decision-making process? Should the law regard teen "consent," given impulsively and under stress, as significant and legally binding?

Perspective

A third trait, perspective, allows someone to frame a decision in context, taking a broader view that would include potential consequences, effect on other people, and the "cost-benefit calculus." Teens demonstrate improvement in abstract and less egocentric thinking until about age seventeen or eighteen.[128] Fischer and others might argue that improvement extends even longer. Research suggests that development of future-time orientation "continues beyond mid-adolescence, at least through the last year of college."[129] Cauffman and Steinberg could not draw firm conclusions regarding perspective and maturity of judgment owing to insufficient correlative research.[130] If there is a correlation, however, one might reasonably conclude that an inability to see "the big picture" could influence a teen's decision to have sex with an adult coworker.

Adolescent Capacity and Physical Appearance

The research regarding adolescent neurological, cognitive, and psychosocial development is relatively new and ongoing. We cannot draw many firm conclusions about physical changes and behavior. Nor do we fully understand the subtle dynamics of behavior, emotions, environment, and physiology. Does any of this really matter, though? Assume for a moment that adolescent "consent" should not be legally binding because adolescents do not have the power, (equal) status, and/or competence to consent to sex with an adult coworker. Will jurists account for adolescent developing capacity, status, and power in their allocation of rights and liabilities?

Donald Kramer and Jennifer Soper suggest that, while many people claim to base the attribution of rights on competency, they often judge competency and assign rights based on physical appearance.[131] Thus, society treats the children who look physically mature as adults, regardless of whether those adolescents are emotionally, neurologically, and psychosocially mature. For an example of this phenomenon, examine the statutory rape defenses. Under this criminal scheme, a minor lacks capacity even if she "consents," so her "consent" is no defense. Her physical maturity, however, might constitute one. In California, the perpetrator's mistake of age, particularly of older victims—arguably based on physical maturity—constitutes a defense.[132]

Even if firm conclusions cannot yet be made regarding adolescent "developing capacity" and judgmental maturity, we should at least avoid confusing physical maturity with neurological and psychosocial maturity as we assign legal rights and duties. Neither the blooming of the adult body or its withering with disease or old age necessarily equates with mental maturity or acuity.

V. Science and the Law

A brief review of adolescent development permits us to come back to the law's treatment of adolescents with a fresh perspective. At the very least, we can begin to evaluate whether the law takes us in the right direction.

The "Rule of Sevens" and the Restatements

Current law, embodied in the "rule of sevens,"[133] explicitly posits the capacity in most teenagers to consent. Under this traditional rule, a minor under age seven cannot give consent, be held liable for negligent conduct, or formulate the requisite mental state to engage in criminal conduct. From seven to fourteen, the law presumes that a minor lacks capacity. From fourteen to twenty-one (now eighteen), a rebuttable presumption declares that minors are competent to consent and responsible for criminal and negligent conduct.[134] Thus, in the context of a civil claim for damages and absent evidence to the contrary, this bright-line rule allows a trier-of-fact to presume that a child over fourteen consents to sexual contact. The science does not support the presumption of capacity for most teenagers consenting to sex with an adult.

Additionally, what the neuroscientists and psychologists have said regarding capacity informs this issue. For example, the *Restatement (Second) of Torts* § 892A cmt. 2(b) explains, "If the person consenting is a child or one of deficient mental capacity, the consent may still be effective if he is capable of appreciating the nature, extent and probable consequences of the conduct consented to." Dr. Abigail Baird, who specializes in adolescent neurological development, suggests that "it may be physically impossible for adolescents to engage in counterfactual reasoning and as a result of this are often unable to effectively foresee the possible consequences of their actions."[135]

As discussed, the *Restatement (Second) of Contracts* § 15 addresses volitional incapacity, suggesting that some incapacitated persons who cannot conform their behavior to societal norms may void their contracts. Dr. Silvia Bunge has compared the prefrontal cortex of children with those adults suffering from injuries who take more risks than do healthy adults. She has determined that children make riskier choices than adults, in part because they enjoy doing so. She tied these choices to activity in the prefrontal cortex. Bunge suggests that teens are less able to resist the temptation of a new reward. She explains, "If your friend says, 'Hey let's try this drug; it will be fun,' you might not be able to use the information you know about the possible negative consequences to resist."[136]

These examples of the law side by side with the science suggest that we need to pay serious attention to traditional legal presumptions about adolescents and consider incorporating more about what is now known concerning adolescent development. A few federal and state courts are doing just that.

Science and the U.S. Supreme Court Precedence

Even the U.S. Supreme Court has noticed the importance of the new science of adolescent development. The Supreme Court's recent *Graham v. Florida* opinion, which relied on amici briefing regarding adolescent neurological and psychosocial development, provides valuable guidance relevant to adolescent maturity, "consent," and legal capacity.[137] The *Graham* decision holds that a life sentence without the possibility of parole for particular juvenile offenders violates the Eighth Amendment protection against cruel and unusual punishment.[138] This decision also reaffirms evidence regarding adolescent neurological and psychosocial development, discussed in *Roper v. Simmons*[139] which invalidated the death penalty for minors. The *Graham* Court noted that "developments in psychology and brain science continue to show fundamental differences between juvenile and adult minds. For example, parts of the brain involved in behavior control continue to mature through late adolescence."[140]

The *Graham* Court found that society might still hold a teenager responsible for his behavior but that "his transgression 'is not as morally reprehensible as that of an adult.'"[141] This distinction between responsibility and moral culpability is important. If a toddler knocks over a vase while stumbling to a table, we might find him responsible but not morally culpable because he did not intend to break the vase and lacked the motor coordination to control his steps and body. Extend this example to a teenager who may be technically "responsible" for saying "yes" to sex but who cannot fully anticipate the consequences of her conduct and may lack the psychosocial skills to control her behavior in context. Remember that this same teenager "consents" not in a vacuum but with an adult who solicits, encourages, or at least abets her behavior. But for the adult's conduct, this adolescent would not have had the opportunity to "consent."

The *Graham* Court highlighted several developmental factors that might influence our decision to spare adolescents from *legal* responsibility for their behavior, even as we recognize their *personal* responsibility. The Court affirmed, "As compared to adults, juveniles have a 'lack of maturity and an underdeveloped sense of responsibility;' they 'are more vulnerable or susceptible to negative influences and outside pressures, including peer pressure;' and their characters are 'not as well formed.'"[142] The Court also noted "juveniles' 'lack of maturity and underdeveloped sense of responsibility . . . often result in impetuous and ill-considered actions and decisions.'"[143]

The *Graham* Court recognized that even a psychological evaluation of a given adolescent, of the type necessitated by the *Tobias* dictum, might not yield enough information for jurists to make critical legal determinations about a youth. The Court stated that "even expert psychologists" might find it difficult to differentiate between adolescent conduct that results from "transient immaturity" and that which reflects "irreparable corruption."[144] This finding suggests that a case-by-case determination of adolescent maturity in a criminal or civil case might produce unsatisfactory or flawed results concerning the capacity of a teenager to control his behavior or consent to sex.

Recent Supreme Court focus on adolescent neurological and psychosocial development and the differences between adolescent and adult conduct emphasizes the need to consider these differences as well as adolescent capacity in contexts other than criminal trials. We need to explore further whether adolescent development and psychosocial maturity should also guide the development of civil law and particularly the law regarding "the age of consent."

VI. Civil Law's Treatment of "Consent"

The neuroscience and psychosocial studies regarding adolescent development continue. Society can expect to hear impressive new revelations in the coming years. Our teenagers cannot wait, however, if waiting means a continuation of the legal status quo.[145] Even if we cannot draw robust causal connections between the neuroscience and behavior, we can evaluate whether the law is at least congruent with what we know about adolescent development. This chapter suggests that it is not and that, as a society, we can do better for our teenagers. The question remains: How do we adapt the law regarding adolescent "consent" to match their developmental capabilities and needs—at least until we know more?

Create a National "Age of Consent"

One proposal for dealing with adolescent "consent" involves nationally synchronizing the "age of consent" with the age of majority at eighteen.[146] We deny juvenile legal capacity until eighteen. We do so even though some minors demonstrate sufficient maturity that might justify legal capacity before that age. Several reasons support this move. First, a bright line in a logical place promotes efficient administration. While we might disagree about where to draw the line (at sixteen, eighteen, or twenty-one), few will dispute that rules are easier to enforce than maturity evaluations are to conduct.

Second, anything but a consistent bright line might lead to a maturity evaluation that puts a minor "on trial." Anticipation of such a trial might cause many minors not to complain later about coercive and exploitative conduct to which they "consented" initially. Third, maturity evaluations—by law-school-trained jurists, untrained jurors, and even well-trained psychologists—are inherently risky. No foolproof maturity test exists, or every department of motor vehicles would use it before issuing a driver's license to a teenager. As noted above, *Graham* confirmed that psychological evaluations to link behavior and maturity might not produce robust results. Additionally, a psychologist, who swears that a minor is mature on the test date, cannot be certain that she was mature months before, on the day she "consented."

Fourth, many adults would rather err on the side of protecting all of our teenagers, even the relatively mature ones, than risk traumatizing or sacrificing the immature ones. The point of the law is to protect those persons who need the protection the most, not to sacrifice those youth because we are concerned about protecting a few mature teenagers who do not really need protection.

I join those people who disfavor this approach, however, because our children need maturing experiences. By setting the "age of consent" at a particular age, we deny younger teenagers many of the experiences that will lead to their neurological and psychosocial development. We also deny them important rights to which they are entitled and which they may need, such as the right to procreate, or not. If we infantilize them until they are eighteen, we may harm the very teenagers we would hope to protect.

Eliminate the "Age of Consent"

While one might craft a variety of solutions to address this concern that adolescent "consent" is different from adult consent, some responses seem patently irrational. The *Tobias* dictum that eliminates the age of consent in the context of civil liability creates more problems than it solves and appears inconsistent with what we know from the expert scientists regarding adolescent development and psychosocial maturity. This chapter's brief review of conflicting laws and U.S. Supreme Court acceptance of the developmental differences between adults and teenagers suggests that the elimination of the "age of the consent" places teenagers at risk—of sexual predation, at least.

Create New Multifactor Standards for Legal Consent

Another approach involves a tripartite or multifaceted scheme.[147] Society might use particular age requirements in certain contexts or for particular privileges, such as smoking or gaming, as the law does now. The law might set higher age requirements tied to objective criteria. Objective considerations might include (1) whether juveniles have less familiarity with the activity, (2) whether power imbalances exist, and (3) whether more serious consequences (than, for example, a financial loss on a lottery ticket) might result for a teenager. Finally, "there may be some contexts in which a focus on the age of consent is more a distraction than anything else." Particularly, "where there really is no discernible disparity in power, or any sense of subtle coercion that can be detected," we might eliminate age requirements.[148]

The risk of mandated maturity evaluations still poses a problem under this tripartite approach. As the *Doe* cases demonstrate, when jurists set fixed age barriers, exceptions occur. As noted, we cannot yet provide convincing results regarding adolescent maturity, and evaluator bias can skew results of such psychosocial evaluations. I worry that lawmakers will eliminate age-of-consent requirements inappropriately, as I argue was done in *Tobias*. However, I agree that legal liability for Romeo and Juliet (or Romeo and Romeo) makes no sense, and I have suggested as much previously.[149]

Not all adolescent "consent" requires formal legal analysis. When a six-year-old steals a kiss from a classmate, the children need adult supervision and age-appropriate parenting guidance, not legal intervention.[150] Arguably, Romeo and Juliet need similar and age-appropriate adult supervision and parenting guidance. By relying on responsible parenting and other informal strategies (such as peer counseling, mentoring by qualified youth leaders, teachers, and coaches), one can sidestep formal legal intervention to avoid the misplaced application of legal rules regarding the "age of consent."

The wholesale elimination of those rules does more harm than good, however. In California and across the nation, legal reform must occur to remedy haphazard and misguided treatment of adolescent "consent" when power imbalances, adult-teen sexual predation, and more serious forms of youth exploitation put adolescents at risk of injury and trauma.

Legal Assent

Rather than eliminate default guidance or attempt to implement myriad separate rules for the regulation of adolescent activities and "consent," society might give adolescent "consent" legal significance when it is in a minor's best interests to do so. To that end, I recommend a concept I call *legal assent*. Unlike medical assent, it requires no associated parental consent or permission. Unlike legal consent, it carries no associated threshold level of legal capacity. Similar to consent by a minor under contract law, legal assent is voidable by the minor. However, legal assent operates somewhat differently from traditional, voidable contract consent by a minor.

If a minor gives legal assent, that "consent" is legally binding unless the minor voids her assent during her minority or during a reasonable time thereafter. Parents cannot void a minor's assent for her. If she successfully voids her assent, a court cannot even admit it into evidence or permit discovery on the matter. A criminal prosecutor might still prosecute an adult who has sex with an assenting minor, however, because the legal assent operates only for the benefit of the *minor*. Voters, legislators, and district attorneys might still act in *society's* best interests. Additionally, parents still would have the authority to discipline their children—even in the context of an assent that the parents disapproved.

Consider an example. Suppose a minor, Doe, assents to sex with her teacher. The district attorney can prosecute him for statutory rape or, in California, unlawful sex with a minor. A successful case results in a vindication for a society that does not want its teachers having sex with their students. If Doe reaffirms her assent, there is no parallel civil case; the legal controversy ends. Certainly, Doe's parents can act domestically to comfort, guide, or discipline their daughter, as they see fit.

If, however, Doe determines that she was duped, coerced, or made a mistake in assenting, she can void her legal assent and bring (through her guardian) a sexual harassment or tort claim against her teacher to recover for her damages. Arguably, sexual intercourse with her teacher (be he Clint Smith, Tim Horton, or Robert Donaldson) is not in her best interests. The court will affirm her revocation, deny any discovery, and exclude admission of evidence (at any phase of trial) regarding Doe's assent if the school raises it as a civil defense in a Title IX or tort case. Society allows Doe to void her assent and hopes that teachers will take warning and stay away from teenaged girls and boys. Criminal sanctions for adults clearly suggest that particular activities are not in a minor's best interests.

Thus Doe makes the first and second choices: to assent and whether to void her assent. Society permits her the second choice to protect her from the bad choices we anticipate she might make *and to facilitate her own correction of her mistake.* If someone (such as Smith, Horton, or Donaldson) challenges the abrogation, the court evaluation focuses not on the moral purity or maturity of the minor but upon whether the *original* assent was in her best interests. The evaluation focuses on the circumstances, not on the individual minor.

Under this approach, all our Does, including *Orangeburg* Doe, could have voided their assent. The *Orangeburg* court could not have allowed evidence of Doe's assent at a subsequent civil trial unless it first determined that it was in fourteen-year-old Doe's best interests to assent to sex with her sixteen-year-old classmate while the coach was gone. Absent that determination, the court would have had to validate Doe abrogation of assent and allowed Roe to pursue the case without the prejudice of Doe's proffered "consent."

This theory of legal assent is consistent with what is known about adolescent development: teenagers need maturing experiences and the opportunity to practice their skills. They may not have the capacity to make every decision, but this approach permits teenagers to make some and avoid those that they later believe were unwise, foolish, or mistaken.[151]

VII. Conclusions

The existing conflicts between criminal and civil law treatment of adolescent "consent" leave teenagers vulnerable, especially to sexual predators. Court conflation of acquiescence, consent, and capacity highlights the need for legal reform and intervention. The new neuroscientific evidence and studies concerning adolescent cognitive and psychosocial development confirm that adolescents are not the physical or functional equivalents of adults. Teenagers are developing capacity. Scientific studies support the call for legal reform. Until adolescent maturity and capacity can be accurately assessed, there needs to be a way to protect teenagers while affording them some measure of legal autonomy and maturing experiences.

An approach that credits *legal assent* by adolescents empowers teenagers to take responsibility. It also permits them to recover from poor choices by voiding their assent within a reasonable period. We must model the behavior that we wish to see from our older children. Let's take responsibility for their welfare and implement a system that challenges, nurtures, and protects teenagers. Until we act civilly, we can expect rude consequences.

NOTES

1. I use quotations with adolescent "consent" because even explicit verbal agreement by a minor may not constitute legal consent and may equate more realistically with acquiescence. *See* Meritor Sav. Bank v. Vinson, 477 U.S. 57, 68 (1986) (holding that acquiescence is not consent in an evaluation of the unwelcomeness of sexual conduct under Title VII of the 1964 Civil Rights Act, 42 U.S.C. § 2000e (a)(1) (2000)).

2. Doe v. Starbucks, Inc., No. SACV 08-0582 AG (CWx), 2009 WL 5183773, at *2 (C.D. Cal. Dec. 18, 2009) (order granting in part and denying in part motions for summary judgment).

3. *Id.* at *6; Cal. Penal Code § 261.5(a) (West 2010).

4. Jennifer Ann Drobac, *Sex and the Workplace: "Consenting" Adolescents and a Conflict of Laws*, 79 *Wash. L. Rev.* 471, 518–519 (2004) (explaining the term, "developing capacity" and distinguishing it from "diminished capacity," a term used to describe juvenile criminal offenders).

5. *Consent Definition*, Dictionary.com, http://dictionary.reference.com/browse/consent (last visited June 10, 2014).

6. *Assent Definition*, Dictionary.com, http://dictionary.reference.com/browse/assent (last visited June 10, 2014).

7. *Acquiesce Definition*, Dictionary.com, http://dictionary.reference.com/browse/acquiesce (last visited June 10, 2014).

8. *Restatement (Second) of Torts* § 892A(2)(a) (1979).

9. *Id.* at § 892A cmt. B (italics added).

10. *Restatement (Second) of Contracts* § 12(2)(a) (1981).

11. *See, e.g.,* Jones v. Dressel, 623 P.2d 370, 373 (Colo. 1981); *Jeffrey T. Ferriell, Understanding Contracts*, 603–604 (2d ed. 2009).

12. *Restatement (Second) of Contracts* § 15 cmt. b. (italics added).

13. *See, e.g.,* Kathryn Lynn Modecki, *"It's a Rush": Psychosocial Content of Antisocial Decision Making*, 33 *Law & Hum. Behav.* 183 (2009).

14. *See* Elizabeth S. Scott & Laurence Steinberg, *Blaming Youth*, 81 *Tex. L. Rev.* 799, 829–836 (2003).

15. 45 C.F.R. § 46.404 (2005).

16. *Id.* at § 46.408(a) (2005).

17. *Id.* at § 46.408(c) (2005).

18. *See, e.g.,* People v. Hillhouse, 1 Cal.Rptr.3d 261, 268 (Cal. Ct. App. 2003) (explaining that "we would not assume—nor would we infer a legislative presumption—that the average 14 year old in our current society does not possess the intelligence capable of understanding the nature and consequences of a sexual act.").

19. *Starbucks*, 2009 WL 5183773, at *2, *4.

20. 42 U.S.C. § 2000e (2)(a)(1) (2000).

21. Faragher v. City of Boca Raton, 524 U.S. 775, 787 (1998) (citing Harris v. Forklift Sys., Inc., 510 U.S. 17, 21–22 (1993)).

22. *See, e.g., Cal. Gov't Code* § 12940 (West 2011).

23. *Starbucks*, 2009 WL 5183773, at *1–5.

24. *Id.* at *2 (quoting Starbucks' Objections to Plaintiff's Evidence 9:9–10:8, *Starbucks*, 2009 WL 5183773).

25. *Id.* at *1 (quoting Doe Declaration ¶ 4, *Starbucks*, 2009 WL 5183773).

26. *Id.* at *2.

27. *Id.* at *3 (quoting Doe Declaration, *supra* note 25, ¶ 20). Doe and Horton engaged in sexual activities regularly through June 2006. In addition to "'vaginal intercourse and oral copulation'" at work and off-site, "'[t]hey exchanged explicit sexual comments and text messages at work.'" *Id.* at *5 (quoting Plaintiff's Statement of Material Facts (hereinafter "PSMF") ¶¶ 25, 20, *Starbucks*, 2009 WL 5183773).

28. *Id.* at 5.

29. *Id.* at *6 (quoting J.M. Deposition 187: 18–24, *Starbucks*, 2009 WL 5183773).

30. *Id.* at *6 (quoting PSMF, *supra* note 27, ¶ 40).

31. *Id.* at *6 (quoting PSMF, *supra* note 27, ¶ 59).

32. People v. Tobias, 106 Cal.Rptr.2d 80 (Cal. 2001).

33. *Id.* at 333–334 (citations and footnotes shortened or omitted) (italics added).

34. *Starbucks*, 2009 WL 5183773, at *7.

35. Not until 1993 did the California legislature modify section 261.5 to make it gender neutral. Cal. Penal Code § 261.5.

36. *See, e.g.*, People v. Verdegreen, 106 Cal. 211 (1895).

37. *Starbucks*, 2009 WL 5183773, at *7 (citing Donaldson v. Department of Real Estate, 36 Cal.Rptr.3d 577 (Cal. Ct. App. 2005)).

38. *Donaldson*, 36 Cal.Rptr.3d at 583 (quoting *Cal. Code of Regs.*, tit.10, § 2910(a)(5)).

39. *Id.* at 578.

40. *Id.* at 584.

41. *Id.* at 586.

42. *Id.* at n.12.

43. *Id.* at 588.

44. *Id.* at 589 (italics in the original) (citing to Cal. Civ. Code § 49, subd. (b)(West 1939)).

45. *Donaldson*, 36 Cal.Rptr.3d at 589.

46. *See Tobias*, 106 Cal.Rptr.2d at 341–342 (George, C.J., concurring).

47. *See* Michael M. v. Sup. Ct. of Sonoma Co., 450 U.S. 464, 469–470 (1981).

48. *Meritor*, 477 U.S. 57.

49. *Id.* at 68.

50. Doe v. Oberweis Dairy (hereinafter *Oberweis*, 456 F.3d), 456 F.3d 704 (7th Cir. 2006).

51. Doe v. Oberweis Dairy (hereinafter *Oberweis*, 2005 WL 782709), 2005 WL 782709, at *1 (N.D. Ill. Apr. 6, 2005).

52. *See, e.g.*, 720 ILCS 5/12–16 (West 2011) (defining criminal sexual abuse for victims under 17).

53. *Oberweis*, 2005 WL 782709, at *6.

54. E-mail from H. Candace Gorman, Esq., counsel for *Oberweis* Doe in Chicago, IL, to Jennifer Drobac, professor of law, Indiana School of Law–Indianapolis (Apr. 29, 2010) (on file with author).

55. *Oberweis*, 2005 WL 782709, at *6.

56. *Oberweis*, 456 F.3d at 704.

57. The court cited to the Illinois statutory rape law. 720 ILCS 5/12–15(c), 16(d).

58. *Oberweis*, 456 F.3d at 713.

59. *Id.*

60. *Id.*

61. *Id.*

62. *Id.* at 714.

63. *Ind. Code* § 35–42–4–9 (West 2007) (sexual misconduct with a minor, establishing the age of consent at 16).

64. 720 *Ill. Comp. Stat.* 5/12–15 (criminal sexual abuse, establishing the age of consent at seventeen); *Wis. Stat.* § 948.09 (West 2005) (sexual intercourse with a child, establishing the age of consent at 18).

65. Drobac, *Sex and the Workplace, supra* note 4, at 485–486.

66. *Id.* at 538–39.

67. A jury acquitted O. J. Simpson of charges for the murder of his ex-wife, Nicole Brown Simpson, and her friend Ronald Goldman. Following a civil trial for wrongful death and survival statute damages, the jury found Simpson liable by a preponderance of the evidence. *See* Rufo v. Simpson, 103 Cal.Rptr.2d 494 (Cal. Ct. App. 2001) (affirming judgments in wrongful death and survival case brought by family members of Nicole Brown Simpson and Ronald Goldman against O. J. Simpson). This case highlights how differing criminal and civil law burdens can lead to seemingly contradictory results.

68. For a fuller discussion of this issue regarding the age of consent, see Jennifer Ann Drobac, *Wake Up and Smell the* Starbuck's *Coffee: How* Doe v. Starbucks *Confirms the End of "the Age of Consent" in California and Perhaps Beyond* (hereinafter "*Wake Up*"), 33 B.C. J.L. & Soc. Just. 1 (2013), and *A Bee Line in the Wrong Direction: Science, Teenagers, and the Sting to "the Age of Consent,"* 20 J.L. & Pol'y 63 (2012).

69. E-mail from Lisa Bredahl, court clerk to the Honorable Andrew J. Guilford, in Santa Ana, CA, to Jennifer Drobac, professor of law, Indiana School of Law–Indianapolis (Aug. 24, 2010) (on file with author).

70. Doe by Roe v. Orangeburg County Sch. Dist., 518 S.E.2d 259 (S.C. 1999).

71. *Id.*

72. Barnes v. Barnes, 603 N.E.2d 1337 (Ind. 1992).

73. *Id.* at 1342.

74. *Orangeburg*, 518 S.E.2d at 261 (quoting *Barnes*, 603 N.E.2d at 1342).

75. *See Fed. R. Evid.* 403 (directing that "[a]lthough relevant, evidence may be excluded if its probative value is substantially outweighed by the danger of unfair prejudice").

76. 20 U.S.C. § 1681 (2000).

77. Doe v. Willits Unified Sch. Dist., 2010 WL 2524587 (N.D. Cal.).
78. *Id.* at *3 (discussing *Fed. R. Evid.* 412, which protects against admission of evidence regarding a plaintiff's sexual history).
79. Mary M. v. N. Lawrence Cmty. Sch. Corp., 131 F.3d 1220, 1227 (7th Cir.1997).
80. Chancellor v. Pottsgrove Sch. Dist., 501 F.Supp.2d 695, 706 (E.D. Pa. 2007).
81. *Willits*, 2010 WL 2524587, at *4.
82. *Id.* at *5.
83. *HealthyChildren.org, Ages and Stages*, www.healthychildren.org/English/ages-stages/gradeschool/puberty/pages/Whats-Happening-to-my-Body.aspx?nfstatus=401&nftoken=00000000-0000-0000-0000-000000000000&nfstatusdescription=ERROR%3a+No+local+token (last visited June 2, 2011).
84. Novella Ruffin, *Adolescent Growth and Development*, Virginia Cooperative Extension, Family and Child Development Publication 350–850 (2009), www.ext.vt.edu/pubs/family/350-850/350-850.html (last visited June 2, 2011).
85. National Institute of Mental Health (hereinafter NIMH), *Teenage Brain: A Work in Progress*, NIMH Publication No. 01-4929, www.pa-fsa.org/Assets/files/Teenage_Brain.pdf (last visited July 17, 2014).
86. N. Jay Giedd et al., *Brain Development During Childhood and Adolescence: A Longitudinal MRI Study*, 2 Nature Neuroscience 861, 861–863 (Oct. 1999).
87. Paul M. Thompson, Jay N. Giedd, et al., *Growth Patterns in the Developing Brain Detected by Using Continuum Mechanical Tensor Maps*, 404 Nature 190–192 (Mar. 9, 2000).
88. NIMH, *Teenage Brain, supra* note 85; *see also* Judith L. Rapoport, N. Jay Giedd, et al., *Progressive Cortical Change during Adolescence in Childhood-Onset Schizophrenia: A Longitudinal Magnetic Resonance Imaging Study*, 56(7) Archives Gen. Psychiatry 649–654 (1999).
89. Interview with Jay Giedd, *Frontline: Inside the Teenage Brain*, www.pbs.org/wgbh/pages/frontline/shows/teenbrain/interviews/giedd.html (last visited June 2, 2011).
90. *Id.*
91. Elizabeth R. Sowell et al., *In Vivo Evidence for Post-adolescent Brain Maturation in Frontal and Striatal Regions*, 2 Nature Neuroscience 859, 860 (Oct. 1999).
92. Sarah Spinks, *Adolescent Brains Are Works in Progress*, in *Frontline: Inside the Teenage Brain*, www.pbs.org/wgbh/pages/frontline/shows/teenbrain/work/adolescent.html (last visited June 2, 2011) (focusing on Dr. Giedd's research).
93. *Id.*
94. *Id.* (Giedd notes that the cerebellum, "involved in coordination of our cognitive process, our thinking processes," does not finish changing until the twenties. He adds, "[a]nd this ability to smooth out all the different intellectual processes to navigate the complicated social life of the teen . . . seems to be a function of the cerebellum."); Interview with Giedd, *supra* note 89 (Dr. Todd Preuss commented here that Giedd's view on the cerebellum is one not widely held by neuroscientists but one "held by a respected minority.").

95. Spinks, *Adolescent Brains Are Works in Progress, supra* note 92.

96. Sarah Spinks, *One Reason Teens Respond Differently to the World: Immature Brain Circuitry*, in *Frontline: Inside the Teenage Brain*, www.pbs.org/wgbh/pages/frontline/shows/teenbrain/work/onereason.html (last visited June 2, 2011) (discussing Deborah Yurgelun-Todd's study); *see also* Interview with Deborah Yurgelun-Todd, *Frontline: Inside the Teenage Brain*, www.pbs.org/wgbh/pages/frontline/shows/teenbrain/interviews/todd.html (last visited June 2, 2011) (Yurgelun-Todd noted that hers was a very small pilot study. She urged caution in the interpretation of the results.); Abigail A. Baird *et al.*, *Functional Magnetic Resonance Imaging of Facial Affect Recognition in Children and Adolescents*, 38(2) *J. Am. Acad. Child & Adolescent Psychiatry* 195 (Feb. 1999).

97. Sowell et al., *In Vivo Evidence for Post-adolescent Brain Maturation in Frontal and Striatal Regions, supra* note 91, at 860.

98. Sharon Begley, *Getting inside a Teen Brain*, Newsweek, Feb. 28, 2000, www.newsweek.com/getting-inside-teen-brain-162273 (last visited June 10, 2014) (quoting Dr. Jay Giedd).

99. Interview with Giedd, *supra* note 89.

100. Spinks, *Adolescent Brains Are Works in Progress, supra* note 92.

101. Interview with Giedd, *supra* note 89.

102. Spinks, *Adolescent Brains Are Works in Progress, supra* note 92. Dr. Preuss stressed here that these assertions come from the scientists' interpretations, not from empirically demonstrated fact.

103. Adam Ortiz, *Adolescence, Brain Development and Legal Culpability*, Juvenile Justice Center, Jan. 2004, www.americanbar.org/content/dam/aba/publishing/criminal_justice_section_newsletter/crimjust_juvjus_Adolescence.authcheckdam.pdf (last visited June 10, 2014).

104. NIMH, *Teenage Brain, supra* note 85, at 2.

105. *Id.; see also* Elizabeth Gudrais, *Modern Myelination: The Brain at Midlife*, 103 Harv. Mag. 9 (2001), http://harvardmagazine.com/2001/05/the-brain-at-midlife-html (last visited June 10, 2014) (discussing Dr. Francine Benes's research) (Benes further explained, "Infants, for example, lack the fine motor coordination to move an index finger independently, since their nerves are insufficiently myelinated." Benes found that myelination growth increased again in the forties, growing fifty percent again by the mid-fifties.).

106. Ruffin, *Adolescent Growth and Development, supra* note 84; *see also* Laurence Steinberg, *Adolescence* (8th ed. 2007).

107. Ruffin, *Adolescent Growth and Development, supra* note 84.

108. *How Much Do We Really Know about the Brain?* in *Frontline: Inside the Teenage Brain*, www.pbs.org/wgbh/pages/frontline/shows/teenbrain/work/how.html (last visited June 10, 2014) (interviewing Dr. Fischer). Dr. Kurt Fischer of the Harvard Graduate School of Education cautions, "Ultimately neuroscience research will contribute enormously to our knowledge about raising and educating children, but right now we know too little to build public policy or advice on brain findings." *Id.*

109. *See, e.g.*, Melinda Schmidt & N. Dickon Reppucci, *Children's Rights and Capacities*, in *Children, Social Science, and the Law* 76, 96 (Bette L. Bottoms et al. eds. 2002) (discussing Lois A. Weithorn & Susan B. Campbell, *The Competency of Children and Adolescents to Make Informed Treatment Decisions*, 53 Child Dev. 1589–1598 (1982)).

110. The John D. & Catherine T. MacArthur Foundation, *The MacArthur Juvenile Adjudicative Competence Study Summary* (hereinafter MacArthur Foundation, *Competence Study Summary*), www.adjj.org/downloads/58competence_study_summary.pdf (last visited June 2, 2011).

111. Temple University, *Many Kids 15 and Younger May Lack Maturity Necessary to Be Competent to Stand Trial, Juvenile Justice Study Finds* (press release, Mar. 3, 2003).

112. MacArthur Foundation, *Competence Study Summary*, supra note 110, at 2.

113. *Id.*

114. Kurt W. Fischer et al., *Narrow Assessments Misrepresent Development and Misguide Policy*, 64 Am. Psychol. 595, 597 (Oct. 2009).

115. *Id.* at 598.

116. Jennifer L. Woolard, *Capacity, Competence, and the Juvenile Defendant*, in *Children, Social Science, and the Law* 270, 283 (Bottoms et al. eds.), *supra* note 109 (citing Elizabeth S. Scott et al., *Evaluating Adolescent Decision Making in Legal Contexts*, 19 Law & Hum. Behav. 221, 221–244 (1995)).

117. *See* Ruffin, *Adolescent Growth and Development*, supra note 84.

118. *See* Elizabeth Cauffman & Laurence Steinberg, *The Cognitive and Affective Influences on Adolescent Decision-Making*, 68 Temp. L. Rev. 1763, 1767 (1995) (providing examples of adolescents' frequent participation in dangerous activities).

119. *Id.* at 1771–1772.

120. *Id.* at 1773.

121. *Id.*

122. *Id.* at 1764–1765.

123. *Id.* at 1766.

124. *Id.* at 1774–1775.

125. *Id.* at 1775.

126. *Id.* at 1780.

127. *Id.* at 1781–1782.

128. *Id.* at 1783–1785.

129. *Id.* at 1787.

130. *Id.*

131. Jennifer Soper, *Straddling the Line: Adolescent Pregnancy and Questions of Capacity*, 23 Law & Psychol. Rev. 195, 199 (1999).

132. Charles A. Phipps, *Children, Adults, Sex and the Criminal Law: In Search of Reason*, 22 Seton Hall Legis. J. 1, 52 n.219 (1997) (citing People v. Hernandez, 393 P.2d 673 (Cal. 1964)).

133. In the criminal system, this rule is also known as the "infancy defense." *See generally* Martin R. Gardner, *Understanding Juvenile Law* 1880–1881 (1997) (discussing the infancy defense and capacity to commit a crime).

134. *Id.*

135. Abigail Baird & Jonathan Fugelsang, *The Emergence of Consequential Thought: Evidence from Neuroscience*, in *Law and the Brain* 254 (Semir Zeki & Oliver Goodenough eds. 2006).

136. *The Adolescent Brain*, in *Science Today at the University of California*, Nov. 17, 2008; *see also* Rachel Tompa, *This is Your Brain on Adolescence: MRI Studies of Teenage Brain Show Why Kids Act before They Think*, in *UC Berkeley News Web Feature*, Oct. 16, 2008, www.berkeley.edu/news/media/releases/2008/10/16_neurolaw.shtml (last visited July 17, 2014).

137. Graham v. Florida, 130 S.Ct. 2011 (2010).

138. *Id.*

139. Roper v. Simmons, 543 U.S. 551 (2005).

140. *Graham*, 130 S.Ct. at 2026 (citing Brief for American Medical Association *et al.* as *Amici Curiae* (AMA Brief) 16–24, Brief for American Psychological Association *et al.* as *Amici Curiae* (APA Brief) 22–27).

141. *Id.* (quoting Thompson v. Oklahoma, 487 U.S. 815, 835 (1988) (plurality opinion)).

142. *Id.* (quoting Roper v. Simmons, 543 U.S. at 569–570 (quoting Johnson v. Texas 509 U.S. 350, 367(1993))).

143. *Id.* at 2028 (quoting *Johnson*, 509 U.S. at 367).

144. *Id.* at 2029 (quoting *Roper*, 543 U.S. at 572).

145. For a thorough, detailed, and updated discussion of the neurological and psychosocial development of teenagers, *see* Jennifer Ann Drobac, *Worldly but Not Yet Wise: Teen Sexual Exploitation, Adolescent Development, and Consent Law* (Univ. Chi. Press, under contract for 2015); *see also* Jennifer Ann Drobac, *"Developing Capacity": Adolescent "Consent" at Work, at Law and in the Sciences of the Mind*, 10 U.C. Davis J. Juvenile L. & Pol'y 1 (2006); and Jennifer Ann Drobac, *I Can't to I Kant: The Sexual Harassment of Working Adolescents, Competing Theories, and Ethical Dilemmas*, 70 Alb. L. Rev. 675 (2007).

146. All states but four set the age of majority at eighteen. In Alabama and Nebraska, persons reach their majority at nineteen. In Pennsylvania and Mississippi, the age is twenty-one. Heather Boonstra and Elizabeth Nash, *Minors and the Right to Consent to Health Care*, 3(4) *The Guttmacher Rep. on Pub. Pol'y* 7 (2000), www.guttmacher.org/pubs/tgr/03/4/gr030404.html (last visited June 2, 2011).

147. I thank Professor R. George Wright for exploring this approach with me.

148. E-mail from Professor R. George Wright, professor of law, Indiana University School of Law–Indianapolis to Jennifer Drobac, professor of law, Indiana University School of Law–Indianapolis (Apr. 30, 2010) (on file with author).

149. *See* Drobac, *Sex and the Workplace*, *supra* note 4, at n.373 and accompanying text.

150. *See, e.g.*, Adam Nossiter, *Six Year Old's Sex Crime: Innocent Peck on the Cheek*, N.Y. Times, Sept. 27, 1996, www.nytimes.com/1996/09/27/

us/6-year-old-s-sex-crime-innocent-peck-on-cheek.html?scp=3&sq=six+year+old+sexual+harassment&st=cse&pagewanted=print (last visited June 2, 2011).

151. Legal assent makes sense for contexts in addition to those involving adolescent consent to sexual activity with an adult. Such situations are beyond the scope of this chapter, however, and will be explored in future academic papers. *See, e.g.*, Jennifer Ann Drobac & Oliver R. Goodenough, *Exposing the Myth of Consent,—Ind. Health L. Rev.*—(forthcoming 2015)(exploring the failure of the neoclassical approach to consent and the myth of legal capacity and recommending a new approach to "consent," *legal assent*).

3

The Wages of Ignorance

FRANKLIN E. ZIMRING

If one were looking for a no-win criminal justice embarrassment equivalent to the U.S. occupation of Iraq, our recent adventures with registration and public notice for juvenile sex offenders would be a worthy contender. The current mix of federal and state legal policies toward juvenile sex offenders is a disaster from a wide variety of different perspectives. Often, those creating public policies directed at crime and criminal offenders must choose between ideas that benefit offenders and harsher policies that might prevent crime. But the "genius" of policies like the federal "Amie's Law,"[1] an expansion of the federal definition of "sex offender" and expansion of the definition of "specified offense against a minor" to include all offenses by child predators, is that they provide double trouble: They harm and stigmatize young sex offenders while misdirecting public resources and providing no benefits to police and prevention efforts.

This essay presents the facts and fallacies of juvenile sex offending in two installments. The first section of my analysis provides basic information on the nature and extent of juvenile sex offending in the United States. The second section considers the central empirical issue relating to registration of juvenile sex offenders—future sexual dangerousness—and discusses how those who wrote the federal law managed to guess so terribly wrong on a matter of such high public importance.

Patterns of Juvenile Sex Offending in the United States

The adolescent years represent a period of high risk for both crime commission and arrest in the United States for a wide variety of crimes. Figure 1, taken from total arrest statistics for the year 2000, shows the percentage of all arrests involving offenders under eighteen by crime

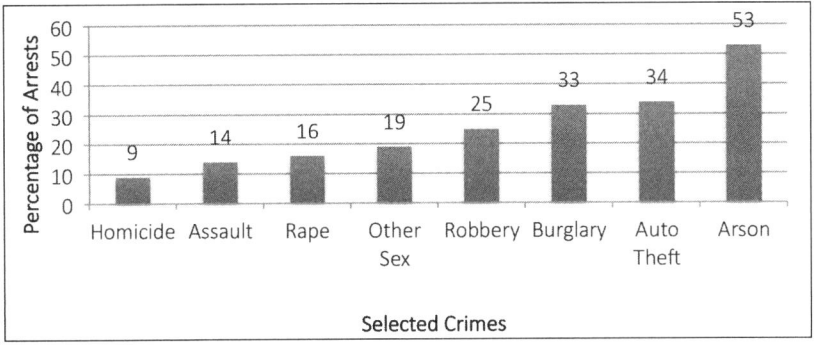

Figure 1. Percentage Distribution for Selected Crimes of U.S. Arrests of Persons under Eighteen during 2000. Source: U.S. Department of Justice, Federal Bureau of Investigation, *Uniform Crime Report* 236 (2000).

type. When compared to the other "index crimes" (i.e., the eight offenses used by the Federal Bureau of Investigation to produce its annual index of reported crimes), we find that persons under eighteen are arrested for a slightly larger share of sex offenses than for homicide and assault but for a much smaller share of sex offenses than for robbery, burglary, auto theft, and arson. Figure 2 shows the types of sex crimes that produce juvenile arrests.

Of the almost sixteen thousand juvenile sex offense arrests in 2000, just under three thousand are for rape charges, and fewer than one thousand are for prostitution and vice crimes. The vast majority of juvenile arrests are for the ambiguous category of "other sex offenses." Among the long list of "other" sex offenses covered in the category are "forcible fondling" (frequently of a child or young person), lewd conduct, and inappropriate sexual contact with young adolescents and children.[2]

The extreme concentration of juvenile sex arrests in the mixed collection of "other sex offenses" means that the fact of an arrest does not tell us much about the seriousness of the offense. The "other sex offenses" category runs a full range of offenses. It encompasses everything from serious sexual offenses such as forced sexual contact to consensual sex among young persons. Likewise, the actual sexual content of the behavior also varies from inappropriate touching to sexual penetration.

In addition to the ambiguous nature of the largest category of offenses, the arrest totals both understate and overstate the extent to

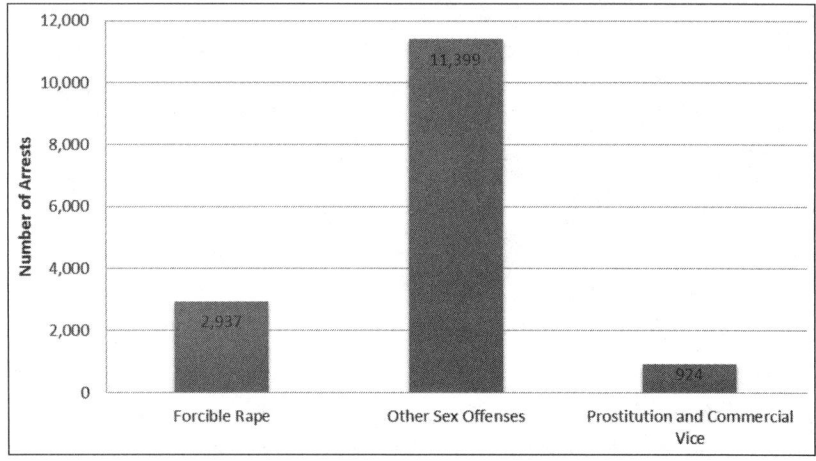

Figure 2. U.S. Arrests of Persons under Eighteen for Three Categories of Sex Crime during 2000. Source: U.S. Department of Justice, Federal Bureau of Investigation, *Uniform Crime Report* 22, tab. 38 (2000).

which juveniles violate criminal laws involving sex. The understatement comes because very few sex law violations, particularly those without complaining victims, result in detection and arrest. The overstatement comes because juveniles often commit crimes in groups much more often than older offenders. Three or four juveniles may be arrested for a single act.

There are two distinctive patterns in the age distribution of juvenile sex offenders and their victims that are worth special emphasis. While most rates of serious juvenile crime are much higher in the older juvenile ages, the rate of arrest among younger ages is much higher for "other sex offenses" than for crimes such as robbery and burglary. Figure 3 shows the relative arrest propensity by age for three "index crimes" and for "other sex offenses" by expressing the arrest rate at each age as a percentage of the rate at age twenty (defined at 100 for each offense).

The relative arrest exposure of younger juveniles is substantial. At ages ten to twelve, the arrest rate for "other sex crimes" is already 29% of the rate at age 20, and the arrest rate for ages thirteen and fourteen is as high for "other sex offenses" as at any time during adolescence. For robbery, by contrast, the arrest rate under twelve is about a tenth of the age twenty rate and less than a tenth of the age eighteen rate. At thirteen and fourteen, robbery arrests are less than half later juvenile age rates. The concentration of highest arrest rates near puberty is found only in this residual sex category (and in arson).[3]

To interpret, the numbers show that "other sex crime" offenders tend to be much younger than other serious juvenile offenders. Interestingly, the corresponding victims of these crimes are also much younger. A study of data from the National Incident Based Reporting System in several states showed that the victims of very young juvenile "other sex crime" offenders were also quite young themselves and that, for the youngest offenders, the most common offensive behavior was defined as "fondling" younger victims. The median age of victims of juveniles in this analysis was eleven years of age, and a third of the victims were under eight years old.[4] More than half of these arrests of juveniles under fifteen were for what the police regarded as "forcible fondling"—seemingly the sexual touching of a younger child.

There are in the statistical pattern of victim and offender reports in the "incident-based" system powerful indications that the youth of victims was a by-product of *when* police chose to arrest young persons. The great majority of victims of the ten-, eleven-, twelve- and thirteen-year-olds arrested were children under eleven, and more than three quarters of the victims of offenders under twelve were under eight. But fewer

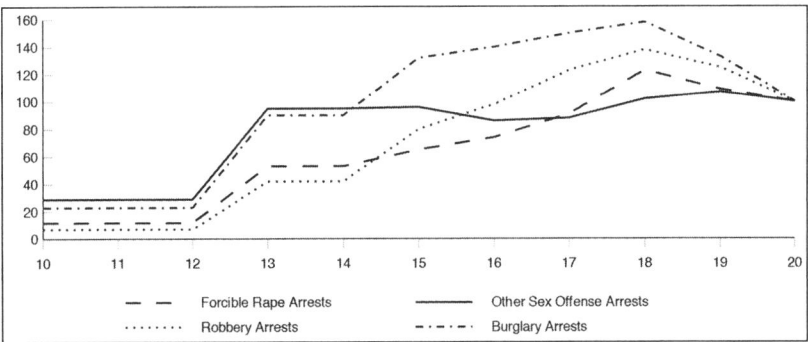

Figure 3. Patterns of Arrests among Teenagers during 2000. Age Twenty = 100.
Sources: U.S. Department of Justice, Federal Bureau of Investigation, *Uniform Crime Reports* (2000); and U.S. Census (2000).

than 13% of the victims of seventeen-year-olds arrested in the same offense category were under eight.[5]

What these data can't tell us is the extent to which today's juvenile sex offenders are tomorrow's adult sex criminals. That is the central question at the heart of registration regimes like Amie's Law—the Sex Offender Registration and Notification Act—in the Adam Walsh Child Protection and Safety Act of 2006. Are there data that answer this question? Why wasn't it addressed in the debates about juvenile registration in the Adam Walsh Act? How did the federal congress stagger into a national juvenile sex offender mandate without utilizing any empirical data on its need or utility? It is the last issue that I address in the next section.

The Mismeasure of Adolescent Sexual Danger

The central paradox of the passing of the Adam Walsh Child Protection and Safety Act of 2006, in which the federal government required the registration of juvenile sex offenders, is the absolute void of any empirical support for the necessity and value of the act itself. When the few analyses of representative samples of juvenile sex offenders are examined, it becomes obvious that juvenile sex offending is a very poor predictor of adult sexual danger.

The available facts on juvenile sex offenders are these: 90% of all juvenile sex offenders are not arrested for sex crimes when followed up for eight years, and over 92% of all the boys who are arrested for sex offenses as adults were not involved in any sex contacts as juveniles. Further, high-arrest juveniles with no sex contacts are twice as likely to become adult sex offenders as boys arrested for a sex offense but few other crimes.[6] Taking these statistics into account, it seems obvious that labeling juveniles as "sex risks" will hinder law enforcement through unnecessary tracking, won't predict dangerousness, doesn't help prevent sex offenses, but will destroy the prospects for youth who are clinically normal and criminologically low risk. How did this mess happen?

A large part of the blame for this symphony of dysfunction goes to the usual suspects: knee-jerk politicians who will climb on any punitive bandwagon without need of evidence. Whatever else may have led to the enactments of Amie's Law and the Adam Walsh Act, it was a clear case of legislative malpractice, yet another example of the political syndrome criminologist Jonathan Simon calls "governing through crime."[7]

But at least two other subgroups not usually responsible for darkside-of-the-moon criminal justice policy contributed sins of omission and sins of commission to the epic misclassification of juvenile sex offenders. For the first group, academics at research universities, the problem was the complete lack of published empirical work on the incidence, prevalence, and predictive value of juvenile sex offending. Here were the sins of omission. The sins of commission were the errors made by therapists with no training in adolescent development.

When I was researching the data and analysis available on juvenile sex offending in 2002, the first and last book on the subject in the English language was by Lewis J. Doshay, M.D., *The Boy Sex Offender and His Later Career*, published in 1943, a comprehensive analysis of juvenile sex offenders in New York City's family court during the first four decades of the twentieth century.[8] His long-term involvement as director of the New York program had left Dr. Doshay cheerful about the clinical status of his clients and their responses to very brief intervention—"male sex delinquency is self-curing"[9]—and he provided substantial statistical data from New York of very low sex recidivism.

What happened next in the study of juvenile sex offenders was absolutely nothing. The topic disappeared from academic radar screens for more than half a century. While juvenile delinquency became a major focus of statistical work on youth and the transition to adulthood, the 2% or so of juvenile arrests for sex offenses of any type were not documented or discussed in the published reports of a series of cohort studies in big and small cities. So data on juvenile sex offending and other phenomena were collected, and the adult histories of juvenile sex offenders were compiled, but they were never the subject of any formal analysis or detailed reporting. Debriefing the empirical data available after 1943 in a 2004 review, I offered the following capsule summary: "The remarkable thing about contemporary writing on juvenile sex offenders by academic specialists in juvenile justice or juvenile court judges is that there isn't any. . . . What one encounters is not so much a paucity of scholarly literature on juvenile sex offenders by juvenile justice experts as a void."[10]

The most powerful evidence on the reason for a zero literature on juvenile sex offenders concerns the absence of data analysis and reports from the sociological studies of birth cohort delinquency. The series of studies started by Thorsten Sellin and Marvin Wolfgang in Philadelphia and continued in a second Philadelphia cohort and in many other cities were the star attraction of empirical criminology in the 1960s and 1970s in the United States, and the principal investigators were very prominent figures in the field.[11] The failure of these reports to put any special focus on sex offenses or to study their predictive value for adult behavior is a clear indication that most juvenile sex offending was regarded as of low importance, not as an indication of clinical problems or future dangerousness. The more than 80% of the 15,000 sex crime arrests each year that were not classified as forcible rape[12] were also never reported in any detail in U.S. crime statistics. Most juvenile sex crime was not regarded as important.

This lack of interest and analysis by criminological scholars may have been caused by a peculiar division of turf between sociology and psychology in the study of criminal behavior and criminal careers. The study of most criminal behavior was dominated in the late twentieth century by scholars with sociological training and attitudes. With the exception of forcible rape, however, there was less interest in sex offending by criminologists of the mainstream than by psychologists.[13] The psychological interest in the treatment and assessment of sex offenders was generated by the conviction that many sex offenders were motivated by a series of clinically distinct abnormalities of sexual desire. The fact that many persons who sexually abuse young children may be also clinically classified as pedophiles creates a strong interest in child molestation on the part of therapists who treat pedophilia and also provides them with a disciplinary comparative advantage over non-psychologists to the extent that offenders in the class exhibit the clinical condition. The tendency of professional groups to associate adult sex offenders with clinical conditions made psychologists and psychiatrists more prominent experts in sex crimes and rendered the sociologically trained criminologist less willing to invade what seems like the turf of the treatment wing of the psychological sciences. One by-product of this division of turf may have been less-diligent attention by the sociologists doing juvenile cohort research to sex offenses and offenders.

The lack of data on juvenile sex offenders and their later careers may not have been consequential until relatively recently because juvenile sex offending wasn't regarded as an enforcement priority. The stakes were not high in most juvenile sex arrests. But when political pressure generated after 1980 put emphasis on sex offenses, particularly child molestation, the stage was set for changes in law and penal policy throughout criminal justice. Reliable data on childhood sex crime victimization are hard to obtain, but there is no reason to believe that the incidence of childhood sexual victimization fluctuates over time to match the wild swings that characterize public and media concern. The 1980s were a peak period for alarm about child molestation, an era that produced the McMartin preschool child molestation trial—the longest criminal trial in the history of the United States, and a trial which resulted in no convictions.[14]

Explosions of media and public concern about sexual predators and children have happened episodically in the United States, but Chrysanthi Leon's study of policy and incarceration in California over seventy years identified two prior panics in California that didn't produce large increases in imprisonment.[15] But the 1980s were a period in the United States where huge expansions in prison population were occurring for a wide variety of offenses—whatever the question, more imprisonment seemed to be the preferred answer. The imprisonment of all sex offenders increased in the United States in the 1980s and 1990s but not in an even pattern. During the seventeen years after 1980, the total number of persons in prison for rape doubled from 13,200 to 27,500.[16] The number of persons imprisoned for the mix of "other sexual assault" offenses that included child molestation and indecent liberties expanded from 7,300 in 1980 to over 64,000 in 1997, a growth of 700% in seventeen years.[17]

The expanded concern with child sex victimization also produced a series of legislative innovations during the last two decades of the twentieth century. One innovation was a species of civil commitment procedures designed to confine sex criminals after their prison terms expired if they met criteria for future dangerousness.[18] Twenty states now have civil sexual predator laws.[19] A second innovation was a combination of registration of persons previously convicted of sexual crimes and public notification of their current place of residence. These registration and public notification requirements are popularly known as Megan's Laws and are now found in some form in all fifty states.

None of these new strategies of social control for sexual offenders had juvenile offenders as their original primary targets or juvenile courts as an important staging area. But the close proximity of juvenile court delinquency cases and the criminal courts often produces attempts to transfer policy when major changes occur in the criminal justice system. Often, but not always, when the criminal justice system sneezes, the juvenile justice system catches cold.

This brings us to the sins of commission committed by sex therapists. The first major incursion from criminal justice approaches to juvenile sex offender policies was the migration of treatment clinicians trained in diagnosis and intervention with adult sex offenders to the diagnosis and treatment of juveniles accused of sex offending. The growth of this new sub-specialty was swift during the 1980s. By 1993, a report by a group of juvenile sex therapists reported that, "whereas there were about 20 [juvenile sex clinicians] identified in 1982, there are now (as of 1993) over 800 specialized treatment programs."[20] Even discounting somewhat the eight-hundred-program estimate for 1993, how could the number of juvenile sex offender clinicians increase twentyfold in eleven years? Where did these hundreds or thousands of new experts come from? There were no university-based training programs giving M.A. and Ph.D. degrees in the etiology and treatment of adolescent sexual misconduct. Relatedly, there were also not many new juvenile sex therapists with credentials and experience in treating other types of juvenile offenders.

The truth is that the major migration into the field of juvenile sex offender clinician was of persons with training and experience in the treatment of adult sex offenders. As a result, the capacity of this group in the diagnosis and treatment of adolescent behavior was rather limited. There was no strong empirical research tradition in American research universities for learning about sex offenders or for training the clinicians who deal with juvenile sex offenders. Sex therapists dealing with adults who sexually abuse children often suspect that pathological mental and emotional sexual conditions are an important element in the motivation for sexual offending and the choice of sexual targets. Presumably, it is knowledge about sexual pathologies that is the comparative advantage of sexual-offense specialists over probation staff, group workers, and juvenile court judges with extensive experience with delinquent youth. But how many juvenile sex offenders suffer from clinically significant paraphilic conditions?

The primary disadvantage of flooding the juvenile courts with adult sex crime specialists is that these folks don't have training or knowledge about the developmental psychology of adolescence as a process and a transition to adulthood. Simple arithmetic suggests the magnitude of the problem of trading knowledge of adult sexual pathology for any knowledge of adolescent development. The proportion of juvenile sex offenders with clear clinical disorders must be rather small—well under 8% of the adolescents arrested for sex offenses.[21] What many of these "experts" do not take into account is that 100% of the juveniles arrested for sex offenses are currently suffering from adolescence, a powerful emotional and physiological condition and the reason that juvenile courts were established across the developed world. The great danger is that persons without training in adolescent development will ignore that important aspect of teen sexual conduct.

This is not just a hypothetical problem. *The Revised Report from the National Task Force on Juvenile Sexual Offending, 1993 of the National Adolescent Perpetrator Network*'s 105-page report, by a network composed of sex-offense specialists, begins by alleging that previous juvenile court policy failed because "sexual behaviors which were clearly exploitative and criminal were often dismissed as 'adolescent adjustment reactions,' a manifestation of emotional disturbance or defined as 'experimentation.'"[22] A few things worry me deeply about this paragraph on the fifth page of a 105-page report by a group seeking to dominate legal policy toward adolescent offenders.

The first problem is the presence of a false dichotomy at the center of the sentence I quoted. This quote displays a disturbing misunderstanding of the core theory of delinquency in American juvenile courts. The Network believes that conduct can either be an "adolescent adjustment reaction" or "exploitative and criminal" but not both at the same time. Conduct *must* be criminal to qualify the accused as a delinquent, yet the criminal nature of harm done is no excuse for either ignoring the conditions associated with the crime or choosing a developmentally appropriate disposition for the juvenile offender. Transitional emotional problems or "experimentation" may suggest different responses to harmful delinquent acts than more deliberate and more chronic crime such as burglary and auto theft. The need for a different response to harmful delinquent acts is the entire reason we have a juvenile delinquency jurisdiction. The Network report thus gets a zero in any quiz on the purpose of juvenile courts.

The second worry I have regarding this quote is its derisive mention of "adolescent adjustment reactions" on page 5 is as the *only* place in this report that the process of adolescent development is mentioned at all. This quote is a single sentence from a very lengthy report containing 387 separate assumptions about the etiology and policy choices for juvenile sex crimes. Without any background in adolescent development, the group that assembled this report seems to have implicitly assumed that adolescence wasn't important to the etiology and control of juvenile sex offenses. The Network doesn't consider any data on this topic, nor does its report make any explicit assumptions about the importance of adolescence in explaining adolescent sex offending. This group merely assumes that because sexual conduct is wrong and harmful, the age and developmental status of the actor is irrelevant to its understanding and control.

This kind of catastrophic error would be outrageous in any era, but it is strategically significant in the era of Meagan's Laws and the Adam Walsh Act. If there is no difference between a fifteen-year-old boy playing with the genitals of his eight-year-old neighbor and the conduct of a repetitive pedophile in his thirties, then the case can be made for a one-size-fits-all regime of sex-offender registration and community notification.

This failure to consider the developmental characteristics of juveniles did have one comic consequence in the Network's report. Among the listed sexual disorders in the report—between "florophilia" and "pedophilia"—is a condition they refer to as "hebophilia," defined by the task force as "sexual interest in adolescents."[23] But since all of the subjects of the Network's reports are adolescent, where is the problem? If adolescents don't have a "sexual interest in adolescents," who should they be sexually interested in?

It is impossible to prove without a doubt that the absurdity of the National Adolescent Perpetrator Network caused the misguided results in Amie's Law. The lack of developmental awareness of groups like the

"Juvenile Perpetrators Network" invited the unjustified generalization of the worst features of the sex crime panic about adult offenders of the 1990s into juvenile justice and adolescent social control. Perhaps politicians' aggressive ignorance of crime in the United States would have overcome even good empirical data and developmentally sophisticated perspectives from the appropriate treatment professionals. That cannot be known. But the lack of data and the epic developmental ignorance of the Adolescent Perpetrator Network certainly did not help when the question of extending registration to juvenile sex offenders emerged. And the failures of the treatment group that assembled the 1993 Network report were sins of commission.

Some Data on Danger

The meticulous data collected in cohort studies from the 1950s onward are, for the most part, still available to investigators now. And while there may be an Alice-in-Wonderland quality to examining some facts about adolescent sexual offending as a prediction of dangerousness only after federal and state policies have been established ("Policy first, facts later"), even belated attention to empirical reality is superior to a jurisprudence of "Policy first, facts never," which seems to be the current approach.

A group of juvenile justice researchers recently published an analysis of data on 13,160 boys born in Philadelphia in 1958, which coded police contacts for ages ten through twenty-seven.[24] The researchers had information not only on the total amount of sex crime (by police account) during the years this group was under eighteen but also of the total amount of sex offending by the groups in the first eight years of legal adulthood.[25] Because the research provides a profile of the group's entire young adult sex offending, it provides a high-quality measure of juvenile sex-offending records as a tool to investigate adult sex crime. As it turns out, the percentage of the adult sexual offending of this group committed by former juvenile sex offenders was 7.8%. According to this result, any attempt to hunt for the sex offenders in this cohort by rounding up the usual juvenile suspects would be wrong 92% of the time. As a repository of information on potential sex offenders among the cohort born in 1958, the juvenile offender file looks useless. But surely that is only because so few boys become police-identified sex offenders as juveniles. Don't some juvenile sex offenders become a very substantial risk to offend in adulthood? Figure 4, which compares a juvenile's contacts with the juvenile justice system to incident of eventual adult sex offenses, provides the critical data on this question. None of the offender groups identified in Figure 4 are at high risk of sex arrest in the eight-year adult exposure period. Those young adults with high arrest rates as juveniles of any kind have the highest chance of a sex arrest as an adult—15.6% and 9.1% for the two high total juvenile arrest groups—one with and one without any sex record as a juvenile. But it is the *length* of a juvenile record rather than the presence or absence of a juvenile sex offense that has the stronger association with adult sex arrests. A youth in Philadelphia who has five or more arrests in total but no sex arrests has twice the risk of an adult sex arrest as a juvenile with a sex record but fewer than five arrests; low-arrest-rate juveniles with no sex offenses under eighteen have the same risk of adult sex offending (4%) as those with a sex arrest as a juvenile but fewer than five total juvenile police contacts.

The use of a juvenile sex offense to trigger registration as a prediction of future sexual danger under these circumstances is both irrational and irresponsible. The actual risk of a juvenile sex offender with less than five contacts reoffending in eight adult years is 4.2%. A statistically identical risk would be identified if juveniles with less than five contacts who were only arrested for theft or curfew were pushed into a sex registry. Of course, putting persons without any juvenile sex offending who have more than five non-sex arrests on a sex registry would be senseless and unfair—but that strategy would identify a group with more than twice the adult sex risk as the juvenile sex offenders with fewer than five total contacts. So perhaps registration for the juvenile sex group is senseless and unfair as well.

We have now analyzed data from two cohort study cities, Philadelphia and Racine, and there is abundant evidence that juvenile sex offenders are not sex-offending specialists and are at low risk of sexual recidivism.[26] Additional cohort samples should be analyzed for data on patterns of juvenile sex offending and later life outcomes. What the Philadelphia data show is that, if a 4% chance of an adult sex arrest should be sufficient to trigger a lifetime prediction of adult sex offense, then *every* male juvenile arrested for *anything* prior to age eighteen should be reg-

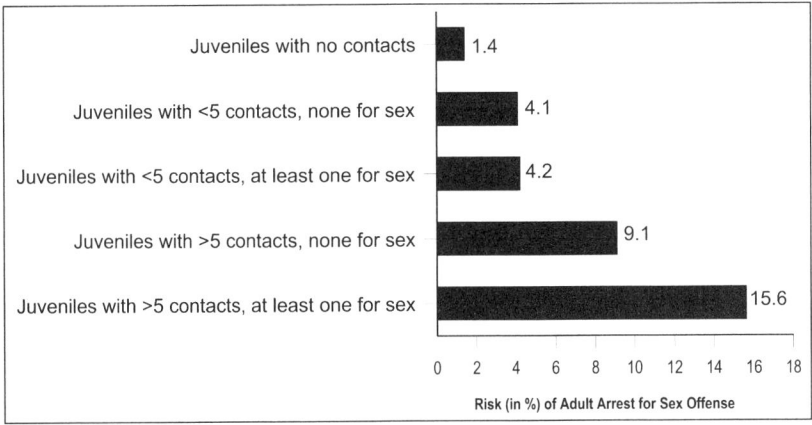

Figure 4. Distinguishing Adult Sex Offenders Based on Juvenile Arrest Record. This graph compares a juvenile's contacts with the juvenile justice system to the incidence of eventual adult sex offenses. Source: Franklin E. Zimring, Wesley G. Jennings, Alex R. Piquero, and Stephanie Hays, *Investigating the Continuity of Sex Offending: Evidence from the Second Philadelphia Birth Cohort*, 26(1) Just. Q. 58, 76 (2009).

istered as at risk for sex offending. If a 4% risk is not sufficient, then all current sex offense registration provisions triggered by a single juvenile sex offense must be abolished.

There is much we still have to learn about the nature of juvenile sex offending and whether there might be small sub-groups that need and would benefit from sex-specific treatment intervention.[27] But the first principle of responding to juvenile sex offenses should be to do no harm. Living up to that precept would be a revolutionary change from current policies.

NOTES

1. Sex Offender Registration and Notification Act, Adam Walsh Child Protection and Safety Act, 42 U.S.C. § 16911 *et seq.* (2006).

2. Franklin E. Zimring, *An American Travesty: Legal Responses to Adolescent Sexual Offending* 43–57 (Univ. Chi. Press 2004).

3. *Id.* at fig. 3.1.

4. *Id.* at 48.

5. *Id.* at 50.

6. Franklin E. Zimring *et al.*, *Investigating the Continuity of Sex Offending: Evidence from the Second Philadelphia Birth Cohort*, 26 Just. Q. 58, 65–67 (2009).

7. Jonathan Simon, *Governing through Crime: How the War on Crime Transformed American Democracy and Created a Culture of Fear* (Oxford Univ. Press 2007).

8. See Lewis J. Doshay, *The Boy Sex Offender and His Later Career* (Grune & Stratton 1943).

9. *Id.* at 168.

10. Zimring, *An American Travesty, supra* note 2, at 112.

11. Marivn E. Wolfgang et al., *Delinquency in a Birth Cohort* (Univ. Chicago Press 1972).

12. Zimring, *An American Travesty, supra* note 2, at 41.

13. *Amir Menachem, Patterns in Forcible Rape* (Univ. Chi. Press 1971).

14. *Paul Eberle & Shirley Eberle, The Abuse of Innocence: The McMartin Preschool Trial* (Prometheus Press 1993).

15. Chrysanthi Leon, Compulsion and Control: Sex Crime and Criminal Justice Policy in California, 1930–2007 (2007) (unpublished Ph.D. dissertation, University of California, Berkeley) (on file with University of California, Berkeley).

16. Zimring, *An American Travesty, supra* note 2, at 35–36.

17. *Id.*

18. Tamara Lave, Constructing and Controlling the Sexually Violent Predator: An American Obsession (2009) (unpublished Ph.D. dissertation, University of California, Berkeley) (on file with University of California, Berkeley).

19. *Id.*

20. *The Revised Report from the National Task Force on Juvenile Sexual Offending, 1993 of the National Adolescent Perpetrator Network*, 44 Juv. & Fam. Ct. J. 1, 3 (1993).

21. Zimring, *An American Travesty, supra* note 2, at 65.

22. *The Revised Report from the National Task Force on Juvenile Sexual Offending, 1993 of the National Adolescent Perpetrator Network, supra* note 20, at 5.

23. *Id.* at 11.

24. Zimring et al., *Investigating the Continuity of Sex Offending, supra* note 6, at 62.

25. *Paul E. Tracy & Kimberly Kempf-Leonard, Continuity and Discontinuity in Criminal Careers* (Plenum Press 1996).

26. Zimring et al., *Investigating the Continuity of Sex Offending, supra* note 6; Franklin E. Zimring et al., *Sexual Delinquency in Racine: Does Early Sex Offending Predict Later Sex Offending in Youth and Young Adulthood?* 6 Criminology & Pub. Pol'y 507 (2007).

27. Zimring, *An American Travesty, supra* note 2.

4

Sugar and Spice and Everything Nice

Definitely Not the Girls in the Juvenile Justice System

ELLEN MARRUS

Mindy is a mom with two daughters, Jill, who is twenty, and Missy, who is fourteen. Jill gave Mindy no problems growing up. She attended school and never cut any classes, had good grades, obeyed curfew, helped out around the house, obeyed all the rules at home and school, and is now attending college. Missy, however, has been a real handful. When Missy was in elementary school she was a sweet girl who all her teachers loved having as a student. She always received good grades, worked hard, and never missed a day of school. Missy was proud that she had all As and perfect attendance. She loved going to school. But something happened when she hit middle school. Mindy thinks that Missy is hanging out with boys too much, particularly one boy, Scott. Missy's grades have gone down, and she had to repeat science and math in summer school. She is cutting classes, receives detention at least a couple of times a week, and the school has threatened to suspend her and send her to an alternative school. It does not appear as if the move to high school is improving the situation. In fact, it seems to be getting worse. At this rate, Missy is likely to become a high school dropout.

Missy's attitude at home is not any better. She stays out pass curfew, won't help around the house, and does not listen to her mom or her stepdad, Stan. Missy stays out with Scott till all hours of the night. Her mom thinks she may be having sex with Scott and is worried that Missy is jeopardizing her health and her future.

Mindy is at her wits' end and has no idea how to handle these problems. She has tried to talk to Scott's parents about the problem. Maybe if they were stricter with Scott and he had a curfew, Missy would go back to following the rules at home. However, Scott's parents do not view any of his actions as problems. They believe boys will be boys. Scott was never a great student, but neither was his dad, and he did okay. Indeed, Scott's dad also stayed out late as a teen, got into trouble at school sometimes, and certainly went after the girls. He turned out okay, and they are sure Scott will, too. Mindy is beginning to wonder if she needs to call social services or the police to see if they can help get Missy back in line.

Regrettably, this is an all-too-common dilemma, one that many parents face: what to do with the "out-of-control" daughter. Oftentimes parents turn to the judicial system to help them in this predicament. This is true even when the girl is demonstrating "acting-out" behavior that is non-criminal in nature, such as Missy's. Boys, in contrast, are viewed differently. As noted in the scenario above, parents often view their sons' "acting out" as "behaving like boys" and that they are only displaying typical adolescent male behavior.

If Mindy calls the police and files a complaint about Missy's behavior, Missy could be picked up as a status offender, a youth in violation of the law only because of her age for actions such as truancy, running away, or violating curfew. However, if Missy then violates any orders of the court, she may become a delinquent. By trying to "help" her daughter, Mindy may be pushing her daughter into the delinquency system, with all the consequences that can follow.

This disparity in the way we view girls and boys escalates as adolescents begin to explore their sexuality. Boys are expected to experiment with sex, to "sow their wild oats," and, certainly, not to be virgins when they get married. This does not mean that adolescent males are not treated harshly for their sexual behavior. As Professor Zimring points out in his chapter, juvenile sex offenders are treated similarly to adult male sex offenders, although their patterns of behavior and recidivism are very different. Girls, however, are expected to remain pure until marriage, not to explore their sexuality, and to look forward to becoming good wives and mothers, in that order. If girls act on their sexual curiosity, they are considered promiscuous, and parents have the responsibility to make sure their daughters are behaving suitably and according to society's standards. Girls are subject to delinquent behavior for acting on their own sexuality.

Just as society and parents react to similar behavior by females and males differently, so does our juvenile justice system. Girls are often referred to the juvenile justice system by different actors and for different reasons than boys, and once in the system they are treated differently than their male counterparts. Additionally, the existing treatment programs that have been designed to rehabilitate juveniles were developed primarily for male offenders, meaning that girls' treatment and rehabilitation needs often go unmet.

The typical male delinquent is viewed as a violent offender who needs punishment rather than rehabilitation. The typical profile of a girl delinquent is different. Although girls may get into fights, they are less likely to use firearms or any type of weapon than boys.[1] Disproportionate minority representation is a factor for both genders, and more than half the girls in the juvenile justice system are of color. Most delinquent girls perform poorly in school, are often truant, and face suspension or expulsion. This may be due to the abuse they have suffered at home or dysfunctional family relationships. Family dynamics also cause girls to run away from home, ending up on the streets and looking for any means of survival. The abuse and trauma suffered at home places girls in the child protective system more often than boys. These girls have been placed in foster homes, often shuffled from one to another, and face possible continued abuse in the foster home. As the foster home placement changes, the child may also change neighborhoods and schools, which causes girls to fall further behind in school and have little or no support network. This may lead the girl to life on the street, prostitution, drugs, and entry into the juvenile justice system.

Pre-juvenile Courts

In colonial times, children were viewed differently than they are today; they were typically considered miniature adults and were treated very similarly to their adult counterparts. Children would often work alongside adults both at home and on the land, taking on the same tasks as adults. They worked the fields and cared for their younger brothers and sisters. Young girls helped with the cleaning, cooking, and other household chores. However, even then girls and boys were viewed differently. Girls were placed in a nurturing role, and females were rarely defined by their unique characteristics or strengths; rather, they were defined by the background and characteristics of the males around them. Children had to answer to and obey their parents and other adults, but other males in the family also dominated girls, including younger siblings.

The expectation for girls was that they would marry young, bear children, care for the home, and work in the fields, if necessary, but not work away from the home. Some girls struggled with these ideas or were concerned about their marriage prospects. Since they could not discuss these fears openly or question their role in society, they would sometimes meet with other girls in secret to discuss these issues. If others found out about these clandestine gatherings or something negative occurred in the community at this time, the girls might be accused of practicing witchcraft. People believed that whatever "magic" they conjured up during the meetings caused the problem, and therefore, they should be punished accordingly. This often led to drowning or hanging.

During this time period, children—boys and girls—were also treated the same as adults when it came to the criminal justice system. Children could be accused of crimes and, if found guilty, could face the same punishments as adults. Children could be imprisoned with adults or even put to death. Since girls were considered weaker and more vulnerable, they were not usually charged with criminal acts. This did not mean that they would not be removed from their family and locked up.

In fact, institutions called "houses of refuge" were designed to bring poor, unfortunate children off the streets and to keep young girls from prostitution or a life of sin. These facilities were to provide children with a better life and the skills necessary to make them more productive citizens. In reality, these were prison-like environments, where children lived in large dormitories and often worked from five in the morning to five at night. Although children were being taught skills for the workplace, they were a source of free or cheap labor. By the 1840s these institutions were declared a failure, and they were replaced by reform schools, which were designed to take immoral children and turn them into upstanding citizens through religious training, education, and training in domestic chores. This training was also meant to help girls become good wives and mothers, and it was considered an important force for keeping the family as a cohesive unit.

For children of color, the "house of refuge" was not a house of refuge, and the reform schools were no better. Children of color were kept separate from their white counterparts. They were trained to take care of the facility. They did the cleaning, cooking, and any repairs, and they were ultimately being trained for the kind of work that they would be expected to do after they left the institutions. In addition, there was a wall kept around the area where children of color were kept. It was not to keep them in but, rather, to keep them separate from the white children who were also placed in the institution. The attitude of the administration was that it might do irreparable harm to the white children to know that they were being kept in the same facility as the children who were of color, as the children of color were not considered worth anything by society.

The first Industrial School for Girls was started in Lancaster, Massachusetts, and again functioned as a place to teach girls about their role in society. Some girls were referred by their parents because the parents were unable to control their daughters, or the parents were not receiving support for the family household from the girls, or the girls were considered "runaways" who were participating in immoral sexual acts. As many of the reform schools were run by the state, parents turned to the courts to help them control their wayward daughters. Girls were charged in court with "vagrancy, running away or staying out all night."[2] During this time period, African American girls were being taken from their families without the parents' consent and placed into indentured servitude. It was not unusual for young girls to be forced to have sexual intercourse with former white slaveholders and to care for their children.[3] In the mid-1800s Philadelphia opened its "Colored Department of the House of Refuge," where African American girls would be able to enjoy "a well-made bed and . . . [would] find themselves for their first time, at a table well-ordered, supplied with wholesome food, and presided over by the head of the family."[4] The judge who made comments at the dedication of the new program made note of the fact that African American girls had to obey all the laws of the country even if they did not enjoy all the rights.[5]

Juvenile Courts

A movement was started by progressives to change the way that the judicial system handled cases that involved children who committed criminal acts. Social workers, psychologists, judges, and policy makers were beginning to recognize that the current system of having children treated the same as adults was not working. They believed there had to be a better way of helping children who were in trouble than punishing them and placing youth in prison with adults. It was with the creation of the juvenile courts in 1899 that at least some people began to recognize the differences between children and adults and that children needed, and deserved, a second chance when they made mistakes. Treatment and rehabilitation could go a long way to making life better for children. This created a major shift in our criminal justice system. Children's cases were heard separately from adult criminal matters, judges were aided by social workers, and it was recommended that judges and their staff have particularized training in child and adolescent development. If children "needed help" or committed a criminal act, they were to be treated and rehabilitated rather than punished. Even the language used in juvenile court was changed in order to reflect this more benevolent approach. Children were not to be indicted or charged with a crime; rather, a petition would be filed alleging a delinquent act. They were not to be arrested but taken into custody instead. They were not to be found guilty of a criminal act but adjudicated as delinquent. And they were not to be sentenced; rather, a disposition was to be made in their best interests. Finally, the biggest change was that children were no longer to be housed with adult criminals. If they were to be committed to an institution, they were to be kept separate from adults. Boys and girls were both intended to be beneficiaries of this new system.

One of the principal goals of this new juvenile system was changing and controlling what society viewed as the immoral sexual behavior of females and stopping wayward girls from misbehaving or living a life of sin. When boys became involved in the system, it was because they committed an act that would be considered criminal in nature. The progressive movement wanted to keep children separate from adults to keep children from being influenced by criminal adult behavior. However, just as the system continues to do now, programs and placements focused on treating and rehabilitating the delinquent boy and not delving into the reasons for what was deemed girls' "inappropriate" behavior or developing procedures that would correct this behavior and alter girls' behavior to one that would be more acceptable by society.

The juvenile justice system that developed with the ideals of helping children—by recognizing the differences between adults and children and building on them to make a better system for youth—still did not distinguish between the differences in adolescent male and female behavior. Furthermore, society's gender biases ensured that girls would not get equal treatment in this system. The courts followed society's biases to protect females more than males. Although one might think this was a good thing, it led to the courts treating what was considered promiscuous behavior and the minor noncriminal behaviors of girls differently than it did of boys. Behavior that might be considered normal adolescent behavior when committed by boys—such as running away, staying out late, getting into family disputes, and engaging in sexual behavior—brought girls who did the same into the juvenile justice system in order for them to be sheltered and pressed into behaving according to society's vision of acceptable female norms. Girls came into the system to be protected from the evil forces around them, and boys came into the system because they committed criminal offenses and society needed to be protected from them. Girls were typically treated more harshly for minor status offenses than boys but would be treated more leniently for more serious offenses.

From the beginning and still today, juvenile courts typically address three types of cases—dependency (child protective services), status offenses, and delinquency. Dependency, or child welfare cases, involve incidents in which children have suffered some type of abuse or neglect at the hands of the primary caregiver. The children may or may not be removed from their home. If removed, they are typically placed in a non-secure setting, such as a foster home or group home, or in some cases a mental health institution if this is considered to be an appropriate placement and in the child's best interests. This is done to protect the child rather than punish, and the child is kept in placements that are separated from delinquents or status offenders.

A status offender is a person who has done something that is only considered criminal in nature because of the age of the offender, that is, running away from home, truancy, incorrigibility, curfew violations, and underage alcohol consumption. According to the 1974 Juvenile Justice and Delinquency Prevention Act (JJDPA), status offenders, if placed out of home, should be placed in non-secure facilities and diverted from delinquency proceedings. With the changes in legislation, status offenders are also placed separately from delinquent youth.

Delinquent youth are children who commit an act that would be considered criminal or a violation of the penal code if committed by an adult. Juveniles who are adjudicated delinquent or are found to be guilty of a criminal act may be placed on probation or placed out of home. Delinquent children who are placed out of home are the most likely group to be placed in a secure facility. When a delinquent is placed in a secure facility it is usually for an indeterminate length of time. The youth will be released either when the child is determined to be rehabilitated or has aged out of the juvenile court's jurisdiction.

While dependency, status, and delinquency courts view children and their actions differently, they often see children who cross over between the three systems. It is not unusual for a dependent child to end up in delinquency court, and vice versa. Status offenders often face delinquency charges when they violate court orders. The problems children face do not stay in separate compartments, even if the courts try to keep the children and their hearings separate. This is particularly true for girls who often get into trouble for running away, for being out past curfew, and for minor infractions that would not be an issue if they were adults. Girls frequently commit these undertakings as a result of problems in the home—abuse (physical or sexual), for example, or miscommunication between the parents and children. Girls who are status offenders or dependents in the child welfare system may run away from their placements. They may miss their home even if their parent or guardian had abused them. They may also face physical, sexual, or emotional abuse in their out-of-home placements and do not want to continue living under those circumstances. Furthermore, many of these girls are very vulnerable, with low self-esteem, and they are easy prey for human traffickers or pimps. If a girl runs away from her non-secure placement where she has been placed as a status offender or dependent, she may become involved with illegal activity, particularly drugs or prostitution, and be pulled into the delinquency system.

Delinquency System

Although girls have always been involved in the juvenile delinquency system in fewer numbers than boys, the number of girls entering the system has greatly increased while the number of boys coming in has continued to decrease. Between 1988 and 1997 the number of female delinquency cases increased 83%. During this time Caucasian girls increased by 74%, African American girls by 106%, and girls of other races by 102%.[6] Saving girls from immoral behavior may have been a focus of the progressive movement, but the programs that were developed concentrated on treating boy delinquents as their numbers were much greater than the number of girls in the system. However, even with the increase of girls in the system in more recent years, the policies and programs of juvenile justice continues to concentrate more on boy delinquents than girls.[7] Prior to discussing some of the various reasons given for the increase in girls' delinquent behavior and the lack of programming for girls, it is important to understand girls' pathway into the system.

Girls' Pathways into Juvenile Court

Prior to a child's interaction with the delinquency system a referral is made from one of several sources—law enforcement, schools, probation, victims, family members, witnesses, or other agencies that may have interaction with the child. Upon a referral an intake officer evaluates the report of the incident, talks to the child, and investigates the family and social history of the child. While boys have typically entered the system in greater numbers than girls, they are usually referred to juvenile court for an act they committed that is criminal in nature. The referral usually comes from law enforcement, probation, schools, or other agencies outside the home. Girls, however, are usually referred to the system by someone in the family unit and for actions that are, at least originally, designated as status-related offenses, such as running away, truancy, or being beyond parental control. The juvenile justice system was designed to handle the types of matters for which boys are referred, violations of the penal code. The family unit would be better to handle the types of incidents that have girls entering the system.

In the early years of the juvenile court the standard charge against girls was "immorality" or "waywardness" or "incorrigibility." Almost 80% of the girls were charged with immorality, primarily based on inappropriate sexual behavior. Incorrigibility or waywardness charges were brought when the court wanted to protect the girl's reputation.[8] Society's concern was to protect females from their own immoral behavior, which could include such minor incidents as "riding in a closed automobile, loitering in a department store, inhabiting a furnished room with a young man, or even shimmying on a roadhouse dance floor."[9]

As girls' sexuality continued to be a problem for society and for parents, the juvenile courts continued to try and resolve the problem. In the first half of the twentieth century, Los Angeles juvenile courts would ask for evidence to show whether or not the girl participated in sexual intercourse. Girls would be asked questions about their sexual activity and were subject to gynecological exams, in which doctors made note of the condition of the girl's hymen when she was charged with immorality in court.[10]

Girls who come into the delinquency system are usually at a different stage in their development than the boys entering the system. Girls are trying to find their own identity and assert their independence. This leads to family conflicts and is often the basis for their pathway into juvenile court. Furthermore, girls' behavior can make them appear to be very needy and more rebellious than their male counterparts in the system.[11]

A referral that is often for non-criminal behavior and is made by a family member causes girls to be treated differently throughout the proceedings. This is where we frequently fail girls by not looking at the deeper reasons for their acting-out behavior or why the person made the referral to the police or probation. Girls often run away because of the abuse they suffer at home. A parent might report a daughter as a runaway because he or she is concerned for her safety, or the parent might be concerned that the girl is going to report the abuse they suffered from the parent. To survive on the streets, many girls will turn to illegal behavior such as prostitution or petty theft. Oftentimes, parents do not know how to control their daughter's "promiscuous" behavior, or they are embarrassed because their daughter is not behaving in a manner that is considered acceptable for females. This may also lead to emotional altercations between parent and child that will lead to the girl leaving home or turning to someone else for support.

Sexual abuse is an even greater problem for girls than physical abuse. Statistics indicate that eight out of ten sexual abuse cases are female, and this may be indicative of why girls are more likely to run from home. Sixty-two percent of females who end up in our juvenile or criminal justice systems have suffered some type of abuse, and out of these, 54.3% have suffered sexual abuse. Most females were under the age of nine when the abuse started, and if they reported the abuse, it either got worse (25.3%), or nothing changed at all (29.9%).[12] Sexual abuse did not just occur once. Rather, for over one-third of the females, it happened between three and ten times, and for 27.4% it occurred eleven times or more.[13]

Coping with this can be difficult at best. For many girls the best coping strategy is to run away from home (20.5%) and/or turning to larceny, petty theft, and stealing food, money, and clothing to survive. Although the girls do not see themselves as delinquents—rather, they consider themselves survivors and victims of sexual abuse—the system criminalizes their actions, failing to delve into the deeper issues causing the behavior, and the girls quickly become statistics in the juvenile delinquency system.

Physical and sexual abuse also cause mental health disorders in females that go untreated or are misdiagnosed, often as oppositional defiant disorder, on account of their aggressive behavior, instead of post-traumatic stress disorder, which stems from the abuse they experienced. To solve their problems, girls often self-medicate or turn to drugs or alcohol to help them face life.[14]

Girls' inability to deal with the abuse, the fact that the system fails to provide them with resources and treatment, and the fact that they often remain in abusive situations facing repeated physical and sexual assaults help to create a situation that has females entering the delinquency system. Girls who have been physically assaulted by family members, boyfriends, or peers tend to respond aggressively when confronted by problems in their lives. They see this aggression as the only possible reaction to a situation that frightens or threatens them, as this is the only response they know.[15]

As runaways, girls are unable to continue in school. They become school dropouts and do not have the skills to get a decent paying job.

Since they have no money and no way to provide for food and shelter, girls tend to turn to the only resource that they have—their bodies—and turn to prostitution. This also increases their likelihood of entering the juvenile justice system through a nonfamily referral.

Girls are also more likely to be referred for assaultive delinquent behavior by a victim's parent. If two girls get into a fight, the parent of the alleged victim will probably want charges brought against the other girl. If two boys get into a fight, the parents are probably going to take the attitude that boys will be boys and he should be able to defend himself. Fighting is not considered acceptable behavior for girls.[16]

Finally, girls also enter the system when they first become status offenders for minor infractions and then violate a court order that had been entered from the status proceeding. A girl may have run away from her placement, been truant from school, or committed any other violation of an order from the status-offender hearing, which places the child in criminal contempt of court and, therefore, labels her a "delinquent."[17] Young girls may also start their interaction with the courts through a dependency action because of the sexual or physical abuse they encountered at home. They may run away from the placement because they miss their home or because they face additional abuse in the dependent care placement. If they run away and had not received counseling for the abuse, they may turn to drugs or alcohol to forget or to illegal activity to survive, as they feel they have no place to turn for help.

Reasons for the Increase of Girls in the System

One reason given for the increase of girls in the system was that the feminist movement encouraged more females to imitate male behavior and that this concept carried over to delinquency behavior. "The departure from the safety of traditional female roles and the testing of uncertain alternative roles coincide with the turmoil of adolescence creating criminogenic risk factors which are bound to increase."[18] However, later studies tended to disprove this theory and found that feminism had little influence on delinquent behavior. In fact, "more delinquent girls were actually less liberated," and although they were not looking toward marriage and children, they also were not "reaching for male-dominated occupations as an alternative."[19] Feminism was "associated with career orientations that . . . had a direct effect on grades, . . . [and] was linked to class and race."[20]

Additionally, girls are also more likely than boys to originally enter the system as status offenders because they are beyond parental control, running away from home or placement, or behaving in a manner that is not considered proper for a female.[21] Females are treated more harshly for status offenses than males and are more likely to be charged with a criminal violation of a court order. Male status offenders who violate a court order and are found to be in contempt are incarcerated at a rate of 4.4%, while female status offenders are incarcerated at a rate of 63.2% when found in contempt.[22] This high numbers of girls being bootstrapped into the delinquency system disproportionately increases the number of girls.

After the changes in JJDPA, which decreased the overall detention of status offenders, jurisdictions found a decline in the number of youth being charged as status offenders. The juvenile justice institutions found other ways to charge girls in order to bring them into the system. This included more often charging them with assault. These assaults tended to be fights between two girls or an altercation between the girl and her parents. This was different from the assaults by boys, as those were usually teen versus adult.[23]

Juvenile Court Proceedings

To further understand the changes in referrals for girls to the system, the increase in the number of girl delinquents, and the lack of programs for girls, it is also important to appreciate how the actors of the juvenile justice system interact with female offenders and how the programs and institutions that exist fail to provide female juvenile offenders with appropriate treatment, education, and rehabilitation. Analyzing these factors will help us develop policies that are more likely to provide programs that are developed specifically for the needs of girls and are more beneficial for them. To do this it is necessary to examine the various steps in juvenile delinquency proceedings and the system's interactions with female offenders.

The first step after the referral is for someone within the juvenile justice system to determine whether the matter can be handled informally, outside of the court process, or if there must be a petition filed charging the minor with a delinquent act. Typically a police officer will review the matter if called to the scene, or a juvenile probation officer will have the opportunity to talk to family members and the child in order to prepare a social history. This social history is completed after the child is brought to the juvenile center and is used to determine if an informal agreement is appropriate for the child. If it is decided to proceed informally, an agreement will be written and the parent(s) or guardian and the child will sign the contract.

For an informal handling of a juvenile matter to be successful, there has to be cooperation among the child, juvenile probation, and the family. Since the majority of female juvenile offenders are referred to probation by a family member, it is unlikely that an informal arrangement will work. Many of these cases may have previously been handled as status offenses, but with the changes in legislation, more states have decreased the number of children falling into the status offense category. This has caused more girls to be brought into delinquency on assault charges because of family altercations or on violation of court orders. Even on first offenses, girls are more often brought up on formal delinquency allegations. Furthermore, if the allegation is based on family conflict between the parent(s) and the child, an informal agreement that depends on cooperation between parent and child would likely be unsuccessful.

A prosecutor will make a decision whether to file a petition based on the police and probation reports. Prosecutors may also display gender bias against female offenders. They are sometimes confused about their role and believe that it is their job to protect the child from her actions and to do what they consider is in the best interests of the child, rather than what justice requires. They may want to provide help to the youth and encourage what they view as more female-like behavior. This may also be the point where the prosecutor and probation decide whether to recommend detention of the juvenile prior to adjudication.

If a parent or guardian is not at the detention hearing, it is unlikely that the juvenile will be released to her home. Females are more likely to be detained for non-serious offenses than males. Again, if the allegations stem from familial conflict—that is, assault or running away—it is unlikely that the parent will come to the detention hearing and request the child be returned home. If there is abuse in the home, and the court learns of the abuse, the judge may be reluctant to allow the girl to return home, even if the parent is present. The judge may see it as his or her job to protect the girl from further abuse.

It is at the detention stage that a defense attorney will probably be appointed. Although the defense attorney should advocate for the expressed interests of the client, defense attorneys can also be confused about their role and may argue best interests instead. Since gender bias is prevalent in society and in the courts, the attorney may also have preconceived notions on how girls should behave.

Since girls are more often brought into the system because of sexual activity, this may also play a role in their detention prior to adjudication. In a study that looked at the juvenile court in Los Angeles from 1920 to 1950, it was found that 77% of the girls were held before their adjudicatory hearing and that their detention was linked to their sexual activity and venereal disease.[24]

The adjudicatory hearing, or the guilt and innocence determination, is the next stage.[25] While the prosecutor can offer diversion at any time, it would be anticipated to occur prior to the start of the adjudicatory hearing. Diversion may be offered more often to girls as the cases against them may be weak and would not be sustained at trial. This actually widens the net for bringing girls into the system because, although the charges might be dismissed at a later point, diversion is a way to keep girls under the supervision of the system. In contrast, when diversion is offered for boy offenders, it is viewed as a proposal of leniency for criminal behavior. The cases against girls that are not diverted are still not going to be the worst of the worse; they are still more minor offenses than the charges brought against boys.[26]

At disposition or sentencing, the courts are to look at the uniqueness of the juvenile offender and offer a disposition that will meet the needs of the juvenile toward rehabilitation and treatment. Since most programs have been developed with the male offender in mind, this is difficult to do for female offenders. Early institutions were built to keep girls and boys in separate facilities. Girls would be kept until marriageable age, and while they were being detained they would learn housekeeping skills in order to ensure they could become good wives and mothers. From 1899 to 1909, half the girls determined to be delinquent would be sent to reformatories, in comparison to only one-fifth of boy delinquents.[27] These disparities continued, and girls were twice as likely to be detained as boys, three times more likely to be sent to reformatories (for their own protection), and stayed five times as long.[28] The study of Los Angeles courts found that although the court would release 61% of all juveniles on probation, only 27% of the girls would be released after their hearing. Approximately 33% of the girls were institutionalized and placed in reformatories for months at a time in order for them to obtain treatment for a variety of venereal diseases.[29] If a girl was lucky enough to be released on probation, she was not sent home; rather, she would be placed in a private home as a domestic or into a private institution such as a home for unmarried mothers.[30] Again, what happened to girls was related to their sexual behavior.

The numbers are worse for girls of color. Half the girls in secure detention are African American, 13% Latina, and 33% Caucasian. Meanwhile, white girls make up 65% of the at-risk female population. When charges are filed against white girls, seven out of ten of the cases will be dismissed, while for African American girls only three out of ten cases will be dismissed.[31] Thus girls of color face a double whammy and are even more likely to not have their needs met through the juvenile justice system.

Juvenile programming continued to concentrate on the needs of boys, and even as the role of women was changing in society, the rehabilitation programs for girls were not being developed with this in mind. Girls are more likely to be placed in inappropriate programs that are not designed to meet the underlying needs of girl offenders. This creates an environment where girls are more likely to reoffend, as they were not given the tools to address the problems they face and are returned to an environment that was not healthy for them originally. As girls reoffend, they will still be placed in programs that are not working for them. The continued failure and recidivism will continue to destroy the girl's self-esteem, making it more difficult for her to succeed in any future placement. In addition, judges tend to show less patience when girls continue to appear in court with new prostitution or drug charges than they do with boys who reoffend.

Another problem within the juvenile justice system is the lack of continuity, making it difficult for the child to develop relationships with the various actors within the system. While this is a problem that affects all juveniles, its adverse affects on girls in the system are stronger as relationship building is more important to females than males. Juveniles will often see one judge who conducts the detention hearing, another judge for the adjudicatory and dispositional hearings, and yet a third judge or master for review hearings. The same may be true for the defense lawyer assigned to the case. Some offices divide the duties by the type of hearing, providing different attorneys at different stages in the proceedings. Furthermore, turnover is frequent in juvenile divisions, so the same lawyer may not be available for the life of the girl's case or still be there if she receives any new charges. The same is true for probation officers and prosecutors. Moreover, if the girl is in both the dependency system and delinquency system, her cases are likely to be heard by different judges, and while a caseworker will be assigned for her dependency case, it will not be the same person as her probation officer from her delinquency case—and the two may never confer.[32]

Improving Outcomes for Girls

There are several steps that could be taken to ensure more quality programs and experiences for girls.

1. *Gender bias awareness.*—All the actors within the juvenile justice system—law enforcement, probation, prosecutors, defense attorneys, and judges—need to acknowledge their own gender biases and be aware of this when they are making determinations about girls. There should be regular trainings to deal with this issue in order to decrease bias in the decision making of these parties.
2. *Communication between defense attorneys and the female juvenile offenders.*—While relationship building is important for any attorney/client relationship, this is particularly true when representing youth and even more so for girls. Studies indicate that girls value their relationships with others and that their self-esteem increases when their opinions and thoughts are valued within the relationships they develop with others. An attorney can help a girl client toward better outcomes by recognizing her strengths, positive behavior, and the steps she is taking to help herself.
3. *Continuity.*—Girls need consistency with the adults in the system in order for them to build relationships. As stated previously, rela-

tionship building is an important aspect of a girl's emotional development. Designing special units within the courts, probation, and defender organizations; recognizing the importance of this work; and having consistency with the actors can go a long way in having delinquent girls think better about and believe in themselves.

4. *Detention.*—Once girls are charged with an offense they are more likely than boys to be detained, even for offenses that are less serious and not violent. Although the benefits of detaining youth pre-adjudication are questionable, it is even more damaging for girls. Girls are also more likely to have been traumatized and victimized prior to the charges being brought against them, and the pending detention makes them more susceptible to the traumatic effects of detention. They face additional distress by being locked up in an environment that is probably not responsive to their needs since the majority of detention centers have been designed with the male offender in mind. For example, in most detention centers, juveniles have no privacy for any aspects of their daily routine. This is very uncomfortable for adolescent girls who typically do not like someone observing them taking care of private hygiene matters. Since many girls have been sexually and physically abused prior to their detention, they may feel as if they are being punished for what has happened to them, rather than because of something they did. Most female offenders see themselves as victims and survivors, as they do not see that they had any other choice but to take whatever actions were necessary to survive. For these reasons it is important for a girl's attorney to strongly advocate for her release.

Since most jurisdictions only look to the parent or legal guardian as the proper party to release the child to, this can further complicate matters for the female offender. The girl's family is likely to be dysfunctional, and there may have been problems between family members. If the girl has been abused, it has likely been at the hands of somebody living in her home. Therefore, the advocate must seek alternative placements for the girl client that does not force her to choose between being in a secure facility or in a dysfunctional, abusive home. If the girl must be detained, it is important to be sure she understands why she is being detained in order for her not to view it as punishment for the abuse she suffered and that she receives appropriate services while in detention.

5. *Placements.*—Female offenders often wait longer for a placement because of the lack of suitable programs for girls and the limited number of slots. Boys outnumber girls in the system, and most jurisdictions do not feel the need to keep slots available for girls. Sixty percent of girls will be detained for more than seven days while waiting for placement, while only 6% of boys will be detained for more than seven days.[33] Follow-up care is very limited in the juvenile system. Girls may need continued counseling, educational opportunities, job training, and parenting skills. These resources are unlikely to be available for the female offender when leaving a placement, and her family situation may remain the same.[34]

6. *Recidivism.*—Girls often fail when they return home because the programs where they are placed do not deal with the underlying issues that the girls face. Abuse—physical and sexual—is often what leads to the delinquent behavior. This ongoing abuse has lowered the girl's self esteem and has not given her the opportunity to learn how to handle relationships and any problems that might arise. She may often look for love and nurturing in all the wrong places and turn to prostitution to provide for herself. Although she may have successfully completed a drug or alcohol abuse program at a placement, since none of her underlying problems have been resolved and she has returned to her dysfunctional family, she is likely to return to drugs or alcohol abuse to ease her problems and pain.[35]

7. *Better programming for girls.*—The juvenile system needs to provide treatment programs that will help girls learn to cope with the abuse they have lived through and that focus on strength-based programming. Many of these girls have faced difficult times and have learned to cope with hardship, becoming stronger from dealing with their situations. What they do not have is a strong sense of how good they are and do not know how to turn the skills that they have obtained to the positive. Building on their existing strengths could help girls develop healthy attachment relationships, help recover from sexual and physical abuse, help them

manage anxiety and depression without substance abuse, be successful in school, have positive self-esteem and a sense for regarding the future, learn effective parenting, and learn to take care of themselves and access good medical care.[36]

Just providing more programming for girls does not guarantee an automatic solution. When there are facilities that are girl-only, the focus appears to be on the girl's sexuality. There is concern about girls being or becoming pregnant, and the facility conducts automatic testing and treatment of girls for venereal diseases. In boy-only facilities, testing for sexually transmitted diseases is only conducted when requested by the juvenile.[37]

8. *More resources for girls' programs.*—State and federal legislators need to allot additional funding for existing girls' programs and for the creation of new systems that meet the needs of girls and are culturally sensitive. Girls need programs that will provide them with treatment, educational opportunities, life skills, and parenting training. In addition to programs supported by the juvenile justice system, developing community-based programing that will provide services for girls who are high risk or are reentering into the community will help keep girls from offending or recidivism.

Many of these suggestions would not take additional resources and would not be that hard to accomplish. However, implementing even some of these programs could make a big difference to girls who do not have much hope. For some girls, just having someone who believes in them could help them turn their lives around.

NOTES

1. Anne Bowen Poulin, *Female Delinquents: Defining Their Place in the Justice System*, 1996 Wis. L. Rev. 541, 557.

2. *Steven Mintz, Huck's Raft: A History of American Childhood* 160–161 (Belknap Press of Harvard University Press 2004).

3. *Id.* at 113–115.

4. Kim Taylor-Thompson, *Girl Talk—Examining Racial and Gender Lines in Juvenile Justice*, 6 Nev. L.J. 1137, 1149 (2006).

5. *Id.*

6. American Bar Association and the National Bar Association, *Justice by Gender: The Lack of Appropriate Prevention, Diversion and Treatment Alternatives for Girls in the Justice System*, 9 Wm. & Mary J. Women & L. 73, 79 (2002).

7. *See* Nancy E. Dowd, *Boys, Masculinities and Juvenile Justice*, 8 J. Korean L. 115, 124 (2008).

8. *D.S. Tanenhaus, Juvenile Justice in the Making* (Oxford Univ. Press 2004).

9. Alison S. Burke, *Girls and the Juvenile Court: An Historical Examination of the Treatment of Girls*, 47(1) Crim. Law Bull. Art. 5 (Winter 2011).

10. *Meda Chesney-Lind & Randall G. Shelden, Girls, Delinquency, and Juvenile Justice* 57 (3rd ed., Wadsworth, Cengage Learning 2004).

11. Bowen Poulin, *Female Delinquents, supra* note 1, at 558–559.

12. *Chesney-Lind & Shelden, Girls, Delinquency, and Juvenile Justice, supra* note 10, at 25.

13. *Id.*

14. Marty Beyer *et al.*, *A Better Way to Spend $500,00: How the Juvenile Justice System Fails Girls*, 18 Wis. Women's L.J. 51, 64 (Spring 2003).

15. *Id.* at 58–59.

16. Bowen Poulin, *Female Delinquents, supra* note 1, at 560–561.

17. D. M. Bishop & C. Frazier, *Gender Bias in Juvenile Justice Processing: Implications of the JJDP Act*, 82 J. Crim. Law & Criminology 1162, 1183 (1992).

18. *Chesney-Lind & Shelden, Girls, Delinquency, and Juvenile Justice, supra* note 10, at 126, quoting *F. Adler, Sisters in Crime* (McGraw-Hill 1975), at 95.

19. *Chesney-Lind & Shelden, Girls, Delinquency, and Juvenile Justice, supra* note 10, at 127.

20. *Id.* at 128.

21. Bowen Poulin, *Female Delinquents, supra* note 1, at 546.

22. Bishop & Frazier, *Gender Bias in Juvenile Justice Processing, supra* note 17, at 1183.

23. *Chesney-Lind & Shelden, Girls, Delinquency, and Juvenile Justice, supra* note 10.

24. *Id.*

25. If a juvenile is to be transferred to criminal court or competency issues are going to be raised, this would occur prior to the adjudicatory hearing. However, these two hearings will not be discussed in this book.

26. Bowen Poulin, *Female Delinquents, supra* note 1, at 553.

27. *Chesney-Lind & Shelden, Girls, Delinquency, and Juvenile Justice, supra* note 10, at 167, 221.

28. *Id.* at 167.

29. *Id.* at 171.

30. *Id.* at 171.

31. *Id.* at 69.

32. Beyer *et al.*, *A Better Way to Spend $500,00, supra* note 14, at 61–62.

33. *Chesney-Lind & Shelden, Girls, Delinquency, and Juvenile Justice, supra* note 10, at 200.

34. Beyer *et al.*, at 63.

35. *Id.* at 64.

36. *Id.* at 71.

37. Meda Chesney-Lind, *Challenging Girls' Invisibility in Juvenile Court*, 564 Annals Am. Acad. Pol. & Soc. Sci. 185, 198 (1999).

5

Sexual Media and American Youth

PIOTR BOBKOWSKI AND AUTUMN SHAFER

Sexual socialization is the process by which individuals come to understand who they are sexually and learn the appropriate behaviors associated with their sexual identities. While parents, siblings, peers, and other individuals in a youth's social settings (e.g., school, religious institutions, etc.) are key agents of sexual socialization, various media also play a role. The average American youth spends more time using media on a daily basis than she does attending school or interacting with parents and family.[1] Sexual themes saturate the media to which many young people attend. With the media landscape increasingly shifting toward interactive and user-generated content (e.g., Facebook, YouTube, texting) it is especially important to consider how youth select, engage, and apply sexual media in their lives.

In this chapter, we focus on media (television, movies, music, magazines, Internet, video games, etc.) and their potential role in teaching young people who to be and what to do sexually. For example, media may influence young people's standards of attractiveness, their sexual and romantic expectations, and their sexual norms and behaviors. This discussion is structured around the media practice model,[2] a conceptual framework that emphasizes young people's active roles in selecting, interacting with, and integrating sexual media content into their developing identities. Sexual media do affect young people, and these effects are often negative. We argue, however, that at least to a certain extent, young people play an active role in regulating these effects.

How Sexual Are the Media Young People Use?

The average eight- to eighteen-year-old American spends 7.5 hours every day using media, a time commitment that stretches to ten hours daily when his or her media multitasking—the simultaneous use of two or more media—is taken into account.³ At 4.5 hours daily, television remains the medium with which young people spend the most time. A comprehensive analysis of more than one thousand American television shows and ten television channels found that more than two-thirds of all programs contained some talk about sex and that more than one-third of the programs depicted sexual behavior.⁴ A separate analysis found that about 90% of television programs that featured teenage characters included some sexual content.⁵ These analyses also showed that when sex was portrayed on television, risks, consequences, or responsibilities associated with sex (e.g., unplanned pregnancies or sexually transmitted infections) were not usually included. Only about 10% of the programs with sexual content included any mention of risks.⁶

Sexual content tends to be even more frequent and explicit in movies than on television.⁷ Popular music, especially rap and hip-hop, contains more sexual references than most television genres.⁸ As with television programs, sexual content in other media in general lacks any serious contextual information. An analysis of four media (music, movies, television, and magazines) used most frequently by early adolescents concluded that less than 1% of the content included any mention of the three C's of sexual health: commitment, contraceptives, or consequences.⁹

The average young American spends about one hour and fifteen minutes a day playing video games.¹⁰ As with other media content, studies have shown that video games regularly portray sexualized characters and situations.¹¹ In addition, the computer takes up approximately 1.5 hours of the average young person's daily non-school media time.¹² While it is difficult to measure the volume of sexual content online, one estimate suggests that more than a third (37%) of all websites are devoted to sexually explicit content.¹³ It is relatively easy for young people to come upon sexually explicit content on the Internet. About one in ten (8%–11%) American adolescents reports intentionally seeking out online pornography,¹⁴ while more than one-fourth (28%) of adolescents report unwillingly coming across such online content.¹⁵

Media Practice Model

In the early days of mass communication and media studies, a common assumption about the media's effect on an audience was that it resembled a "hypodermic needle" or a "magic bullet." A media message was thought to inject itself into a naïve and passive audience, resulting in a direct and uniform effect on all its members. Media researchers now have generally disavowed this traditional paradigm for being overly simplistic. It is still echoed, however, each time that a movie or a song gains popular attention for the potential harm it might inflict on its audience, especially on young people.

Today we know that media messages affect audiences in much less linear and homogeneous ways. Not all members of an audience are uniformly receptive to the media they use. Individuals often take active roles in moderating and even blocking the effects of media messages. In today's new interactive media environment, media users may be more involved than ever before in controlling their media. The media practice model[16] was designed to organize and illustrate this "active audience" perspective. In this chapter, we use the model to integrate and present what we know about young people's use of the media in the context of their sexual development and the media's role in affecting this aspect of young people's development.

The media practice model is structured around three "moments" that transpire in young people's encounters with sexual media: *selection*, *engagement*, and *application*. Each moment in the model, which can last a literal moment or considerably longer, comprises a number of processes that shape an individual's encounter with a media message and its effects. Each moment influences the subsequent moment in a cycle that is repeated over time and exposures. Peer-generated media and mass media are interwoven at each moment.[17]

Empirical evidence in the domain of sexual media provides support for the model's moments. Longitudinal studies show that young people become attuned to sexual content in the media when they enter puberty.[18] The sexual content to which they expose themselves at this stage influences their sexual norms and scripts. Continued exposure to sexual content may further increase the salience of this content. Heavier users of sexually permissive content may come to think of early and unprotected sexual intercourse as being normal for their age group. Particularly in the absence of negative consequences, positive portrayals of sexual acts may promote the premature initiation of sexual behavior.[19] In the following sections, we discuss each of the "moments"—selection, engagement, and application—and summarize research that demonstrates how each of these operates.

The First Moment: Selection
Personal Characteristics

Media consumers' first task is to choose specific media and content from among a vast and growing set of media options. Both personal and contextual factors can influence a young person's decision to use specific sexual media. For some teens, there may be a biological basis to their interest in such media. A study of white male teens, for instance, showed that individuals with high testosterone levels were more likely to have engaged in sexual intercourse than young men with low testosterone levels.[20] It is likely, therefore, that youth with high testosterone levels would also be more interested in sexual media than their low-testosterone peers. In a separate study, teenage girls who entered puberty earlier than their peers expressed more interest in sexual media than girls who matured later.[21]

Young people's social factors, such as family characteristics, peer groups, and religious involvement, can moderate the extent to which their biological predispositions lead to sexual behaviors. A follow-up to the testosterone study cited above showed that high-testosterone boys who did not attend religious services were most likely to initiate sex over a three-year period; low-testosterone boys who attended religious services frequently were the least likely to be sexually active during the same period.[22]

The backgrounds of young people—the way they were brought up—likely also influence their interest in consuming sexual media. Some youth appear to shield themselves from sexual content that conflicts with their sexual values. In a national survey, for example, teens who were more religious and who had less permissive attitudes about premarital sex reported liking less mature (including less sexual) television programs than their peers who were not as religious.[23] Family and home characteristics can also increase the amount of sexual media that young people consume. Teens who had a television in their bedroom and teens who spent more unsupervised time at home consumed more sexual content.[24]

Sexual Scripts

Young people actively select the media they use based on the characters, scripts, and storylines these media present. Guided by their sexual self-concepts and their attitudes about romantic and sexual relationships, specific segments of youth will select the types of sexual scripts they find more or less compelling. A traditional heterosexual script dominates romantic and sexual storylines on prime-time television, reality dating shows, and teen dramas and in popular music and music videos.[25] In this script, male characters actively and aggressively pursue sex, and female characters willingly objectify themselves and are judged for their sexual conduct. Gender-oriented magazines that many youth are exposed to—*Maxim* and *FHM* for men, *Cleo* and *Cosmo* for women—suggest that sex for men is primarily for pleasure and recreation and that it is normal for men to have many sexual partners.[26] Media scripts also inform young people about desirable partner characteristics, long-term relationships, and the appropriate timing of sex.[27]

The experiences of many youth may not resonate with this dominant script, however. Members of racial and sexual minorities may prefer media that better reflect their lives. African American adolescents, for instance, prefer television shows with black characters.[28] Such preferences based on cultural and social group affiliations also likely affect young people's other media selections. Models of romantic relationships differ between African American, Latino, and European American youth,[29] and these differences are likely reflected in the media scripts members of these groups endorse. Finally, although gay and lesbian relationships are depicted more often in the media now than in the past, these relationships are rarely shown as being overtly sexual,[30] which suggests that gay and lesbian youth may be more likely than their straight peers to turn to alternative and niche media for sexual scripts that reflect their identities and experiences.

This overview of factors that influence young people's media selections should make clear that exposure to sexual media is unlikely to result in uniform effects across the adolescent population. By their dispositions, young people may be drawn to some media and disregard other media. In accord with who they see themselves being and becoming, they may actively select some genres and messages while ignoring others. Once selected, the effects of sexual media on their audiences are further complicated by how users engage with the media and how they apply the lessons of these media in their lives.

The Second Moment: Engagement

Engagement encompasses the psychological, interpretative, and physical interactions young people can have with sexual media content. Since youth engage with media differently across media platforms and exposure contexts, the effects of sexual media exposure tend not to be direct or uniform among individuals exposed to the same sexual content. The same sexual message may even have a different effect on a single individual if it is presented under two unique circumstances. For example, each adolescent in a carful of joyriding friends would engage differently with a popular song being blasted from the car radio. Each teen's experience with the song would also be different if he or she was listening to the radio alone at home or if the song played in the background as he or she played a video game. Media research suggests that the way that individuals engage with media content influences the effects that content may have on its users.

What Happens during Exposure?

A number of psychological and physical factors that transpire during an individual's exposure to media influence that individual's engagement with the media message and the ultimate effect of the message. The following discussion reviews several aspects of message processing that occurs during exposure. These include attention, involvement, arousal, character evaluation, narrative transportation, counterarguing, and reactance. Each of these can suppress or enhance the effects of sexual media content. It is important to note that some of these aspects of processing are conscious and controllable, while others occur automatically and beyond our awareness.

An adolescent must devote some level of attention to process any message presented in the media. Research on attention, memory, and processing has found, however, that we have a limited amount of cognitive resources available to process messages.[31] When our cognitive resources are taxed, our ability to scrutinize the merits of a message is reduced.[32] The relationship between attention, cognitive resources, and processing is especially important for adolescents because they tend to be heavy multitaskers, often using more than one media at a time.[33]

Media multitasking may intensify the role that sexual media play in adolescents' development. It is theorized that a multitasking adolescent will have fewer resources to counterargue or criticize a sexual media message, thus processing it with little or no resistance.[34] One study found that watching television while surfing the Internet increased the sexual effects of media for adolescents.[35] A study of media/non-media multitasking (e.g., listening to a sexually explicit song while driving), however, found that adolescents who frequently engaged in media/non-media multitasking were less affected by sexual media than adolescents who engaged in less media/non-media multitasking.[36]

A key factor in message processing is the media user's level of involvement with the message, which encompasses both attention and interest. When highly involved, an audience member should be highly motivated to process the message.[37] Correlational studies have found that involvement in sexual media is positively associated with recreational attitudes toward sex, increased normative beliefs about peer sexual activity, and beliefs that men are motivated by sex and that physical appearance is important.[38] One study even found that the amount of television youth watched was less predictive of sexual attitudes and expectations than their involvement in the sexual media they used.[39] This suggests that *how* youth watch television may be more important than how *much* television they watch.

Another element of processing sexual media content is arousal, which may be general (e.g., anticipation or excitement) or specifically sexual in nature.[40] When aroused, the audience member is likely to be intensely focused on the arousing content, which is likely to increase memory and accessibility of the content. For instance, teens aroused while watching online pornography are more likely to think about sexual activities after exposure than teens who were not aroused.[41]

Psychological aspects of message processing, such as character evaluations and narrative transportation, can also affect engagement. Most media messages include characters, and many are presented in a narrative format. A number of communication and psychology theories assert that our perceptions and attachments to characters and the story influence media effects. Social cognitive theory, for example, suggests that the more an audience member perceives a character to be similar to her, the more likely she is to imitate that character's behavior.[42] In addition, the message interpretation process model states that perceived realism of a media portrayal influences perceptions of similarity and identification with the character, which in turn affects relevant behavioral intentions and behavior.[43] Research suggests that the more realistic (or authentic) characters and a story line are perceived to be, and the more an audience member feels he is similar to and can identify with the story's characters, the more likely he is to manifest story-consistent beliefs and behaviors.

For example, suppose that a teen watches a television show that he perceives to be authentic and which includes a character with whom the teen identifies. In the show, the character is rewarded by high fives from other male characters when he is sexually aggressive toward women. This teen may come to believe that acting sexually aggressive is positive, expected, and likely to result in admiration from his friends. If this stereotypical media portrayal occurs repeatedly over time and across multiple media platforms, then it is even more likely to become engrained in the audience member.

For narratives, research suggests that the more transported into the story a reader or viewer becomes, the more likely she will develop story-consistent beliefs and attitudes.[44] Transportation into a story means that the reader or viewer is highly absorbed into the story and is essentially "transported" into the story world. Transportation is said to result in less counterarguing with the story content, greater identification, increased attention to the story, and decreased attention to the non-media events happening during exposure. Transportation is also theorized to promote post-viewing discussion and thinking about the story.[45] Although little research has thus far examined the impact of transportation into sexual media content, one study found that when readers were transported into a story about a gay man experiencing discrimination at his fraternity reunion, they were more likely to believe fraternities were homophobic.[46]

An important aspect of message processing and persuasion is whether an audience member engages in resistance to persuasion during exposure. The two most common forms of resistance to persuasion are counterarguing and reactance. When watching, reading, or listening to a media message, counterarguing happens when the audience member has contradictory or argumentative thoughts about the message.[47] For example, a teen reading a magazine article about how to attract a boyfriend may disagree with the advice in the article and actively generate thoughts that dispute that advice (e.g., "that would never work" or "most guys don't act like that"). Greater counterarguing should result in less message acceptance. Reactance occurs when a reader, viewer, or listener experiences a negative emotional or logical reaction to a message that is portrayed as threatening his or her freedoms.[48]

A teen may experience reactance when he watches a television show about teen sexual relationships that is overtly educational rather than entertaining. In this instance, the teen may feel like the show's creators are trying to preach to him and limit his freedom of choice or influence him. Reactance is likely to lead to message rejection. An experiment that examined effects of portrayals of condom use in a teen television program found that greater reactance to a scene in which characters positively discussed using condoms resulted in lower intentions to practice safe sex.[49]

In sum, much happens at the moment of exposure to a sexual media message. The level of attention and involvement, the extent of arousal, the degree of identification with storylines and characters, the level of transportation, and the amount of counterarguing and reactance—all these elements have the potential to temper or inflate the effect of a sexual media message on an individual's thoughts or behaviors. While many of these aspects of message processing are likely present for adolescents and adults, there is reason to believe that there are also some differences. For instance, as discussed, adolescents are particularly prone to media multitasking that affects their attention level; adolescents likely differ from adults in the types of content they find arousing and the types of characters with which they identify; and adolescents may be especially disposed to experiencing reactance because they dislike being told what they should do.[50]

Formation of Attitudes and Beliefs

Young people who use sexual media do not simply enact behaviors they learn from these media. Exposure to sexual content on television or in song lyrics is likely to first stimulate in young people certain sexual attitudes, norms, expectations, and assessments of self-efficacy, that is, how sexually able they feel themselves to be. It is these attitudes and beliefs that may then influence the type of sexual actions, if any, in which young people engage.

Young people's attitudes about the nature of sex and sexual relationships can be influenced by the attitudes modeled to them in the media. Teens who watched more prime-time television featuring sexual content thought of sex as being recreational rather than relational, in contrast to their peers who watched such programs less frequently.[51] Increased exposure to sexy music videos has been associated with more positive attitudes about premarital sex.[52] Young adults who viewed advertisements that featured sexual themes reported more sexually aggressive attitudes than their peers who viewed ads depicting women in progressive roles.[53] Studies have found that sexual attitudes informed by television content are an important precursor to sexual behavior.[54]

Sexual media inform young people's social norms—whether, with whom, and how often it is normal for people their age to have sex, for instance. Frequent television viewers tended to overestimate rates of sexual activity and pregnancy among young people.[55] Teens with heavier sexual media "diets" felt stronger pressure to have sex than those who did not consume as much sexual media.[56] Among college men, exposure to sexual portrayals in the media was associated with perceptions of peers' sexual activity, which were in turn associated with casual sexual behavior.[57] Similarly, reading men's magazines (e.g., *Maxim*) and watching movies was associated with estimating higher rates of sexual risk taking among peers and with more permissive sexual attitudes.[58] These perceptions of peers' behaviors and sexual attitudes were, in turn, associated with earlier sexual debut.

Sexual media can also influence young people's expectations about the appropriate timing of sex and the consequences of having sex. Females who watched television frequently, for example, reported expecting sex to occur earlier in the course of a relationship than females who did not watch as much television.[59] Two studies that measured media exposure and teens' expectations about sexual outcomes over time showed that teens who consumed more sexual media had more permissive expectations, which are likely to lead to sexual behavior.[60] In these studies, young people with heavy sexual media diets were more likely to believe that sex would lead to feeling more grown-up and that it would prevent a relationship from ending. They were also less likely to think that sex could ruin someone's reputation or result in pregnancy.

Adolescents for whom movies, Internet, or magazines were the primary sources of information about sex expressed greater self-efficacy for having sex despite possible obstacles (e.g., upset parents) than adolescents who primarily relied on non-media sources for their sexual information.[61] Teens with heavy sexual media diets had greater self-efficacy for practicing safe sex than teens with lighter sexual media diets.[62] Self-efficacy for practicing safe sex was associated with actually practicing safe sex.

Media Effect Theories

Several theories have been proposed to account for the cognitive processes by which media content affects media users' norms, self-concepts, beliefs, intentions, and ultimately, behaviors. These include social cognitive theory, cultivation theory, uses and gratifications, and priming. The following discussion briefly summarizes each of these, focusing on how each may operate within the context of sexual media. While each of these theories proposes a mechanism that links media messages and their potential effects on audience members, the moderators we discussed previously (e.g., attention, arousal, etc.) could interrupt or enhance the functioning of these mechanisms.

According to social cognitive theory,[63] media characters model sexual beliefs, attitudes, and behaviors for audiences. Central for this theory is the portrayal or absence of consequences associated with media characters' sexual behaviors. Young people are more likely to imitate media attitudes or behaviors that are rewarded; they are less likely to do so if the behaviors are not rewarded or are punished. Several further characteristics may temper or intensify this association. The more similar viewers perceive themselves to the media characters, the more likely they will be to imitate the modeled attitudes and behaviors. The more capable of performing a specific action viewers perceive themselves to be (i.e., self-efficacy), the more likely they will be to carry out this action.[64] Media messages may also steer individuals toward specific social settings or networks that support and reinforce the attitudes and behaviors modeled in the media.[65] In one survey, adolescents who relied on friends and media for their sexual information had greater self-efficacy for having sex than their peers who used other sources for sexual information.[66]

Cultivation theory[67] suggests that the repeated exposure to similar media content cultivates in viewers a vision of the world that is more consistent with the world portrayed in the media than with reality. As ideas and scripts about relationships and sexual behavior are echoed in various media (e.g., it's normal to hook up with many people), these become salient and accessible in the minds of media consumers.[68] As a result, young people's beliefs and expectations about relationships and sex may reflect more the distorted view of reality presented in the media than actual reality.

According to the uses and gratifications perspective,[69] media users' motivations for using specific media are related to what they anticipate to take away from these media. College males who watched sexual television intending to gain knowledge from these programs reported expecting a wider variety of sexual behaviors within a romantic relationship than their peers who watched such programs without an intention to learn.[70] Women who used television programs as a source of learning and entertainment were more likely to adhere to traditional gender roles and to hold stereotypical attitudes about sex and dating than those with different motives for television use.[71]

According to priming theory, specific media content activates related scripts in the minds of viewers.[72] Once primed, individuals might respond to various stimuli differently than they would without the priming. For instance, college students who listened to sexually provocative lyrics before evaluating online dating profiles were more likely to focus on the sexual characteristics of the owners of the profiles than those who listened to innocuous music before viewing the online profiles.[73]

Same Content, Different Interpretation

As we all know, messages can often have multiple meanings and are frequently subject to interpretation. Adolescents have agency in how they interpret the sexual content they select and engage with. Interpretation is often influenced by a teen's identity and sexual beliefs. Studies have found that sexual content in media popular with teens is often not explicit and frequently contains innuendos. Music lyrics, for instance, are frequently found to contain sexual innuendos, which invites multiple interpretations. A study of Madonna's early music video "Papa Don't Preach" illustrates both points when Madonna sings, "Papa don't preach, I'm in trouble deep, I'm going to keep my baby." Race and gender were found to be factors in how teens interpreted this lyric. For example, African American males thought the "baby" line meant that Madonna wanted to stay with her boyfriend despite her father's objections, but white females thought Madonna was singing about being pregnant and wanting to keep her child.[74] For African American males this song might influence their beliefs about romantic relationships, while white females would interpret it as a message supportive of not having an abortion.

In sum, engagement is a crucial point when considering the potential effects of sexual media on young people. How youth engage with sexual media at the moment of exposure is likely to influence the outcome of that exposure. Media users' attention, involvement, arousal, identification with characters, transportation, and resistance to persuasion can regulate the various mechanisms through which media messages influence their lives. The influence of sexual media may manifest itself first in attitudes, norms, outcome expectancies, and a sense of sexual self-efficacy. These attitudes and beliefs, in turn, shape whether and how young people apply media messages and the types of sexual behaviors they enact.

The Third Moment: Application

Testing Sexual Behaviors

After engaging with sexual media, young people may apply what they have gleaned from the media messages to their lives and identities. In the application stage, young people may test sexual behaviors they learned in the media, consider how well these fit with their expectations, and gauge their peers' reactions to these behaviors. Such behaviors may not only include sexual intercourse but also pre-coital behaviors such the overall treatment of a romantic partner, sexual talk, and sexual touching. Application may also take the form of production, as users create and distribute their own sexual media to their peers.

Studies show that exposure to sexual media affects young people's sexual behavior, including pre-coital behaviors, the timing of sexual debut, and the number of sexual partners.[75] The evidence of media's effect on the timing of sexual debut appears particularly compelling. In a study of North Carolina adolescents, white twelve- to fourteen-year-olds with heavier sexual media diets (television, music, movies, and magazines) were more than twice as likely to have had sex by sixteen than their peers who did not consume as much sexual media.[76] In a national study that assessed teens' consumption of sexual content on television, heavy viewers were twice as likely as light viewers to initiate sex within a year of the original survey.[77]

Other sexual behaviors linked to increased exposure to sexual media include lower rates of birth control use,[78] more uncommitted sexual relationships,[79] increased perpetration of sexual harassment,[80] and sexual violence.[81] Among teen girls, studies have also shown associations between heavier sexual media use and pregnancy,[82] as well as testing positive for a sexually transmitted infection.[83] Statistical tests of these associations accounted for various demographic and social characteristics that may have contributed to these sexual outcomes. Even so, the links between exposure to sexual media and sexual outcomes persisted.

Associations between sexual media exposure and sexual behavior outcomes may be reciprocal. One study, for instance, showed that adolescents who were sexually active during an initial survey reported heavier exposure to sexual media in a later survey than their peers who initially were not sexually active.[84] Those with higher exposure to sexual media, in turn, had an increased probability of progressing in the level of their sexual activity within the following year.

Youth as Distributors and Creators of Sexual Media

In recent years, easy access to media production and dissemination platforms has expanded young people's opportunities for applying sexual media in their lives. In the past, we characterized teens hanging posters of scantily clad actors and models on their bedroom walls as part of the application arch of the media practice model.[85] Today, young people can post photographs of themselves in suggestive poses on Facebook, send sexual text messages to one or more friends, or create mash-up videos of sexy celebrities on YouTube. Such actions of sexual self-disclosure move teens beyond their bedrooms and into the vast digital domain where they become producers and disseminators of sexual media content. In the following discussion, we address two questions: Who are the young people who engage in mediated sexual self-disclosure? and What are the implications of sexual self-disclosure for these youth?

Young people whose sexual self-concept is a prominent component of their identities are more likely to present themselves sexually than those youth for whom sexuality is not an important characteristic. One study has shown, for instance, that sexually active young adults and those with a history of casual sex were more likely to self-disclose sexually in their MySpace profiles than their peers who were not as sexually active.[86] In another study, girls who had suffered sexual abuse were more likely to select sexier characters (i.e., avatars) in an experimental online game than girls without a history of abuse.[87] In sum, youth for whom sex is a more prominent component of their identities, as measured by a history of sexual behavior, appear to be more likely to disclose sexually in online contexts.

Personal dispositions such as extraversion and self-monitoring may moderate the extent to which young people engage in self-disclosure. Extraverts are generally more talkative and assertive in offline contexts,[88] and these characteristics also carry over to self-disclosure in online settings.[89] Self-monitors, meanwhile, are concerned about presenting themselves in ways that are appropriate for the situation, as opposed to accurately presenting their self-attributes.[90] Thus, while extraverts might be more likely to present themselves sexually online, self-monitors may be more likely to do so only if they determine that such presentations are contextually appropriate.

Audience-related goals may also shape the extent to which young people portray themselves sexually. Friends and other offline acquaintances tend to make up the audience for young people's online self-disclosures.[91] Many young people strive for their offline identities to match their online personas, so the way they present themselves offline corresponds to the way they appear online. Others may be guided by the self-presentation norms of their friendship groups. For example, in an analysis of religious self-disclosure in MySpace, users whose friends were religious were three times as likely as users who had no religious friends to identify religiously in their profiles, regardless of how religious they were personally.[92] The standards and opinions of those who are meant to receive the self-disclosure play an important role in the characteristics of the self-disclosure.

The online environment does allow users who desire for their online selves to diverge from their offline identities to selectively tailor their self-presentations.[93] For instance, individuals who are committed to a particular identity but who feel they have not fully conformed to this identity may present themselves using symbols that signify that identity.[94] Individuals who think of themselves as sexy may symbolically communicate this identity using online media. Conversely, those who want to tone down their offline sexual identities or reputations may use online self-presentations to do so.

We now turn to the second question: What happens when youth produce sexual media content? Communicating about sex with strangers online increases young people's risk of receiving aggressive sexual solicitations.[95] Internally, online sexual self-disclosure may reinforce the centrality of the sexual self within one's identity. Studies have shown that stating a position or performing a behavior in offline contexts leads to the internalization of that position or behavior, particularly if the assertion or behavior is public.[96] Evidence shows that internalization also occurs when the identity is enacted in an online environment.[97] In one experiment, for example, participants who viewed virtual characters who looked like them and who were shown exercising, reported exercising more in the subsequent twenty-four-hour period than participants who viewed virtual characters who looked like them but did not exercise.[98] Although the internalization effect has not been tested in the context of sexual self-disclosure, evidence suggests it may lead to a sexualization of the self-concept.

Feedback from audience members plays an important role in today's interactive digital media. Facebook photos, text messages, and YouTube videos are all subject to being "liked," commented on, and re-posted. A supportive feedback message may increase the probability that a publicly presented identity will be internalized,[99] while no feedback or negative feedback may forestall such an identity shift. Negative feedback may have negative consequences for the presenter's self-esteem, and it may, in some cases, rise to the level of cyber bullying.[100] Whether negative or positive, feedback is a unique and important characteristic of new media environments. It can have important implications for young people's sexual self-disclosures in these environments.

In addition to the potentially negative effects of sexual self-disclosure, new media may play a constructive role in young people's sexual development. The Internet allows like-minded but physically remote individuals to connect, communicate, explore, and affirm their identities. Gay and lesbian youth who lack offline support structures, for instance, may find positive peers and mentors in online communities and virtually rehearse their sexual identities, relationships, and behaviors.[101] In sum, while not all youth will engage in sexual self-disclosure in online settings, those who do may face a host of negative and positive consequences.

There are various ways in which young people can apply in their lives what they pick up in sexual media. Sexual debut and sexual intercourse are some of the behaviors that have been linked to sexual media exposure. Watching and listening to sexual media may also influence pre-coital behaviors, including the overall way in which youth relate to potential and real relationship partners. In the new media environment, sexual media application can also take the form of producing and distributing sexual media. With easy access to inexpensive production hardware (e.g., digital cameras), editing software, and dissemination platforms (e.g., social media), young people are free to digitally present their sexual selves to their online friends and to the wider virtual world.

Conclusion

Many internal, environmental, and situation-specific factors influence the extent to which sexual media affect how young people think about their sexual selves and how they act sexually. We have discussed these factors in terms of how young people select the media they use, how they engage these media, and how they apply the media's messages to their lives. The effects of sexual media, therefore, may differ from one individual to the next and from one situation to another. It is important to recognize these potential differences when predicting or evaluating the media's effects on young people's sexual socialization.

Given the amount of time young people spend with media and the volume of sexual content in the media, it is clear that the media play an important role in teaching young people about sex and sexuality. In light of both scientific evidence and anecdotal concerns about the media's role in sexual socialization, policies and regulations have been suggested and adopted to mitigate potential harmful effects of sexual media content and to create opportunities for healthy effects. The mostly voluntary ratings systems that have been developed for movies, television, and video games, specifying the amount and sometimes kind of sexual content, however, have been criticized for being applied inconsistently, being misunderstood by parents, and for potentially making sexually explicit programs more appealing to youth who want to be seen as mature and who dislike being told what to do.[102]

Policy statements from the American Academy of Pediatrics and the American Medical Association call on parents, medical professionals, and the entertainment media to limit children's exposure to unhealthy media messages about sex and to increase young people's access to information about contraceptives and healthy sexuality.[103] Media watchdog groups, like Common Sense Media, promote policy and technology improvements that would allow for greater parental monitoring of media consumption. Scholars have suggested that increasing the availability of sexual education and media literacy are strategies that may help youth be better informed about sexual health and the impact of media on their lives. Curricula may need to be updated to include information about potential consequences of creating and distributing sexual content.

Even in light of current and proposed policies and regulations, it is unlikely (and perhaps undesirable) that adolescents will ever be completely shielded from exposure to sexual content in media. What may be important is not eliminating opportunities for exposure to sexual content but, rather, increasing opportunities for adolescents to learn about sexual health, discuss what they see or hear in media with their parents, and have outlets to criticize and call for improvements in content. The goal may be the promotion of development of a healthy sense of sexual self-concept so adolescents have more agency in the media they select, how they engage with it, and how they apply it to their lives.

NOTES

1. V. Rideout et al., *The Henry J. Kaiser Fam. Found., Generation M²: Media in the Lives of 8–18 Year-Olds* (2010).

2. J.D. Brown, *Adolescents' Sexual Media Diets*, 27 J. Adolescent Health 35 (2000); A. Shafer et al., *Sexual Media Practice: How Adolescents Select, Engage with, and Are Affected by Sexual Media*, in The Oxford Handbook of Media Psychology 223–251 (Karen E. Dill, ed., Oxford Univ. Press 2012); J.R. Steele, *Teenage Sexuality and Media Practice: Factoring in the Influences of Family, Friends and School*, 36 J. Sex Res. 331 (1999); J.R. Steele & J.D. Brown, *Adolescent Room Culture: Studying Media in the Context of Everyday Life*, 24 J. Youth & Adolescence 551 (1995).

3. Rideout et al., *Generation M²*, supra note 1.

4. D. Kunkel et al., *The Henry J. Kaiser Fam. Found., Sex on TV 4: A Biennial Report to the Kaiser Family Foundation* (2005).

5. J.S. Aubrey, *Sex and Punishment: An Examination of Sexual Consequences and the Sexual Double Standard in Teen Programming*, 50 Sex Roles 505 (2004).

6. Kunkel et al., *Sex on TV 4*, supra note 4.

7. H. Gunasekera et al., *Sex and Drugs in Popular Movies: An Analysis of the Top 200 Films*, 9 J. Royal Soc'y Med. 464 (2005); C.J. Pardun et al., *Linking Exposure to Outcomes: Early Adolescents' Consumption of Sexual Content in Six Media*, 8 Mass Comm. & Soc'y 75 (2005).

8. Pardun et al., *Linking Exposure to Outcomes*, supra note 7.

9. *Id.*

10. Rideout et al., *Generation M²*, supra note 1.

11. J.D. Ivory, *Still a Man's Game: Gender Representation in Online Reviews of Video Games*, 9 Mass Comm. & Soc'y 103 (2006); E. Scharrer, *Virtual Violence: Gender and Aggression in Video Game Advertisements*, 7 Mass Comm. & Soc'y 393 (2004).

12. Rideout et al., *Generation M²*, supra note 1.

13. Optenet, *More than One Third of Web Pages Are Pornographic* (press release, June 16, 2010), www.optenet.com/en-us/new.asp?id=270 (last visited June 13, 2014).

14. M.L. Ybarra & K.J. Mitchell, *Exposure to Internet Pornography among Children and Adolescents: A National Survey*, 8 Cyber Psychol. & Behav. 437 (2005); M.L. Ybarra et al., *X-Rated Material and Perpetration of Sexually Aggressive Behavior among Children and Adolescents: Is There a Link?* 37 Aggressive Behav. 1 (2011) .

15. J. Wolak et al., *Does Online Harassment Constitute Bullying? An Exploration of Online Harassment by Known Peers and Online-Only Contacts*, 41 J. Adolescent Health 51 (2007).

16. Brown, *Adolescents' Sexual Media Diets*, supra note 2; Steele, *Teenage Sexuality and Media Practice*, supra note 2; Steele & Brown, *Adolescent Room Culture*, supra note 2.

17. Shafer et al., *Sexual Media Practice*, supra note 2.

18. A. Bleakley et al., *It Works Both Ways: The Relationship between Exposure to Sexual Content in the Media and Adolescent Sexual Behavior*, 11 Media Psychol. 443 (2008); J.L. Kim et al., *Sexual Readiness, Household Policies, and Other Predictors of Adolescents' Exposure to Sexual Content in Mainstream Entertainment Television*, 8 Media Psychol. 449 (2006).

19. P. Wright, *Mass Media Effects on Youth Sexual Behavior: Assessing the Claim for Causality*, in *Communication Yearbook* 343–386 (C.T Salmon ed., Routledge Press 2011).

20. J. Udry, *Hormonal and Social Determinants of Adolescent Sexual Initiation*, in *Adolescence and Puberty* 70–87 (J. Bancroft & J. Reinisch eds., Oxford Univ. Press 1990).

21. J.D. Brown et al., *Mass Media as a Sexual Super Peer for Early Maturing Girls*, 36 J. Adolescent Health 420 (2005).

22. C. Halpern et al., *Testosterone and Religiosity as Predictors of Sexual Attitudes and Activity among Adolescent Males: A Biosocial Model*, 26 J. Biosocial Sci. 217 (1994).

23. P.S. Bobkowski, *Adolescent Religiosity and Selective Exposure to Television*, 8 J. Media & Religion 55 (2009).

24. Kim et al., *Sexual Readiness*, supra note 18.

25. Aubrey, *Sex and Punishment*, supra note 5; R.L. Dukes et al., *Expressions of Love, Sex, and Hurt in Popular Songs: A Content Analysis of All-Time Greatest Hits*, 40 Soc. Sci. J. 643 (2003); A.L. Ferris et al., *The Content of Reality Dating Shows and Viewer Perceptions of Dating*, 57 J. Comm. 490 (2007); M. Kelly, *Virginity Loss Narratives in "Teen Drama" Television Programs*, 47 J. Sex Res. 479 (2010); J.L. Kim et al., *From Sex to Sexuality: Exposing the Heterosexual Script on Primetime Network Television*, 44 J. Sex Res. 145 (2007); B.A. Primack et al., *Degrading and Non-degrading Sex in Popular Music: A Content Analysis*, 123 Pub. Health Rep. 593 (2008).

26. P. Farvid & V. Braun, *"Most of Us Guys Are Raring to Go Anytime, Anyplace, Anywhere": Male and Female Sexuality in Cleo and Cosmo*, 55 Sex Roles 295 (2006); L.D. Taylor, *Effects of Visual and Verbal Sexual Television Content and Perceived Realism on Attitudes and Beliefs*, 42 J. Sex Res. 130 (2005).

27. Ferris et al., *The Content of Reality Dating Shows and Viewer Perceptions of Dating*, supra note 25; K.R. Johnson & B.M. Holmes, *Contradictory Messages: A Content*

Analysis of Hollywood-Produced Romantic Comedy Feature Films, 57 Comm. Q. 352 (2009); C. Segrin & R. Nabi, *Does Television Viewing Cultivate Unrealistic Expectations about Marriage?* 52 J. Comm. 247 (2002).

28. J.D. Brown & C.J. Pardun, *Little in Common: Racial and Gender Differences in Adolescents' Television Diets*, 48 J. Broadcasting & Electronic Media 266 (2004).

29. C. Milbrath et al., *Analyzing Cultural Models in Adolescent Accounts of Romantic Relationship*, 19 J. Res. Adolescence 313 (2009).

30. D.A. Fisher et al., *Gay, Lesbian, and Bisexual Content on Television: A Quantitative Analysis across Two Seasons*, 52 J. Homosexuality 167 (2007).

31. A. Lang, *The Limited Capacity Model of Mediated Message Processing*, 50 J. Comm. 46 (2000).

32. D.T. Gilbert, *How Mental Systems Believe*, 46 Am. Psychologist 107 (1991).

33. S.H. Jeong & M. Fishbein, *Predictors of Multitasking with Media: Media Factors and Audience Factors*, 10 Media Psychol. 364 (2007).

34. R.L. Collins, *Media Multitasking: Issues Posed in Measuring the Effects of Television Sexual Content Exposure*, 2 Comm. Methods & Measures 65 (2008).

35. *Id.*

36. S.H. Jeong et al., *Effects of Exposure to Sexual Content in the Media on Adolescent Sexual Behaviors: The Moderating Role of Multitasking with Media*, 13 Media Psychol. 222 (2010).

37. J. Peter & P. M. Valkenburg, *Adolescents' Use of Sexually Explicit Internet Material and Sexual Uncertainty: The Role of Involvement and Gender*, 77 Comm. Monographs 357 (2010); L.M. Ward & R. Rivadeneyra, *Contributions of Entertainment Television to Adolescents' Sexual Attitudes and Expectations: The Role of Viewing Amount versus Viewer Involvement*, 36 J. Sex. Res. 237 (1999).

38. Ward & Rivadeneyra, *Contributions of Entertainment Television to Adolescents' Sexual Attitudes and Expectations*, supra note 37; E.L. Zurbriggen & E.M. Morgan, *Who Wants to Marry a Millionaire? Reality Dating Television Programs, Attitudes towards Sex, and Sexual Behaviors*, 54 Sex Roles 1 (2006).

39. Ward & Rivadeneyra, *Contributions of Entertainment Television to Adolescents' Sexual Attitudes and Expectations*, supra note 37.

40. C.H. Hansen & W. Krygowski, *Arousal-Augmented Priming Effects: Rock Music Videos and Sex Object Schemas*, 21 Comm. Res. 24 (1994).

41. J. Peter & P.M. Valkenburg, *Adolescents' Exposure to Sexually Explicit Internet Material and Sexual Preoccupancy: A Three-Way Panel Study*, 11 Media Psychol. 207 (2008).

42. A. Bandura, *Social Foundations of Thought and Action: A Social Cognitive Theory* (Prentice-Hall 1986).

43. E.W. Austin & C.S. Knaus, *Predicting the Potential for Risky Behavior among Those Too Young to Drink, as the Result of Appealing Advertising*, 5 J. Health Comm. 13 (2000); E.W. Austin & H.K. Meili, *Effects of Interpretations of Televised Alcohol Portrayals on Children's Alcohol Beliefs*, 38 J. Broadcasting & Electronic Media 417 (1994); B.E. Pinkleton et al., *A Statewide Evaluation of the Effectiveness of Media*

Literacy Training to Prevent Tobacco Use among Adolescents, 21 Health Comm. 23 (2007).

44. M.C. Green & T.C. Brock, *The Role of Transportation in the Persuasiveness of Public Narratives*, 79 J. Personality and Soc. Psychol. 701 (2000).

45. M. Slater & D. Rouner, *Entertainment-Education and Elaboration Likelihood: Understanding the Processing of Narrative Persuasion*, 12 Comm. Theory 173 (2002).

46. M.C. Green, *Transportation into Narrative Worlds: The Role of Prior Knowledge and Perceived Realism*, 38 Discourse Processes 247 (2004).

47. J.T. Cacioppo, *Effects of Exogenous Changes in Heart Rate on Facilitation of Thoughts and Resistance to Persuasion*, 37 J. Personality & Soc. Psychol. 489 (1979).

48. S.S. Brehm & J.W. Brehm, *Psychological Reactance: A Theory of Freedom and Control* (Academic Press 1981); J.P. Dillard & L. Shen, *On the Nature of Reactance and Its Role in Persuasive Health Communication*, 72 Comm. Monographs 144 (2005).

49. E. Moyer-Gusé & R. Nabi, *Explaining the Effects of Narrative in an Entertainment Television Program: Overcoming Resistance to Persuasion*, 36 Hum. Comm. Res. 26 (2010).

50. J. Zeman et al., *Measurement Issues in Emotion Research with Children and Adolescents*, 14 Clinical Psychol.: Sci. & Prac. 377 (2007).

51. L. M. Ward & K. Friedman, *Using TV as a Guide: Associations between Television Viewing and Adolescents' Sexual Attitudes and Behavior*, 16 J. Res. Adolescence 133 (2006).

52. L.E. Greeson & R.A. Williams, *Social Implications of Music Videos for Youth: An Analysis of the Content and Effects of MTV*, 18 Youth & Soc'y 177 (1986).

53. N.J. MacKay & K. Covell, *The Impact of Women in Advertisement on Attitudes toward Women*, 36 Sex Roles 573 (1997).

54. L.M. Ward, *Understanding the Role of Entertainment Media in the Sexual Socialization of American Youth: A Review of Empirical Research*, 23 Developmental Rev. 347 (2003).

55. S. Davis & M.-L. Mares, *Effects of Talk Show Viewing on Adolescents*, 48 J. Comm. 69 (1998).

56. Bleakley et al., *It Works Both Ways*, supra note 18.

57. S.C. Chia & A.C. Gunther, *How Media Contribute to Misperceptions of Social Norms about Sex*, 9 Mass Comm. & Soc'y 301 (2006).

58. L.M. Ward et al., *Men's Media Use, Sexual Cognitions, and Sexual Risk Behavior: Testing a Mediational Model*, 47 Developmental Psychol. 592 (2011).

59. J.S. Aubrey et al., *Variety versus Timing: Gender Differences in College Students' Expectations as Predicted by Exposure to Sexually Oriented Television*, 30 Comm. Res. 432 (2003).

60. D.A. Fisher et al., *Televised Sexual Content and Parental Mediation: Influences on Adolescent Sexuality*, 12 Media Psychol. 121 (2009); S. Martino et al., *Social Cognitive Processes Mediating the Relationship between Exposure to Television's Sexual Content and Adolescents' Sexual Behavior*, 89 J. Personality & Soc. Psychol. 914 (2005).

61. A. Bleakley et al., *How Sources of Sexual Information Relate to Adolescents' Beliefs about Sex*, 33 Am. J. Health Behav. 37 (2009).

62. Martino et al., *Social Cognitive Processes Mediating the Relationship between Exposure to Television's Sexual Content and Adolescents' Sexual Behavior*, supra note 60.

63. Bandura, Social Foundations of Thought and Action, supra note 42.

64. A. Bandura, *Self-Efficacy: The Exercise of Control* (Freeman 1997).

65. A. Bandura, *Social Cognitive Theory for Personal and Social Change by Enabling Media*, in Entertainment-Education and Social Change: History, Research, and Practice 75–96 (A. Singhal et al. eds., Lawrence Erlbaum 2004).

66. Bleakley et al., *How Sources of Sexual Information Relate to Adolescents' Beliefs about Sex*, supra note 61.

67. G. Gerbner & L. Gross, *Living with Television: The Violence Profile*, 26 J. Comm. 172 (1976).

68. L.J. Shrum, *Psychological Processes underlying Cultivation Effects Further Tests of Construct Accessibility*, 22 Hum. Comm. Res. 482 (1996).

69. A. Rubin, *Ritualized and Instrumental Television Viewing*, 34 J. Comm. 67 (1984).

70. Aubrey et al., *Variety versus Timing*, supra note 59.

71. L.M. Ward, *Does Television Exposure Affect Emerging Adults' Attitudes and Assumptions about Sexual Relationship? Correlational and Experimental Confirmation*, 31 J. Youth & Adolescence 1 (2002).

72. L.R. Huesmann, *An Information Processing Model for the Development of Aggression*, 14 Aggressive Behav. 13 (1988).

73. F. Dillman-Carpentier et al., *Naughty versus Nice: Suggestive Pop Music Influences on Perceptions of Potential Romantic Partners*, 9 Media Psychol. 1 (2007).

74. J.D. Brown & L. Schulze, *The Effects of Race, Gender, and Fandom on Audience Interpretations of Madonna's Music Videos*, 40 J. Comm. 88 (1990).

75. *See* Am. Acad. Pediatrics, *Policy Statement: Sexuality, Contraception, and the Media*, 126 Pediatrics 576 (2010); Wright, *Mass Media Effects on Youth Sexual Behavior*, supra note 19.

76. J.D. Brown et al., *Sexy Media Matter: Exposure to Sexual Content in Music, Movies, Television, and Magazines Predicts Black and White Adolescents' Sexual Behavior*, 117 Pediatrics 1018 (2006).

77. R.L. Collins et al., *Watching Sex on Television Predicts Adolescent Initiation of Sexual Behavior*, 114 Pediatrics 280 (2004).

78. R.H. DuRant et al., *Viewing Professional Wrestling on Television and Engaging in Violent and Other Health Risk Behaviors by a National Sample of Adolescents*, 101 S. Med. J. 129 (2008).

79. Peter & Valkenburg, *Adolescents' Use of Sexually Explicit Internet Material and Sexual Uncertainty*, supra note 37.

80. J.D. Brown & K.L. L'Engle, *X-Rated: Sexual Attitudes and Behaviors Associated with U.S. Early Adolescents' Exposure to Sexually Explicit Media*, 35 Comm. Res. 129 (2009).

81. Ybarra *et al.*, *X-Rated Material and Perpetration of Sexually Aggressive Behavior among Children and Adolescents*, supra note 14.

82. A. Chandra *et al.*, *Does Watching Sex on Television Predict Teen Pregnancy? Findings from a National Longitudinal Survey of Youth*, 122 Pediatrics 1047 (2008).

83. G.M. Wingood *et al.*, *A Prospective Study of Exposure to Rap Music Videos and African American Female Adolescents' Health*, 93 Am. J. Pub. Health 437 (2003).

84. Bleakley *et al.*, *It Works Both Ways*, supra note 18.

85. Steele & Brown, *Adolescent Room Culture*, supra note 2.

86. P.S. Bobkowski *et al.*, *"Hit Me Up and We Can Get Down": Youth Risk Behaviors and Sexual Self-Disclosure in MySpace Profiles*, 6 J. Child. & Media 119 (2012).

87. J.G. Noll *et al.*, *Childhood Abuse, Avatar Choices, and Other Risk Factors Associated with Internet-Initiated Victimization of Adolescent Girls*, 123 Pediatrics 1078 (2009).

88. J. Wilt & W. Revelle, *Extraversion*, in *Handbook of Individual Differences in Social Behavior* 27–45 (M.R. Leary & R.H. Hoyle eds., Guilford Press 2009).

89. J. Peter *et al.*, *Developing a Model of Adolescent Friendship Formation on the Internet*, 8 Cyber Psychol. & Behav. 423 (2005); A.P. Schouten *et al.*, *Precursors and Underlying Processes of Adolescents' Online Self-Disclosure: Developing and Testing an "Internet-Attribute-Perception" Model*, 10 Media Psychol. 292 (2008); P.M. Valkenburg & J. Peter, *Social Consequences of the Internet for Adolescents: A Decade of Research*, 18 Current Directions Psychol. Sci. 1 (2009).

90. P.T. Fuglestad & M. Snyder, *Self-Monitoring*, in *Handbook of Individual Differences in Social Behavior* (Leary & Hoyle eds.), supra note 88.

91. A.M. Manago *et al.*, *Self-Presentation and Gender on MySpace*, 29 J. Applied Developmental Psychol. 446 (2008); K. Subrahmanyam *et al.*, *Online and Offline Social Networks: Use of Social Networking Site by Emerging Adults*, 29 J. Applied Developmental Psychol. 420 (2008).

92. P.S. Bobkowski & L.D. Pearce, *Baring Their Souls in Online Profiles or Not: Religious Self-Disclosure in Social Media*, 50 J. Sci. Study Religion 744 (2011).

93. J.B. Walther, *Computer-Mediated Communication: Impersonal, Interpersonal, and Hyperpersonal Interaction*, 23 Comm. Res. 3 (1996).

94. R.A. Wicklund & P.M. Gollwitzer, *Symbolic Self-Completion* (Lawrence Erlbaum Associates 1982).

95. J. Wolak *et al.*, *Online "Predators" and Their Victims: Myths, Realities, and Implications for Prevention and Treatment*, 63 Am. Psychologist 111 (2008).

96. *E.g.*, R.H. Fazio *et al.*, *Self-Perceptions following Social Interaction*, 41 J. Personality & Soc. Psychol. 232 (1981); A.E. Kelly & R.R. Rodriguez, *Publicly Committing Oneself to an Identity*, 28 Basic & Applied Soc. Psychol. 185 (2006).

97. A.L. Gonzales & J.T. Hancock, *Identity Shift in Computer-Mediated Environments*, 11 Media Psychol. 167 (2008).

98. J. Fox & J.N. Bailenson, *Virtual Self-Modeling: The Effects of Vicarious Reinforcement and Identification on Exercise Behaviors*, 12 Media Psychol. 1 (2009).

99. *E.g.*, J.B. Walther *et al.*, *The Effect of Feedback on Identity Shift in Computer-Mediated Communication*, 14 Media Psychol. 1 (2011).

100. R.S. Tokunaga, *Following You Home from School: A Critical Review and Synthesis of Research on Cyberbullying Victimization*, 26 Computers Hum. Behav. 277 (2010).

101. L. Hillier & L. Harrison, *Building Realities Less Limited than Their Own: Young People Practicing Same-Sex Attraction on the Internet*, 10 Sexualities 82 (2007).

102. D.A. Gentile, *The Rating Systems for Media Products*, in *Handbook of Children, Media, and Development* 527–551 (S. Calvert & B. Wilson eds., Blackwell Publishing 2008).

103. Am. Acad. Pediatrics, *Policy Statement, supra* note 75.

6

Sex, Laws, and Videophones

The Problem of Juvenile Sexting Prosecutions

SETH F. KREIMER

Self-portraitists usually risk no legal liability. Yet as modern digital image capabilities encounter teenage hormones and impulsiveness, young digital self-portraitists find themselves prosecuted as child pornographers.

In the twenty-first century, teenagers armed with cell-phone cameras have acquired increasing capacities to capture and share nude images of themselves and their sexual partners. The act of appending sexualized digital images to e-mails or text messages has become common enough to acquire its own moniker: "sexting." Concern about the phenomenon began in turn to approach epidemic momentum toward the end of the last decade. A widely publicized online survey of teens aged thirteen to nineteen in late 2008 found that 20% of the sample had sent or posted "a nude or semi-nude picture or video" of themselves and that 31% had received or shared such an image.[1] As sexting burst into popular consciousness, scandalized prosecutors dragged its teenaged practitioners into court, bringing to bear child pornography statutes drafted to address the threat of adult pedophiles from a pre-digital era.

This essay discusses my experiences with one example of the phenomenon, *Miller v. Skumanick*,[2] the first federal case addressing the problem of sexting. It moves on to set the case in the broader context of twenty-first-century law, technology, and culture. It concludes with reflections on the proper scope of legal intervention.

Trouble in Tunkhannock

Tunkhannock, Pennsylvania, home to 1,911 people, lies twenty-five miles north of Wilkes-Barre, in Wyoming County. The county's ten thousand households are spread across 405 square miles, and Tunkhannock Area School District enrolls 3,100 students.

In October 2008, a girl in the Tunkhannock High School lunchroom encountered a boy to whom she had sent a nude picture of herself. He was, to her displeasure, displaying the photo on his cell phone to his friends. The girl emptied a carton of milk on the head of her faithless companion, and both were sent to the principal's office. The principal flipped through the phone—I leave to one side the question of whether this was a Fourth Amendment violation[3]—and encountered other pictures of what were referred to as "nude or semi-nude" girls in "sexually suggestive poses."

Fearing trouble in Tunkhannock, school officials called in the police and the local district attorney, a forty-seven-year old lawyer by the name of George Skumanick who had served in that office for the last twenty years.

Law enforcement investigated and discovered that sexting had come to north central Pennsylvania. By the beginning of November, police had confiscated five cell phones from students aged eleven to seventeen containing roughly a hundred pictures of girls in various states of undress. They discovered that some Tunkhannock girls treated sending racy cell-phone pictures of themselves as "the new flirting" and that some boys at Tunkhannock High School and Tunkhannock Middle School had been trading cell phone photos of "nude or semi-nude" girls. With the help of the Pennsylvania State Police, computer crime lab investigators identified ten of the local girls under the age of eighteen whose photos appeared in the collections.

Over the next three months, the Tunkhannock officials prepared a campaign to meet the newly discovered threat. They sent letters to parents. They warned that once released into the digital environment images could make their way into the hands of child predators. They cautioned that possession of what were referred to as "inappropriate" images at school could result in expulsion. They announced that producing, possessing, or disseminating "inappropriate" images of minors could lead to prosecution on felony child pornography charges. "We're not out to ruin anyone's life, but at the same time this has to stop and we won't tolerate it,"[4] thundered Skumanick at one school assembly in November, shortly after he had announced the beginning of his campaign for re-election. A student who objected that prosecuting an eleven-year-old on child pornography charges was in fact likely to ruin his life was escorted out of the auditorium.

In February 2009, District Attorney Skumanick sent identical letters to the parents of the five owners of the confiscated cell phones and ten of the girls who had been identified as appearing in "inappropriate" photos. The letter warned parents that their children had been identified in an investigation of "the possession and/or dissemination of child pornography." It announced that "charges would be filed" unless their children agreed to a six-month rehabilitation program involving confession and atonement for their misdeeeds, suspicionless drug testing, and education on the dangers of sexual violence and sexual harassment. Twelve of the families took the deal.

One of the recipients of these letters, however, was Mary Jo Miller, a special education teacher at Tunkhannock High School, whose youngest daughter Marissa had just turned fifteen. Marissa denied to her mother any knowledge of or involvement in child pornography. When Mary Jo and her ex-husband met with the district attorney, Skumanick displayed the offending image to them. The Millers recognized a digital photo taken at a slumber party three years earlier. It depicted twelve-year-old Marissa and her thirteen-year-old friend Grace Kelly from the waist up, talking on cell phones while reclining on a bed, clad in white opaque bras. Challenged to explain how this could constitute child pornography, Skumanick took the position that the picture was "provocative." In a public meeting he adopted the same stance with respect to another photo which involved a full frontal view of a girl in a bikini. Mary Jo was outraged. She consulted her daughter. Marissa was equally adamant in her refusal to accede to Skumanick's demands for confession and repentance. Mary Jo called the Pennsylvania American Civil Liberties Union (ACLU), which asked me to consult on the case.

At one level, Marissa's case presented straightforward issues under Pennsylvania law. Pennsylvania's child pornography statute, like many contemporary child pornography laws, imposes felony liability on any person who produces, displays, or possesses images "depicting a child under the age of 18 years engaging in a prohibited sexual act."[5] Prohibited sexual acts include the activities that one might expect: "sexual intercourse, masturbation, sadism, masochism, bestiality, fellatio, cunnilingus." The prohibition also covers "lewd exhibition of the genitals or nudity . . . depicted for the purpose of sexual stimulation or gratification" of the viewer.

Nude pictures of minors "produced for the purpose of sexual stimulation or gratification" could fall within the statute. So could pictures of minors "lewdly" exhibiting clothed genitals.[6] Skumanick claimed the slumber party photo was "provocative." It is conceivable that to an aging pedophile or a hormone-wracked teenage boy it might be, though there is substantial doubt about whether it would qualify under the Pennsylvania case law as either "lewd" or produced "for the purpose of sexual stimulation or gratification" of the viewer. But in any case, the photo did not depict a "prohibited sexual act" as defined by the statute. The pictures portrayed no sexual contact. A view of Marissa and Grace from the waist up involved no exhibition of the genitals. And clad in opaque white bras, Marissa and Grace were not nude. Q.E.D.

As it turned out, things were not quite so simple.

Skumanick refused to drop his threatened prosecution. Facing the prospect of felony charges and possible listing on a sex-offender registry, Mary Jo and Marissa were not inclined to trust Marissa's future to litigation before a juvenile court judge in central Pennsylvania in the midst of a moral panic over sexting.

Moreover, the Pennsylvania ACLU had also been contacted by another mother who had received the Skumanick letter. Jane Doe, who chose to remain anonymous in the litigation, was the mother of seventeen-year-old Nancy Doe. Nancy's image had been captured digitally a year before with a white towel wrapped around her body, just below the breasts. In the picture, it appeared that she had just emerged from a shower. For Nancy Doe, the "nudity" condition of the statute was arguably met, which meant that the applicability of the statute turned on whether the photograph was "produced for the purpose of sexual stimulation or gratification of the viewer," whether minors could be prosecuted as "victims" of their own self-portraiture, and proof that Nancy had herself produced, possessed, or distributed the picture found on another student's phone. Jane and Nancy were also disinclined to trust Nancy's future to state court.

The ACLU team decided to investigate federal constitutional challenges to Skumanick's threats to prosecute the girls and his demands that they enter his rehabilitation program. We concluded that there were viable claims, and on March 30, 2008, Judge James Munley agreed with us and issued a temporary restraining order barring prosecution.[7] The case garnered national publicity, as Skumanick appeared regularly in the media touting his concern for the welfare of the children of central Pennsylvania. The voters of Tunkhannock were less enthusiastic: in November 2009 they refused to return Skumanick to office. Skumanick's opponent Jeff Mitchell garnered 56% of the vote.

Newly elected District Attorney Mitchell continued to litigate the case against Nancy Doe on appeal but represented to the Third Circuit that his office would not pursue charges against Mary Jo and Marissa. When the Third Circuit affirmed Judge Munley's order, Mitchell agreed to a permanent injunction barring future prosecution of the girls.[8]

Twentieth-Century Constitutional Context

Modern First Amendment analysis protects photography no less than painting as a medium of expression.[9] The Court has recognized that private communication no less than public debate falls within that protection.[10] Doctrine established in the 1970s holds that "'nudity alone' does not place otherwise protected material outside the mantle of the First Amendment."[11] So on its face, sexting appears to be protected speech.

There are, however, exceptions.

Distribution of "obscene" material may be prosecuted, free-speech guaranties notwithstanding. Since *Miller v. California* in 1973, images (and words) can be prosecuted as "obscene" where three conditions are met: a finder of fact must determine that

(a) ... "the average person, applying contemporary community standards" would find that the work, taken as a whole, appeals to the prurient interest ... ;
(b) ... the work depicts ... in a patently offensive way, sexual conduct specifically defined by the applicable state law; and
(c) ... the work, taken as a whole, lacks serious literary, artistic, political, or scientific value.[12]

Further, for sexual material distributed to minors, the "government's interest in the 'well-being of its youth' . . . can justif[y] the regulation of otherwise protected expression."[13] The test parallels *Miller*: material can be "obscene as to minors" if it depicts "nudity" in a fashion that

> (i) predominantly appeals to the prurient . . . interest of minors, and (ii) is patently offensive to prevailing standards in the adult community as a whole with respect to what is suitable material for minors, and (iii) [lacks serious literary, artistic, political, or scientific value] for minors.[14]

An obscenity prosecution for sexting would face both the challenge of prevailing on the issue of "patent offensiveness" and prurience[15] before the finder of fact and the hurdle that personal romantic correspondence, which is the context of much sexting, has independent constitutional value.[16]

"Child pornography" is accorded less protection. The last three decades witnessed the disturbing spread of sexual images that cater to the tastes of pedophiles—images produced by the abuse of children. In response, the Supreme Court determined that dissemination of images constituting "child pornography" can be prohibited without demonstrating the absence of redeeming value, prurience, or patent offensiveness. And unlike "obscenity," the government can punish private possession of such images.

In 1982, *New York v. Ferber*[17] upheld a statute punishing production or distribution of images of minors depicting "actual or simulated [sexual activity] . . . or lewd exhibition of the genitals." "The prevention of the sexual exploitation and abuse of children," the Court observed, "constitutes an objective of surpassing importance" whose vindication would not impinge on legitimate speech.[18] Producing the images involved committing criminal child exploitation; if a prohibition of child exploitation were effectively enforced, there would be no child pornography images to be circulated in the first place. The Court therefore approved prosecution of "child pornography" without showing either patent offensiveness or the absence of serious value.

Eight years later, in *Osborne v. Ohio*,[19] the Court observed that "much of the child pornography market has been driven underground; as a result, it is now difficult, if not impossible, to solve the child pornography problem by only attacking production and distribution."[20] In order to "dry up the market" for child pornography and its attendant abuse, the Court upheld a statute punishing possession of nude images of a minor involving "a lewd exhibition or . . . a graphic focus on the genitals,"[21] notwithstanding the right to possess adult images that were merely "obscene."

The Digital Revolution

The *Miller-Ferber-Osborne* regime was crafted to deal with pornography disseminated through largely commercial (though often illicit) networks distributing photographs, films, or videotape. But technological developments have converged to generate a new reality in the twenty-first century.

Digital cameras, introduced to the public in 1997, drove the marginal cost of recording, editing, and saving images toward zero. Video cameras, introduced as a rare luxury in 1992, are pervasively embedded in inexpensive and personal digital devices. Cell-phone cameras, introduced in the United States in 2002, today accompany Americans constantly. Three quarters of contemporary American teens own cell phones, and almost all have digital image capabilities.[22] Once captured, digital images today are like any other data; they can flow from cameras to e-mail, web pages, and social media. And during the last decade, web-based media for distribution of images have expanded exponentially. Increasingly high bandwidth combines with social networking sites like Facebook (2004), caching sites like Flickr (2004) and YouTube (2005), easier blogging technology, and Twitter (2006) to enable any holder of an image to make it instantly available to individual correspondents or the world at large.

Legal efforts to constrain pornography have struggled to play catch-up. The 1996 Communications Decency Act, which imposed a federal ban on the dissemination of "indecent" material that was "harmful to minors" over the Internet, was invalidated on First Amendment over-breadth grounds in 1997.[23] Its successor, the Child Online Protection Act of 1998 (COPA) narrowed the federal prohibition of Internet smut to commercially produced material "obscene as to minors" but was enjoined on First Amendment grounds for failing to use the "least restrictive alternative" to accomplish its goal. After two trips to the Supreme Court[24] COPA finally expired when the Supreme Court refused to grant certiorari a third time in 2009.[25]

By the time the COPA saga concluded, the 2008 trial of the case established that "1 percent of all Web pages on the Surface Web (amounting to approximately 275 million to 700 million Web pages) are sexually explicit."[26] Protecting children by prosecuting obscenity on the Internet had become a lost cause.

Efforts to prosecute the narrower class of child pornography, however, have proven hardier. State and federal statutes levy increasingly draconian penalties on those who produce, possess, or disseminate child pornography. State police have established computer crime task forces to identify and track down distributors and viewers of child pornography, and annual federal child pornography prosecutions jumped from 30 in 1995 to more than 2,200.[27]

A decade ago, in *Ashcroft v. Free Speech Coalition*,[28] the Court invalidated portions of the Child Pornography Protection Act, adopted in 1996 by the same Congress that passed the Communications Decency Act. The Child Pornography Protection Act sought to punish possession of "virtual" child pornography produced by computer image manipulation without involving real children. Justice Kennedy's majority opinion held that—unlike the child pornography prohibitions upheld in *Osborne* and *Ferber*—the images at issue were not "intrinsically related to the abuse of children."[29] Child pornography involving real children is unprotected because of "how it was made, not what it communicated."[30] Computer-generated child pornography by contrast is "speech that records no crime and creates no victims by its production."[31] According to a majority of the Court, the potentially repellant audience or use of such images did not warrant an exception to the general First Amendment rule that the government "cannot constitutionally premise legislation on the desirability of controlling a person's private thoughts."[32]

Child pornography prosecutions involving images of real children, however, have continued apace, augmented by private causes of action available to individuals whose images are captured.[33] The Court recently upheld the "pandering" provisions of the PROTECT Act of 2003, which punish the distribution, promotion, or solicitation of material in a manner "intended to cause another to believe that the material contains" images of an actual minor engaged in sexually explicit conduct. *United States v. Williams*[34] affirmed the conviction of a man who posted a message to an Internet chatroom offering to provide pictures of men molesting his four-year-old daughter. The Court held that, even if no images of real children existed, the statute was not overbroad because "offers to engage in illegal activity are categorically excluded from the First Amendment."

Youth, Sexuality, and Sexting in Modern America

Teenagers have always engaged in sexual experimentation and never more so than the last generation. In 2005, the Centers for Disease Control reported that over a quarter of fifteen-year-old girls in the United States had experienced vaginal intercourse and another 10% had some other form of sexual contact involving penetration; the incidence of vaginal intercourse rose to 50% among seventeen-year-olds, with an additional 15% reporting some other form of sexual interaction.[35] Among boys, the rate of intercourse was similar, with an additional 20% reporting other varieties of sexual experience.[36] In contemporary America, if one chooses a teenager at random in the fifteen- to seventeen-year-old cohort, the chances that he or she will have engaged in sexual contact are better than 50%. While a minority of these liaisons constitute statutory rape, in most states sexual experimentation between consenting teenagers is shielded from prosecution by some variant of Romeo and Juliet laws.[37]

In recent years, teens have increasingly captured sexual experimentation in visual images, and scandalized prosecutors have turned to child pornography statutes. In 1996 a Florida appeals court affirmed the child pornography conviction of a fifteen-year-old boy who videotaped himself and a younger girl "engaged in nude sexual foreplay" and played the tape for a friend.[38] Four years later a Washington appeals court upheld the child pornography conviction of a fifteen-year-old boy who brought a video camera with him to high school and persuaded three of his fifteen-year-old fellow students to expose their breasts for the camera.[39]

The expansion of the Internet broadened concern. In addition to prosecuting teenaged videographers, prosecutors discovered a set of youthful "cam-girls" and "cam-boys" who displayed their own nude images or sexual activities on websites to remunerative patrons. The 2005 *New York Times* exposé of the activities of eighteen-year-old Justin Berry highlighted the problem.[40] Berry began his odyssey at age thirteen with a playful agreement to remove his shirt in front of his home web camera for $50 and gradually slid into a series of activities that included PayPal reimbursement for sexual acts performed for an online Internet audience and recruiting other youngsters to expose themselves for paying online voyeurs.

Fortified by concerns about "self-exploitation" and calls for prosecution from aggressive anti-child pornography advocates,[41] a wider array of prosecutors moved to invoke child pornography statutes against teens who captured, shared, and posted their own digital images.[42] In 2007, a Florida appellate court reviewed the adjudication of delinquency for child pornography of a sixteen-year-old girl who had taken 117 digital photos of herself and her seventeen-year-old boyfriend "naked and engaged in sexual behavior" at her boyfriend's house in 2004 and e-mailed the images to her home computer. The underlying sexual encounter violated no valid state law, but the Florida judges upheld the adjudication by a vote of two to one.[43]

By the time that Skumanick decided to threaten prosecution in February 2009, similar child pornography prosecutions had sprouted around the country.[44] They ranged from the seventeen-year-old football player living near Rochester, New York, who was subjected to child pornography prosecution for receiving and retaining a video e-mailed by a fourteen-year-old cheerleader of herself performing a strip tease,[45] to the fourteen- and fifteen-year-old girls in Greensburg, Pennsylvania, who drew child pornography charges for sending nude cell phone photos of themselves to three fifteen-year-old boys.[46]

Sexting and Child Pornography

Prevalence of Sexting

How widespread is "sexting" among twenty-first century youth? The first broadly noted survey in 2008 reported that 20% of respondents age thirteen to nineteen had sent or posted a "nude or semi-nude picture or video" of themselves and that 31% had received such an image.[47]

The vast majority of these images were sent to boyfriends, girlfriends, or contemporaries on whom the sender had a "crush."[48]

The survey is methodologically flawed: it involved a self-selected group of online volunteers, some of whom were legally adults. Later studies suggest that the actual incidence of sexting youth at risk of prosecution is probably somewhat lower, but the order of magnitude is similar. A more sophisticated randomized online survey of 655 teens aged thirteen to eighteen in April 2009 found that 9% of thirteen-year-olds had either sent or received sexually suggestive nude or nearly nude digital images by text message or e-mail, rising to 24% of seventeen-year-olds.[49] Again, the vast majority of images were conveyed in the context of teenage romance.[50] A second online interview study in 2009 estimated that 24% of fourteen- to seventeen-year-olds had either sent or received such images.[51] In late 2009, a national phone survey of eight hundred teens identified 4% of cell-phone-owning respondents ages twelve to seventeen who sent nude or nearly nude images of themselves and 15% who had received such images by text message.[52] A 2010 survey of 23,187 Massachusetts students in twenty-four high schools found that 25% of respondents had received nude explicit photos while 10% had sent, forwarded, or posted them.[53] The most recent 2012 study suggests that sexting behavior is more prevalent than previously reported, with 27.6% of 1,042 high school student participants having sent a naked picture of themselves through text or e-mail.[54]

The Propriety of Prosecution

If child pornography laws are properly deployed against sexting, then American teenagers constitute a vast sea of actual and potential child pornographers who are vulnerable to the draconian penalties that have been put in place to suppress child abuse and imprison pedophiles. The more reasonable conclusion is that those laws and penalties should not be so deployed.

Nude Self-Portraits

The primary harm at which child pornography statutes are directed is the exploitation of children. Children who are forced or inveigled into sex by adults who hope to display the children's images are monstrously abused. The harsh penalties levied against such conduct attests to our societal revulsion. The proliferating web of sex-offender registries betokens the perception of the dangers its perpetrators pose to children.

Minors who take nude pictures of themselves, however, are not necessarily or even often victims of abuse by others. They may be engaging in play, fantasy, exploration, or identity formation. One commentator observed that the canonical women's empowerment book "Our Bodies Ourselves" recommends that young women examine their genitalia through the use of a mirror.[55] Under the Skumanick interpretation of child pornography statutes, a woman under the age of eighteen who substitutes a digital camera for a mirror could find herself subject to felony prosecution. To claim that such conduct is the production of child pornography is a category mistake. Nor is it serious to believe that a teen who invites an age-mate to go along on a vacation at a French beach and then records their topless frolics on an iPhone is engaged, or likely to engage, in child abuse.

To be sure, prosecutors are less likely to target images of personal health care or photos in family scrapbooks than racier images. "Sexting" involves the transmission of images to others and, in many instances, the transmission is tinged with sexual energy. The most prevalent sexting identified by surveys of youth is the sharing of images within actual or prospective romantic relationships. When a minor voluntarily disseminates his image to an actual or prospective romantic interest of a similar age, however, he is neither facilitating a web of pedophila nor subjecting himself to abuse.[56]

Deploying child pornography statutes against teenagers who take or send sexualized pictures of themselves raises substantial First Amendment questions. Adults have protected First Amendment rights to produce, possess, and share nude images of themselves with partners, and "in most circumstances, the values protected by the First Amendment are no less applicable when government seeks to control the flow of information to minors."[57] The arguments that have justified excluding "child pornography" from constitutional protection do not apply to the situation of most sexting youth. In contrast to images obtained by persuading a child to subject himself to sexual abuse, images produced by romantic teenage sexting, at least where there is no statutory prohibition against the underlying conduct recorded, resemble the computer-generated images protected in *Ashcroft v. Free Speech Coalition*. They constitute speech that "records no crime and creates no victims by its production."[58]

This is not to say that sharing nude digital images is sensible or without risk. Teenage romance is notoriously unstable, and disappointed or malicious former partners are hardly reliable custodians of intimate images. Digital dissemination of "sexts" by faithless or careless friends and lovers can be devastating.

Shortly after the trouble in Tunkhannock, an eighth-grade girl in Lacey, Washington, sent a nude digital self-portrait of herself snapped in a bathroom mirror to her boyfriend. The couple broke up, and the boyfriend forwarded the picture to another fourteen-year-old girl. The recipient, a former friend and current social antagonist of the subject

> slapped a text message on it. "Ho Alert!" she typed, "If you think this girl is a whore, then text this to all of your friends," then she clicked open the long list of contacts on her phone and pressed "send." [59]

Misery followed, as the subject became the target of text messages, e-mails, and hallway harassment. The picture and ostracism followed her when she changed schools.

Across the continent, in Ruskin, Florida, Hope Witsell began her last week of seventh grade by sending a digital photograph of her breasts to a boy in her grade to whom she was attracted. A social rival of Hope's borrowed the phone from the recipient, found the image and forwarded it; the image quickly spread through Hope's middle school. Hope was brutally taunted at school, and school authorities suspended her for the first week of eighth grade. Two weeks after she returned, Hope committed suicide.[60]

These harms result not from digital self-portraiture itself but from its subsequent redistribution. They are neither unique to minors nor to sexualized images. The other celebrated sexting suicide of the decade involved Jessica Logan of Cincinnati, age eighteen, whose estranged high school boyfriend forwarded her nude digital picture, initiating a chain of redistribution, and precipitating a cycle of harassment and humiliation in school and online.[61] Logan's age placed her image beyond the "child pornography" rubric though her pain was no less real. Conversely, vicious "cyberbullying" can and does lead to teen suicide without relying on sexual images. Words can be as hurtful as sexualized images, but potentially ruinous impact does not suspend the First Amendment.[62]

To be sure, the constitutional protections provided to minors differ from those of adults. Minors are more likely to show a "lack of maturity" and are "more vulnerable or susceptible to negative influences and outside pressures"; their "character . . . is not as well formed as that of an adult."[63] Minors can be required to seek either parental or judicial approval before obtaining abortions.[64] Statutory rape statutes may constrain minors' sexuality.[65] The Court has recognized rights for same-sex relations with stipulation that the relations did not involve minors.[66] And, of course, material to which adults are entitled can be "obscene as to minors."

But the Court recently and forcefully rejected the argument that those differences justify abandoning First Amendment hostility to censorship where minors are involved. In *Brown v. Entertainment Merchants Association*, the state of California sought to prevent the sale of violent video games to minors, arguing that the risk of psychological and emotional harm from such games outweighed any intrusion on free expression.[67] Justice Thomas's dissent maintained that children had no rights "to access speech without their parents consent," while Justice Breyer's dissent relied on minors' lack of maturity and vulnerability to undergird a special power of the state to control their conduct.[68] Justice Scalia's majority rejected these claims that any test short of strict scrutiny could justify the prohibition:

> That is unprecedented and mistaken. [M]inors are entitled to a significant measure of First Amendment protection, and only in relatively narrow and well-defined circumstances may government bar public dissemination of protected materials to them. . . . No doubt a State possesses legitimate power to protect children from harm, but that does not include a free-floating power to restrict the ideas to which children may be exposed.[69]

The *Brown* majority reaffirmed the proposition that the categorical exclusion of "obscenity" from full First Amendment protection can be adjusted "to ensure that a definition that is designed for adults is not applied uncritically to children" and that children can be denied "sexual material that would be obscene from the perspective of a child."[70] Some sexting may in fact be found "prurient" rather than "healthy," patently offensive as to minors and lack redeeming value. But given the centrality of romance to sexting teenagers and the status of sexualized images in the culture at large, it is difficult to say that sexting entirely lacks protection. Even if could be shown that risk of harm is substantial, it is certainly not clear that prosecution of digital self-portraitists is the least intrusive means of avoiding the risk.

If constitutional objections are not determinative, policy concerns counsel strongly against Skumanick-style prosecutions of underage creators or initial recipients of digital self-portraits. Indeed, even the most aggressive scholars acknowledge that decisions to prosecute the authors of digital self-portraits are usually bad policy, risking the destruction of youthful lives for little likely societal gain.[71]

Child pornography prosecutions of these youth are unlikely to abate threats of actual child abuse, and the nature of the penalties are simply not calibrated to the conduct at issue. Child pornography penalties and sex-offender registration are keyed to the dangers of child exploitation and adult predators. Indeed, if the reason for imposing limitations on sexting is the reduced capacity of minors to make reasoned choices, the same reasoning should apply to reduce punishment. States have begun to acknowledge this proposition, as many of the actual and proposed statutes addressing sexting youth lower penalties to juvenile adjudication, misdemeanor, or diversion.[72]

Some prosecutors, however, claim the right to use the threat of the draconian penalties and stigma associated with child pornography statutes to reach otherwise inattentive teenagers who ignore the risk of promiscuous redistribution of their images. In an era in which the cell phone has replaced the diary as the repository of teenage fantasy and transgressive impulse, an enormous swathe of the teenaged population is subject to those threats.[73]

With due respect to thoughtful district attorneys who may exercise prosecutorial discretion with wisdom and sensitivity, the magnitude of the available penalties is likely to tempt others to impose idiosyncratic moral enthusiasms—often in place of the judgment of parents and always to the detriment of the self-determination of the youths involved. The temptation is rendered more potent by the fact that refusal to accede to prosecutorial demands will subject embarrassing intimate images of the minor to review and public disclosure by adults with whom she is at daggers drawn. Unless the teens in question are backed by parents like Mary Jo Miller and have access to effective and aggressive counsel, prosecutors can extract almost any concessions from sexting teens they decide to target.

The example of Tunkhannock suggests caution in making these weapons available, and Skumanick is not alone in his approach. Shortly after Skumanick left office, a grand jury in Washington County, Oregon, indicted twenty-year-old Antjuanece Brown on child pornography charges when her seventeen-year-old girlfriend's mother found "provocative" photos of the two on the younger girl's cell phone and turned the phone over to police.[74] Brown pleaded guilty to lesser charges to avoid the risk of being placed on a sex-offender registry.

Skumanick's approach has a final defect: if the willing minor subject of a nude digital image is guilty of conspiracy to produce child pornography, true victims of pornographic abuse risk prosecution when they report their abusers. A major impediment to prosecution of child pornographers is the reluctance of their subjects to report the abuse because of the victims' belief that they are guilty or complicit. Law enforcement does not further the effort to suppress child abuse if it propagates this message. And the young person who finds herself the victim of "cyberbullying" as a result of the recirculation of a nude image initially shared in a romantic context should not be deterred from seeking official assistance by statutes that put her at risk of prosecution.[75] If the goal is protect these minors, making them liable to draconian punishment associated with child pornography is a most peculiar way to go about it.

Notwithstanding the reactions of scandalized prosecutors, teenagers sexting nude pictures of themselves to a boyfriend or a girlfriend should be treated no differently than their predecessors a generation ago who handed an inamorata a nude self portrait in charcoal or oil paint: the matter should be confided to parental discipline and education.[76]

Away from Voluntary Self-Portraiture

The picture changes when sexting moves beyond the central case of consensual romantic interaction between age-mates. If there is doubt regarding the voluntary consent of the subject, concerns about exploitation become more plausible, and the arguments for prosecution more pressing. The same is true where images originally created for romantic interaction are distributed or redistributed outside of the relationship.

Impaired or Absent Consent

Where intimate sexual acts or nude images are captured without the consent of the subject, the initial intrusion is unproblematically liable to legal sanction whether the subject is a child or an adult, and subsequent distribution of the image can claim little protection.[77] So, too, where the nude images are procured by misrepresentation[78] or under threat of coercion,[79] the person who exercises such influence should be subject to prosecution.

The consent of a child differs from the consent of an adult; children's cognitive capacities are less developed, and they act from a state of relative vulnerability that may cast doubt on their volition. This is the basis for statutory rape laws, and the threat of child exploitation provides substantial basis for prosecuting adults who induce young children to send nude photographs. A later turn in the Tunkhannock saga raises the issue in stark form. In response to Skumanick's anti-sexting initiatives, the mother of a fourteen-year-old Tunkhannock girl examined her daughter's cell phone. She discovered semi-nude images of her daughter, as well as correspondence with a fifty-two-year-old man in Hiawassee, Georgia. The mother reported the information to the local authorities, and having uncovered a real threat of sexual predation Skumanick contacted the Federal Bureau of Investigation (FBI). After an FBI sting, the Georgia man was arrested and pleaded guilty to child pornography charges.[80]

As with statutory rape laws, it seems plausible to say that a middle-aged adult who seeks and obtains sexualized images from a minor partner could be subject to prosecution under properly drawn statutes; the perpetrator rather than the victim should be the defendant. Things become more complicated as the ages of the participants converge, but as a first approximation, the rules on sexting should be no more strict than the rules on statutory rape: a young person who may seek sexual contact should not be punished for seeking sexualized photos of an actual or prospective partner.[81] Conversely, the penalties for recording sexual interaction should be keyed to the relative seriousness of sexting and sex.

The cognitive and emotional capacities of youth, combined with the dynamics of teenage life, raise a second question about consent. Even among age-mates, threats that would not suffice to constitute coercion of an adult may be all but irresistible to a vulnerable young teen.

Consider *Clark v. Roccanova*,[82] which upheld a private action seeking damages under federal child pornography statutes against a motion to dismiss. According to the complaint in the case,[83] in the fall of 2005, the plaintiff Natalie Clark enrolled in eighth grade at the Montessori Middle School of Kentucky. During the year, Clark was hospitalized for anorexia, and on her return she developed a crush on her classmate Nick Roccanova. Rocccanova importuned Clark for "a video . . . showing herself pleasuring herself," which he "said he would use when he masturbated" and "told her that if she did not produce the sexually explicit video he would not be her friend at Lexington Catholic High School" the next fall. Clark acceded, and the video clip which she sent by cell phone was distributed to students at Lexington Catholic High School and three neighboring high schools.

On the one hand, Roccanova's conduct was manifestly reprehensible. For an adult, the threat to "not be her friend" would not suffice to vitiate consent, but for a vulnerable eighth-grade girl it evoked something quite different from a passing request or romantic inquiry. On the other hand, the spectrum running from Roccanova's conduct through sexual negotiation, experimentation, and flirtation to generalized peer pressure is tinged with shades of gray too subtle for the criminal justice system. If a growing percentages of teenagers are not to be put at risk of prosecution for adolescent experimentation, emotional pressure should not suffice to impose criminal liability for inducing an age-mate to share sexually explicit photos.

Third-Party Distribution

Roccanova's subsequent distribution of the photos, however, clearly exceeded any plausible consent and stands on quite a different footing. Sharing sexualized images with legitimate actual or potential romantic partners can be a part of a flourishing teenage life, and its potential harms are usually speculative. It is much harder, both as a matter of constitutional law and policy, to make arguments that there should be a right to redistribute such images without legal liability. Digital images, unlike charcoal sketches, can be distributed easily and widely beyond the context of teenage romance. A major part of the real danger of sexting is the prospect that, instead of an "electronic hickey,"[84] impulsive minors will end up with the equivalent of a "cybertattoo": that the diffusion of humiliating images over the Internet will mark them for life.

The proper response to a teenager who wants to give himself a tattoo is to persuade him that this is a foolish act he is likely to regret, rather than to subject him to prosecution. But we prohibit tattoo shops from serving minors without parental consent—occasionally upon pain of criminal prosecution. Once the image of a minor passes beyond the initial sharing with age-mate partners, the free-expression interest in dissemination to third, fourth, and hundredth parties decreases. Distribution among age-mates is not child pornography, but third-party distribution is not part of a personal relationship, which can claim strong constitutional protection.

Consider *Doe v. Peterson*,[85] a saga that began in 2007 when, according to plaintiffs' account, Jane Doe, four months shy of her eighteenth birthday, took several sexually explicit digital photos of herself, transferred them to her father's computer, and sent them via a social networking site to her eighteen-year-old boyfriend, who was serving in the army.

A year and a half later, Jane Doe was informed that the images had been posted on the website imagebeaver.com. She contacted the website and informed them that she was a minor at the time of the photos. The site removed the images. In April 2009, the images reappeared on Erik Peterson's commercial website exgfpics.com, which "encourages men to submit nude photos of their ex-girlfriends, ex-wives, current girlfriend or wife." After a series of fruitless efforts to have the pictures removed,

Jane Doe filed suit under the civil provisions of the federal child pornography statutes. The pictures were removed the next day.

After motions, discovery and briefing, the trial judge denied defendants' summary judgment motions. Notwithstanding his conclusion that Jane Doe "clear[ly] is guilty of violating federal laws prohibiting the production and distribution of child pornography" the judge struck the defendants' *in pari delicto* defense because "plaintiff is a member of the class [the statute] was designed to protect—minors."[86] He observed that because Doe "did not consent to Defendants possession or use of the photos," she fell clearly within the ambit of the cause of action the statute provides to "victims."

In order to conclude that Jane Doe's privacy interest outweighed the rights of Erik Peterson, proprietor of exgfpics.com, or the individuals who posted and distributed the photos without her consent, one need not invoke the "child pornography" exception to the First Amendment. A minor (like an adult) can have a protectable interest in preventing dissemination of an image that she shares in confidence with a boyfriend. In *Cohen v. Cowles Media*,[87] the Court upheld a damage action for a newspaper's breach of a confidentiality agreement. In *Globe Newspaper Co. v. Superior Court of Norfolk County*,[88] the Court held that a State's interest in the physical and psychological well-being of a minor victim was sufficient to justify depriving the press and public of the right to attend criminal trials. In *Bartnicki v. Vopper*,[89] the Court strongly suggested that redistribution of illicitly obtained intimate photos would be unprotected. Suitably tailored statutes could properly punish redistribution of prurient pictures of minors by those unable to prove that the minor had authorized the distribution.[90] Such a statute would, unlike broad-brush child pornography statutes, target the second and third parties who inflict the harm, rather than the first party who is its victim.[91]

The statutory response to sexting remains by and large aggressively punitive, with most states deferring to their child pornography laws to address this conduct. According to the National Conference of State Legislatures, since 2009, at least twenty states have enacted bills specifically to address youth sexting.[92] However, only a handful have taken steps to more carefully tailor the penalties for minors who create, distribute, and possess sexually explicit images to the nature of the offense and the offenders, with most statutes continuing to advance a policy of protection through prosecution. Most relevant to the analysis in this chapter, Pennsylvania recently enacted a sexting statute under which youths age twelve to seventeen who send, view, or disseminate sexually explicit images can be charged with a misdemeanor or summary offense, depending on the circumstances.[93] Instead of a felony conviction and registration as a sex offender, youth, in most cases, will be allowed to enter a diversionary educational program and afterward have their records wiped clean. Described by opponents as a "law in search of a crime," the statute still provides for more severe criminal prosecution of youth who engage in sexting with the intent to harm, leaving some youth still subject to the overly harsh penalties of child pornography laws.[94]

Conclusion

While sexting among age-mates may be unattractive, it is not child pornography. As the Court reminds us in *Brown*, "[D]isgust is not a valid basis for restricting expression."[95] Likewise, while sexted images can result in harms, Marissa Miller and Antjuanece Brown differ from Nick Roccanova and Erik Peterson. Statutes and prosecutors should not confuse them. To quote *Brown* again, "[E]ven where the protection of children is the object, constitutional limits on governmental action apply."[96] And even where the constitutional concerns are not determinative, common sense along with a recollection of the trouble in Tunkhannock suggests that enabling draconian prosecution of sexting youth is bad policy.

NOTES

1. The National Campaign to Prevent Teen and Unplanned Pregnancy & Cosmogirl.com, *Sex and Tech: Results from a Survey of Teens and Young Adults* 1, 11–12 (2008), www.afim.org/SexTech_Summary.pdf (last visited 16 June 2014).
2. Miller v. Skumanick, 605 F. Supp. 2d 634, 647 (M.D. Pa. 2009), *aff'd* Miller v. Mitchell, 598 F.3d 139, 143 (3d Cir. 2010).
3. *See* N.N. v. Tunkhannock Area Sch. Dist., No. 3-10-CV-01080, 2011 U.S. Dist. LEXIS 73637 (M.D. Pa. July 8, 2011) (denying motion to dismiss Fourth Amendment challenge to examination of student's cell phone photos).
4. Josh Mrozinski, *Students Warned about Dangers of Cell Phone Use*, Wyoming County Press Examiner, Nov. 19, 2008, http://archives.wcexaminer.com/index.

php/2008/11/19/students-warned-about-dangers-of-cell-phone-use (last visited 16 June 2014).

5. 18 Pa. Cons. Stat. Ann. § 6312 (2009).

6. Federal courts have long held that the parallel prohibition of "lewd exhibition" does not require nudity. *E.g.*, United States v. Knox, 32 F.3d 733, 745 (3d Cir. 1994).

7. Miller v. Skumanick, 605 F. Supp. 2d 634, 647 (M.D. Pa. 2009).

8. Miller v. Mitchell, 598 F.3d 139 (3d Cir. 2010), remanded to 2010 U.S. Dist. LEXIS 42512 (M. D. Pa. 2010) (granting permanent injunction). The affirmance rested on the Circuit's understanding of the absence of factual basis for prosecuting Doe:

> assuming that the sexual abuse of children law applies to a minor depicted . . . and that the photo in question could constitute a "prohibited sexual act" (issues on which we need not opine), we discern no indication from this record that the District Attorney had any evidence that Doe ever possessed or distributed the photo.

Id. at 153–154. The demand that "Nancy" attend Skumanick's classes therefore was held to violate her First Amendment rights and those of her parents.

9. *See, e.g.*, Kaplan v. California, 413 U.S. 115, 119–120 (1973) (holding that the First Amendment applies "to moving pictures, to photographs, and to words in book"); Seth F. Kreimer, *Pervasive Image Capture and the First Amendment: Memory, Discourse and the Right to Record*, 159 *U. Pa. L. Rev.* 335, 373–374 (2011).

10. *E.g.*, Bartnicki v. Vopper, 532 U.S. 514, 533 (2001) (noting the importance of private conversations); Procunier v. Martinez 416 U.S. 396, 409 (1974) (protecting private letters); Redmond v. United States, 384 U.S. 264, 264–65 (1966) (per curiam) (dismissing obscenity prosecution of a husband and wife who mailed "undeveloped films of each other posing in the nude to an out-of-state firm for developing"); *cf.* Stanford v. Texas, 379 U.S. 476, 486 (1965) (requiring heightened protection against searches of private correspondence). Intimate sexual speech can also invoke the privacy and autonomy protections of Lawrence v. Texas, 539 U.S. 558 (2003).

11. Schad v. Borough of Mount Ephraim, 452 U.S. 61, 66 (1981) (quoting Jenkins v. Georgia, 418 U.S. 153, 161 (1974)); Erznoznik v. City of Jacksonville, 422 U.S. 205, 213 (1975).

12. Miller v. California, 413 U.S. 15, 24 (1973). Even for images properly classified as obscene, the government cannot prohibit simple possession in a private residence. Stanley v. Georgia, 394 U.S. 557, 567 (1969). *See also* United States v. Williams, 553 U.S. 285, 288 (2008) ("[G]overnment may . . . not criminalize the mere possession of obscene material involving adults.").

13. FCC v. Pacifica Found., 438 U.S. 726,749 (1978) (quoting Ginsberg v. New York, 390 U.S. 629, 640 639 (1968)). *Cf.* FCC v. Fox TV Stations, Inc., 129 S. Ct. 1800, 1813–1814 (2009) (quoting *Pacifica*).

14. Ginsberg v. New York, 390 U.S. 629, 646 (1968); Brown v. Entm't Merchs. Ass'n, 131 S. Ct. 2729, 2743 (2011).

15. Brockett v. Spokane Arcades, Inc., 472 U.S. 491, 504–505 (1985) (distinguishing "normal" from prurient, *i.e.*, "shameful or morbid" interest in sex, and holding

overbroad an obscenity statute prohibiting publications that appeal to "normal interest in sex").

16. For one recent case concluding that sexting was unprotected obscenity, however, *see* State v. Canal, 773 N.W. 2d 528, 529 (Iowa 2009) (affirming conviction of eighteen-year-old who sent a fourteen-year-old friend an e-mail containing a picture of his erect penis "as a joke" after she had requested such a picture three times in a single telephone call). Canal was fined $250, sentenced to nineteen days in jail, placed on probation, and required to register as a sex offender.

17. 458 U.S. 747 (1982).

18. New York v. Ferber, 458 U.S. 747, 757 (1982).

19. 495 U.S. 103 (1990).

20. Osborne v. Ohio, 495 U.S. 103, 110 (1990).

21. *Id.* at 113.

22. Lenhart et al., *Teens and Mobile Phones*, Pew Internet and American Life Project (Apr. 20, 2010), http://pewinternet.org/Reports/2010/Teens-and-Mobile-Phones/Summary-of-findings.aspx (last visited June 16, 2014).

23. Reno v. ACLU, 521 U.S. 844 (1997).

24. Ashcroft v. ACLU, 535 U.S. 564 (2002); Ashcroft v. ACLU, 542 U.S. 656 (2004).

25. Mukasey v. ACLU, 129 S. Ct. 1032 (2009).

26. ACLU v. Gonzales, 478 F. Supp. 2d. 775, 788 (E.D. Pa. 2007).

27. U.S. Department of Justice, *Fact Sheet: Project Safe Childhood* (press release, Sept. 23, 2008), www.usdoj.gov/opa/pr/2008/September/08-opa-845.html (last visited June 16, 2014); Tracey Kyckelhahn & Mark Motivans, *Federal Prosecution of Child Sex Exploitation Offenders, 2006* (Dec. 1, 2007), http://bjs.ojp.usdoj.gov/index.cfm?ty=pbdetail&iid=886 (last visited June 16, 2014).

28. 535 U.S. 234 (2002).

29. Ashcroft v. Free Speech Coalition, 535 U.S. 234, 236 (2002).

30. *Id.* at 250–251.

31. *Id.* at 250.

32. *Id.* at 253 (quoting Stanley v. Georgia, 394 U.S. 557, 566 (1969)).

33. 18 U.S.C. §2255(a) authorizes private actions by "victims" injured by federal child pornography violations, with presumed damages of $150,000. *See, e.g.*, Tilton v. Playboy Entm't Group, Inc., 554 F.3d 1371, 1374 (11th Cir. 2009) (rejecting claim based on "videos and photographs of plaintiff participating in activities during spring break in Daytona Beach, Florida, when she was seventeen years and ten months old"); Clark v. Roccanova, 772 F. Supp. 2d 844 (E.D. Ky. 2011) (discussed *infra* note 83); Doe v. Peterson, No. 2:09-CV-13138-PDB-PJ, 2011 U.S. Dist. LEXIS 30637 (E.D. Mich. Mar. 24, 2011) (discussed *infra* note 85). Actions for compensatory and punitive damages by "persons aggrieved" are authorized by 18 U.S.C. § 2252A(f).

34. 553 U.S. 285 (2008).

35. W. Mosher, A. Chandra, & J. Jones, *Sexual Behavior and Selected Health Measures: Men and Women 15–44 years of Age, United States, 2002* (2005), http://cdc.gov/nchs/data/ad/ad362.pdf (last visited June 16, 2014).

36. *Id.*; *cf.* Centers for Disease Control, *Youth Risk Behavior Surveillance—United States, 2009, Morbidity & Mortality Weekly Report,* June 4, 2010, at table 61, www.cdc.gov/mmwr/pdf/ss/ss5905.pdf (last visited June 16, 2014) (reporting 31% of ninth graders have had sexual intercourse, as well as 62% of twelfth graders); Guttmacher Institute, *Facts on American Teens' Sexual and Reproductive Health* (Jan. 2011), http://web.archive.org/web/20110602055401/http://www.guttmacher.org/pubs/FB-ATSRH.html (last visited Aug. 5, 2014) (stating that at the age of nineteen, 70% of individuals have had intercourse); Kaiser Family Foundation, *Sexual Health Statistics for Teenagers* (2006), http://web.archive.org/web/20110607170054/http://www.kff.org/womenshealth/upload/3040-03.pdf (last visited Aug. 5, 2014) (reporting that over half of teenage males and females have had oral sex by age nineteen).

37. *E.g.*, Charles A. Phipps, *Misdirected Reform: On Regulating Consensual Sexual Activity between Teenagers,* 12 Cornell J.L. & Pub. Pol'y 373 app. A (2003) (reporting the age of consent in thirty eight states). *Cf.* Jennifer Drobac, *Sex and the Workplace: Consenting Adolescents and a Conflict of Laws,* 79 Wash. L. Rev. 471, 546 (2004) (noting conflicting legal treatment of age of consent laws between neighboring states).

38. State v. A.R.S., 684 So. 2d 1383 (Fla. Dist. Ct. App. 1st Dist. 1996).

39. State v. D.H., 102 Wash. App. 620 (Wash App. 2000).

40. *See* David France, *Saving Justin Berry,* N.Y. Mag., Oct. 27, 2007, http://nymag.com/guides/money/2007/39957 (last visited June 16, 2014); Kurt Eichenwald, *Through His Webcam, a Boy Joins a Sordid Online World,* N.Y. Times, Dec. 19, 2005, www.nytimes.com/2005/12/19/national/19kids.ready.html?_r=1&oref=slogin (last visited June 16, 2014).

41. *E.g.*, Mary G. Leary, *Self Produced Child Pornography: The Appropriate Societal Response to Juvenile Self-Sexual Exploitation,* 15 Va. J. Soc. Pol'y & L. 1 (2007). Leary, the former director of the National Center for the Prosecution of Child Abuse, has since clarified her position to advocate prosecution of youth only in "rare" and "extreme" cases. Mary G. Leary, *Sexting or Self Produced Child Pornography: The Dialogue Continues—Structured Prosecutorial Discretion within a Multidisciplinary Response,* 17 Va. J. Soc. Pol'y & L. 486, 489–490, 509n97, 549 (2010) (usually excluding from prosecution the youthful creators of voluntary self-portraits, though recommending prosecution of the "child who is refusing to alter his destructive behavior").

42. *E.g.*, Stephanie Reitz, *Teens Sending Nude Photos via Cell Phone,* Assoc. Press (June 4, 2008) www.msnbc.msn.com/id/24970829 (reporting cases in Colorado, New Jersey, New York, Alabama, Utah, Pennsylvania, Texas, Connecticut and Wisconsin) (last visited June 16, 2014).

43. A.H. v. State, 949 So.2d 234 (Fla. Dist. Ct App 1st. Dist.2007).

44. Judith Levine, *What's the Matter with Teen Sexting? American Prospect* (Feb. 2009), http://prospect.org/cs/articles?article=whats_the_matter_with_teen_sexting (citing "arrests in Alabama, Connecticut, Florida, New Jersey, New York, Michigan, Ohio, Pennsylvania, Texas, and Utah . . . for sending or posting soft-core photo or video self-portraits").

45. Nancy Rommelmann, *Anatomy of a Child Pornographer, Reason.com* (July 2009), at 30–37, http://reason.com/archives/2009/06/04/anatomy-of-a-child-pornographe (last visited June 16, 2014).

46. Mike Brunker, *"Sexting" Surprise: Teens Face Child Porn Charges* (Jan. 15, 2009), www.msnbc.msn.com/id/28679588/ns/technology_and_science-tech_and_gadgets/t/sexting-surprise-teens-face-child-porn-charges (last visited June 16, 2014).

47. National Campaign to Prevent Teen and Unplanned Pregnancy & Cosmogirl.com, *Sex and Tech, supra* note 1.

48. *Id.* at 12 (reporting that, of the teenagers who sent nude photos of themselves, 69% sent these pictures to boyfriend or girlfriend and 29% to a "crush").

49. Cox Communications, *2009 Cox Teen Online & Wireless Safety Survey: Cyberbullying, Sexing and Parental Controls* 36, 41 (2009), www.scribd.com/doc/20023365/2009-Cox-Teen-Online-Wireless-Safety-Survey-Cyberbullying-Sexting-and-Parental-Controls (last visited June 16, 2014).

50. *Id.* at 34 (reporting that of the 19% of teens that sexted at least once, 9% sent, 17% received, and 3% forwarded; 60% sent a sext to a boyfriend/girlfriend, 21% sent one to a "crush" while 75% received from boyfriend/girlfriend, 49% received from a crush, and that girls are almost twice as likely to send as boys).

51. Knowledge Networks, *The MTV-Associated Press Poll: Digital Abuse Survey Conducted by Knowledge Networks* (Sept. 23, 2009), www.athinline.org/MTV-AP_Digital_Abuse_Study_Full.pdf (last visited June 16, 2014); MTV & the Associated Press, *A Thin Line: 2009 AP-MTV Digital Abuse Study* (2009), www.athinline.org/MTV-AP_Digital_Abuse_Study_Executive_Summary.pdf (last visited June 16, 2014). Together, these reports indicate that 33% of respondents age eighteen to twenty four and 24% of respondents age fourteen to seventeen had sent or received a naked image by text message or e-mail. Ten percent of the respondents had sent a naked image of themselves, and the majority of the images were transmitted to actual or potential romantic partners. *Cf.* Arnold Cole & Pamela Caudill Ovwigho, *Research Findings on Scriptural Engagement, Communication with God, and Behavior among Young Believers: Implications for Discipleship*, presented at the Children's Spirituality Conference fig. 4 (June 2009), www.billion.tv/uploads/resources/resources/Back-to-the-Bible.pdf (finding that out of a sample of one thousand children from an online panel age eight to twelve, 4.8% "sext" while 10.2% have sex and 5.7% smoke) (last visited June 16, 2014).

52. Amanda Lenhart, *Teens and Sexting: How and Why Minor Teens Are Sending Sexually Suggestive Nude or Nearly Nude Images via Text Messaging*, Pew Internet and American Life Project, 2 (Dec. 15, 2009), www.pewinternet.org/~/media//Files/Reports/2009/PIP_Teens_and_Sexting.pdf (last visited June 16, 2014).

53. MetroWest Community Health Care Foundation, *Highlights from the MetroWest Adolescent Health Survey* 4 (2011), www.mwhealth.org/Portals/0/Uploads/Documents/Adolescent_Health_Survey_High_School_2010.pdf (last visited Aug. 5, 2014).

54. Jeff R. Temple, Jonathan A. Paul, Patricia van den Berg, Vi Donna Lee, Amy McElhany, & Brian W. Temple, *Teen Sexting and Its Association with Sexual Behaviors*, 166(9) *Archives of Pediatrics & Adolescent Med.* 828 (2012).

55. Tracy Clark-Flory, *The New Pornographers*, Salon.com, Feb. 20, 2009, www.salon.com/mwt/feature/2009/02/20/sexting_teens/index.html (last visited June 16, 2014). *See Boston Women's Health Book Collective, Our Bodies, Ourselves: A New Edition for a New Era* 591 (2005).

56. The analysis of the Canadian Supreme Court in R. v. Sharpe, [2001] 1 S.C.R. 45; 2001 SCC 2; 2001 S.C.R. LEXIS 2, which established constitutional protection for the creation and first-party possession of materials created by minors and shared in romantic relationships, is illuminating:

> [paragraph 109].[V]isual recordings made by a person of him- or herself alone . . . may be of significance to adolescent self-fulfillment, self-actualization and sexual exploration and identity. Similar considerations apply . . . where lawful sexual acts are documented in a visual recording . . . , and held privately by the participants exclusively for their own private use. . . . [T]wo adolescents might arguably deepen a loving and respectful relationship through erotic pictures of themselves engaged in sexual activity. The cost of including such materials to the right of free expression outweighs any tenuous benefit it might confer in preventing harm to children.

For recent reviews of the Canadian approach, *see* R. v. Keogh [2011] A.J. No. 89, 2011 ABQB 48; Andea Slane, *From Scanning to Sexting: The Scope of Protection of Dignity-Based Privacy in Canadian Child Pornography Law*, 48 Osgoode Hall L.J. 3 (2010), http://papers.ssrn.com/sol3/papers.cfm?abstract_id=1800047 (last visited June 16, 2014).

57. Erznoznik v. Jacksonville, 422 U.S. 205, 213 (1975). *See* Brown v. Entm't Merchs. Ass'n, 131 S. Ct. 2729, 2735 (2011) (quoting Erznoznik with approval); Bolger v. Youngs Drug Prods. Corp., 463 U.S. 60, 74n30 (1983) ("The right to privacy in matters affecting procreation also applies to minors"); Planned Parenthood of Central Missouri v. Danforth, 428 U.S. 52, 72–75 (1976) (holding that the State could not ban the distribution of contraceptives to minors); and Carey v. Population Services International, 431 U.S. 678, 694 (1977) (plurality opinion)).

58. *Free Speech Coalition*, 535 U.S. at 250. *See also id.* at 250 ("child pornography" exception to First Amendment doctrine rests on the proposition that the material in question is "the product of sexual abuse"), *id.* at 249 ("production of the work not its content was the target of the statute").

Leary argues that by reserving the question of "morphed" images of real children *Free Speech Coalition* requires the conclusion that all images of real children are categorically unprotected. But even Leary acknowledges that in *United States v. Stevens*, 130 S. Ct. 1577, 1586 (2010), the Court characterized the child pornography exception as based on production being "intrinsically related to the sexual abuse of children," and she concludes that "the significance of Stevens . . . remains to be seen." Leary, *Self Produced Child Pornography, supra* note 41.

59. Jan Hoffman, *A Girl's Nude Photo, and Altered Lives*, N.Y. Times, Mar. 26, 2011, www.nytimes.com/2011/03/27/us/27sexting.html (last visited June 16, 2014).

60. Andrew Meacham, *Sexting Related Bullying Cited in Hillborough Teen's Suicide, St. Petersburg Times*, Nov. 20, 2009, www.tampabay.com/news/humaninterest/article1054895.ece (last visited June 16, 2014).

61. Cindy Kranz, *Nude Photo Led to Suicide, Cincinnati Enquirer*, Mar. 22, 2009, http://news.cincinnati.com/article/20090322/NEWS01/903220312/Nude-photo-led-suicide (last visited June 16, 2014); Logan v. Sycamore Cmty. Sch. Bd. of Educ., NO. 1:09-CV-00885, 2011 U.S. Dist. LEXIS 10505 (S.D. Ohio, Feb. 3, 2011) (action seeking damages for suicide from school, police officers, and students involved).

62. *See* Snyder v. Phelps, 131 S. Ct. 1207 (2011) (abusive statements about decedent at funeral); Florida Star v. B. J. F., 491 U.S. 524 (1989) (name of rape victim was published in the newspaper); Cox Broadcasting Corp. v. Cohn, 420 U.S. 469 (1975) (same).

63. Roper v. Simmons, 543 U. S. 551, 569–570 (2005).

64. *E.g.*, Ayotte v. Planned Parenthood, 546 U.S. 320, 326 (2006) ("States unquestionably have the right to require parental involvement when a minor considers terminating her pregnancy").

65. Michael M. v. Superior Court of Sonoma County, 450 U.S. 464, 472 n8 (1981).

66. Lawrence v. Texas, 539 U.S. 558, 578 (2003) ("The present case does not involve minors").

67. Brown v. Entm't Merchs. Ass'n, 131 S. Ct. 2729 (2011).

68. *Id.* at 2751 (Thomas, J., dissenting); *id.* at 2767 (Breyer, J. dissenting).

69. *Id.*at 2735–2736 (citations omitted).

70. *Id.*at 2735.

71. Leary, *Sexting or Self Produced Child Pornography, supra* note 41, at 508 (distinction between "youth who takes a picture himself . . . and sends it to one person . . . and an adult predator is obvious . . . [the two] should not be equated"); *id.* at n92.

72. Statutes adopting lesser sanctions include Vt. Code. Ann. § 13–2802B; Illinois Public Act 096–1087, Section 3–40, available at www.ilga.gov/legislation/fulltext.asp?DocName=&SessionId=76&GA=96&DocTypeId=HB&DocNum=4583&GAID=10&LegID=48264&SpecSess=&Session= (Counseling and community service) (last visited June 16, 2014); Utah U.C.A. 1953 § 76–10–1204 (persons sixteen or seventeen years of age are guilty of a class A misdemeanor, and persons younger than sixteen years of age are guilty of a class B misdemeanor), and statutes canvassed *infra* note 91. For a current account of state laws, *see* National Conference of State Legislatures, *2011 Legislation Related to Sexting* (Jan. 23, 2012), www.ncsl.org/default.aspx?tabid=22127 (last visited June 16, 2014).

One difficulty with this emerging state consensus is that federal child pornography statutes still apply to images conveyed over the Internet.

73. *Cf.* Janis Wolak & David Finkelhor, *Sexting: A Typology*, Crimes against Children Research Center (Mar. 2011), www.unh.edu/ccrc/pdf/CV231_Sexting%20Typology%20Bulletin_4-6-11_revised.pdf (last visited June 16, 2014) (describing survey of a sample of law enforcement agencies identifying 550 cases involving sexting during 2008 and 2009, promising future analysis of data).

74. Beth Slovic, *Sexting Crimes, Williamette Week*, Dec. 1, 2010, http://wweek.com/portland/article-16544-sext_crimes.html (last visited June 16, 2014). For other recent prosecutions of first-party sexters *see, e.g.*, Lori Fullbright, *Sexting Could Land Vedigris Teens on Sex Offender List, NewsOn6.com* (Apr. 12, 2011), www.newson6.com/story/14433694/sexting (Oklahoma) (last visited June 16, 2014); Ken Kosky, *Middle School Students Charged in "Sexting" Case, NWI.com* (Jan. 28, 2010), www.nwitimes.com/news/local/porter/article_bf8bdbf3-952e-5382-9f2e-6224eefaa3c2.html (Indiana) (last visited June 16, 2014); CBS Chicago, *Valparaiso, Ind. Police Investigate Teen Sexting* (May 26, 2011), http://chicago.cbslocal.com/2011/05/26/valparaiso-ind-police-investigate-teens-for-sexting (Indiana) (last visited June 16, 2014).

75. *See* Logan v. Sycamore Cmty. Sch. Bd. of Educ., NO. 1:09-CV-0088, 2011 U.S. Dist. LEXIS 10505 (S.D. Ohio, Feb. 3, 2011) (police officer in Jessica Logan case "contacted a prosecutor, who told him there was no criminal case to pursue, unless both the male student who had forwarded the image and the female student who had created the image were both prosecuted"); *cf.* Lauren Whetzel, *Two Pa. Bills Target Sexting and Cyberbullying, York Dispatch*, May 5, 2011 (comparing first party and third party liability, child welfare advocate "believes under [first-party] bill, fewer girls would report being victims of cyberbullying because they'd fear being prosecuted").

76. Canadian law has taken this approach as a matter of constitutional law. *See supra* note 56. Likewise, some states have adopted statutes treating sexting among age-mates as a summary offense, 13 V.S.A. § 2802b, or providing affirmative defenses for voluntary first-party age-mate sexting. Neb. Rev. Stat. § 28–813.01 (2010).

Some of the images at issue in these cases, to be sure, go well beyond nudity to sexual congress. Younger children are in no condition to tender legitimate consent to sexual contact. But where state law treats teenagers as adults for purposes of sexual consent, it is at best anomalous and at worst an invitation to prosecutorial evasion of the terms of state consent statutes to hold participants who record that conduct criminally liable, though it must be conceded that courts have upheld such prosecutions. *E.g.*, A.H. v. State, 949 So.2d 234 (Fla. Dist. Ct App 1st. Dist. 2007).

77. E.g., State v. Schaller, 15 So. 3d 1046 (La. App 2009) (criminal defendant secretly videotaped the sexual acts between a teenage girl and her boyfriend); State v. Huffman, 847 N.E.2d 58 (Ohio App. 2006) (criminal defendant installed a hidden camera in a tanning room); In re Marriage of Tigges, 758 N.W.2d 824, 830 (Iowa 2008) (civil action against a husband who surreptitiously videotaped his wife in their marital bedroom); Lewis v. LeGrow, 670 N.W.2d 675, 680 (Mich. Ct. App. 2003) (civil action against a man who secretly videotaped a series of consensual sexual encounters with ex-girlfriends). *See* Bartnicki v. Vopper, 532 U.S. 514, 540 (2001) (Breyer, J., concurring) (no First Amendment protection "in situations where the media publicizes truly private matters [such as] broadcast of videotape recording of sexual relations").

78. E.g., Ryan Smith, *Sexting Hell: Man Posing as Girl on Facebook Blackmails Boys into Sex, CBS News.com* (July 15, 2009), www.cbsnews.com/news/sexting-hell-man-posing-as-girl-on-facebook-blackmails-boys-into-sex (eighteen-year-old male

Wisconsin high school student posed as a girl on Facebook, induced boys to send him nude images, then "blackmailed them into sex acts") (last visited June 17, 2014).

79. *E.g.*, U.S. Attorney's Office, District of Massachusetts, *Framingham Man Charged with Threatening Victims by Posting Photo Online* (Apr. 15, 2011), www.justice.gov/usao/ma/news/2011/April/PizetteJoshuaPR.html (indictment alleging twenty-two-year-old defendant threatened to post naked pictures of the victim online and "threatened to send copies of the [her naked] pictures to the victim's boyfriend if the victim did not send Pizette 10 additional naked pictures") (last visited June 17, 2014); Lauren Leamanczyk, *Sentence in Whitnall Sexting Case*, Jan. 13, 2010, www.620wtmj.com/news/local/81355282.html (fifteen-year-old blackmailed "high school girls into texting him sexually explicit photos; if they refused, he would threaten to expose their friends, spread rumors or release digitally altered pictures of them") (last visited June 17, 2014).

80. Robert Baker, *Georgia Man Sentenced in "Sexting" Case Involving Tunkhannock Area Student*, Oct. 8, 2010, http://thetimes-tribune.com/news/georgia-man-sentenced-in-sexting-case-involving-tunkhannock-area-student-1.1045619# (last visited June 17, 2014).

81. For statutes focusing on age-mates *see, e.g.*, 2010 Conn. Public Acts 10–191, available at www.cga.ct.gov/2010/ACT/PA/2010PA-00191-R00HB-05533-PA.htm (misdemeanor offense for " person who is thirteen years of age or older but under eighteen years of age" possessing or transmitting image "knowingly and voluntarily transmitted . . . in which the subject of such visual depiction is a person thirteen years of age or older but under sixteen years of age") (last visited June 17, 2014); S.B. 277, 74th Leg. (Nev. 2011), available at http://www.leg.state.nv.us/74th/bills/SB/SB277.pdf ("another minor who is older than, the same age as or not more than four years younger than the minor transmitting the sexual image") (last visited June 17, 2014).

82. 772 F. Supp. 2d 844 (E.D. Ky. 2011).

83. Clark v. Roccanova, 5:10 -cv-00155-JBC -REW (complaint filed 5/05/10).

84. Hoffman, *A Girl's Nude Photo, and Altered Lives, supra* note 59 ("Having a naked picture of your significant other on your cellphone is an advertisement that you're sexually active . . . ," said Rick Peters, a senior deputy prosecuting attorney for Thurston County. . . . "It's an electronic hickey.")

85. Doe v. Peterson, No. 2:09-cv-13138-PDB-PJK, 2011 U.S. Dist. LEXIS 30635 (E.D. Mich. Mar. 24, 2011); Doe v. Peterson, 784 F. Supp. 2d 831 (E.D. Mich. 2011).

86. Doe v. Peterson, 784 F. Supp. 2d 831, 838–39 (E.D. Mich. 2011).

87. 501 U.S. 663 (1991).

88. 457 U.S. 596, 607 (1982).

89. *See* Bartnicki v. Vopper, 532 U.S. 514, 540 (2001) (Breyer, J., concurring)

90. Some states already prohibit similar conduct regardless of age. *E.g.*, N.J. Rev. Stat. § 2C:14–9 1 c ("discloses . . . any . . . reproduction of the image of another person whose intimate parts are exposed or who is engaged in an act of sexual penetration or sexual contact, unless that person has consented to such disclosure"); North Dakota Cent. Code 12.1–27.1–03.3 (2009), amended 2011 North Dakota Laws Ch. 99 (H.B. 1371) ("Without written consent from each individual who has a reasonable expectation of

privacy in the image, surreptitiously creates or willfully possesses a sexually expressive image that was surreptitiously created; or b. Distributes or publishes . . . a sexually expressive image with the intent to cause emotional harm or humiliation . . . or after being given notice . . . the individual . . . does not consent to the distribution").

91. For sexting statutes targeting retransmission, *see* Ariz. Rev. Stat. § 8-309 (2010) (petty offense for juvenile possession of distributed image or distribution to one, misdemeanor for distribution to more); LA R.S. 14:81.1.1 (juvenile supervision for first-person transmission, $250 fine/ten days for possession of transmitted images or retransmission); Nevada, SB 277, adopted June 3, 2011 (distinguishing first-party transmission (child in need of supervision for first offense), possession of images of another (same), and retransmission (misdemeanor)).

92. National Conference of State Legislatures, *2012 Sexting Legislation: Year-End Summary* (Dec. 14, 2012), www.ncsl.org/issues-research/telecom/sexting-legislation-2012.aspx (last visited June 17, 2014).

93. *Offense of Sexual Abuse of Children and Offense of Transmission of Sexually Explicit Images by Minor*, Crimes Code, 18 PA.C.S., Act of Oct. 25, 2012, P.L. 1623, No. 198, Cl. 18, Session of 2012, No. 2012-198, HB 815, www.legis.state.pa.us/WU01/LI/LI/US/HTM/2012/0/0198..HTM (last visited June 17, 2014).

94. Marsha Levick, *Sexting Bill Victimizes Pennsylvania Teens, Patriot-News Op-Ed*, Oct. 23, 2012, www.pennlive.com/opinion/index.ssf/2012/10/sexting_bill_victimizes_pennsylvania_teens.html (last visited June 17, 2014). For a more thorough exploration of the widening effect of prosecution of juveniles, even with diminished penalties as in Pennsylvania, *see* Marsha Levick & Christina Moon, *Prosecuting Sexting as Child Pornography*, 44 *Val. U.L. Rev.* 1035 (2010). And consider In re C. S., 2012 Pa. Dist. & Cnty. Dec. LEXIS 407, 1–2 (Pa. County Ct. 2012), reversed and remanded on other grounds, In the Interest of C.S., 84 A.3d 698, 2014 Pa. LEXIS 232 (Pa. 2014):

> The juvenile, C.S., has been charged with crimes that could be interpreted as those committed by a deviant sexual offender. What heinous acts has she allegedly committed: the posting to her Facebook page of the consensual sexual acts of L.C. and M.T., who are ages sixteen (16) and seventeen (17). . . . L.C. agreed to allow M.T. to record their sexual assignation. It appears, however, that sometime after doing so M.T. was indiscreet and sexted his recording to others. One of the recipients of the sexting was C.S., who then posted the video to her Facebook page. . . . [T]eenagers, unless prosecuted, would be clueless that their conduct falls within the parameters of the Sexual Abuse of Children statute.

95. Brown v. Entm't Merchs. Ass'n, 131 S. Ct. 2729, 2741 (2011).

96. *Id.*

7

The Right to Comprehensive Sex Education

HAZEL G. BEH

In this chapter, I consider efforts to construct a rights-based argument that children, particularly adolescents, are entitled to accurate and non-discriminatory sex education in schools. Traditionally, debates about education have focused on the rights of parents to raise their child as they see fit versus the interests of the state to educate its citizenry. For example, conflicts have tested the limits of the state right to control educational content and compel education against claims by parents that the state has infringed upon their parental rights or free exercise of religion.[1] Often these competing claims are resolved by balancing the rights of the parents with interests of the state, with scant attention to the child.[2]

Over the last several decades, the federal government and conservative religious organizations have joined together to develop and implement abstinence-only sex education within the public schools. These curricula have been regarded by some as so overtly deceptive, narrowly focused, and discriminatory as to be harmful to children. Framing the debate about sex education in terms of parental rights or state interests deflects us from important issues. In considering the legitimacy of a sex education curriculum, a children's rights perspective holds more currency.

Placing the sex education debate within the context of children's rights does not yield simple answers. The historian Steven Mintz observes that children's rights must accommodate two distinct concepts, "protective rights" and "civil, liberty, or autonomy rights."[3] Proponents of abstinence-only sex education claim that a narrow curriculum protects children by shielding them from a sexually permissive message. Proponents of a comprehensive approach argue that knowledge about sexuality empowers children to realize the liberty and autonomy rights they possess. Thus, even when the debate is shorn of political rhetoric and focused only on the child, what children are taught about sex exposes the friction that exists at the margin between protection and empowerment and provides an opportunity to explore hard questions about children's rights.

A Brief History of Adolescence and Sex Education in the United States

As America transformed to an industrial nation, the transition from childhood to adulthood transformed as well. While puberty as a biological process kept to its own timetable, a distinct developmental stage of life known as adolescence emerged as a social phenomenon.[4]

Adolescence marks a prolonged period of transition from childhood to adulthood. It is largely a modern invention resulting from changes industrialization brought to work and family. The historian Jeffrey Moran observes that the construction of adolescence "rested on three important material changes in the nineteenth century" that prolonged and solidified an adolescent identity.[5] First, the modern educational system segregated youth by age and in doing so forged them with a strong group identity.[6] Second, changes in lifestyle caused American youth to sexually mature at an increasingly younger age.[7] As "the period of training and education for young men, especially, grew longer," American youth were expected to delay marriage.[8] As a result of these changes, modern youth experience a lengthy period in which, despite sexual maturity, they lack adult status and full sexual rights. A substantial portion of these years is spent in an age-segregated subculture within schools, making sexuality an issue that the educational system cannot ignore.

Characteristics of adolescence as a distinct developmental stage of life include a peer identity and culture separate from adulthood and without adult privileges, a prolonged course of schooling, career postponement, and delayed marriage. As a result of delayed adulthood, a period of time exists in which sexual capacity is not co-extensive with the liberty and privacy surrounding sexuality traditionally accorded to adults. Because schools began to take on a greater role in the life of children, sex education, including the inculcation of sexual morals, moved from the more private sphere of family and religion to the educational arena.[9]

Early sex education sought to "promote and restore Victorian values" and to discourage promiscuity, conveying the message that sex outside of marriage was both morally evil and dangerous to one's health.[10] In the first half of the twentieth century, owing in part to recognition of the sexual health needs of American soldiers during two world wars, an era of education that discouraged sex outside of marriage but also emphasized social hygiene and disease prevention emerged as the dominant trend in public education.

The sexual revolution that began in the 1960s, together with an increasing acceptance of sound public health principles, contributed to even more changes to the sex education curriculum.[11] Thus, in the second half of the twentieth century sex education not only provided preventive and practical information but also "became more forthright, increasingly comprehensive, and accepted a more positive view of human sexuality."[12]

The comprehensive approach came under attack beginning in the 1980s, as the federal government's interest in influencing sex education programs in America's schools grew.[13] Over the next three decades, the federal government provided funds to states and community groups to develop and promote a curriculum of instruction entitled "abstinence-only sex education."[14] Abstinence-only sex education rejects a factually comprehensive curriculum in favor of one that focuses exclusively on the benefits of abstinence and the risks of sex outside of traditional marriage. This approach is based on a concern that providing comprehensive information conveys permissiveness. Beginning in 2000, the federal government increased spending and provided grants to religious and conservative community organizations to develop and provide abstinence-only sex education. Although these funds were not supposed to be used to promote a religious message, the values espoused in abstinence-only classes through these "faith-based initiatives" were compatible with the religious convictions of these organizations.[15]

Abstinence-only sex education lost some ground as a federal policy in recent years with the election of President Barrack Obama. Notably, even in the waning months of President George W. Bush's term in office, an increasing number of states, concerned that abstinence-only education was hurting students, began to reject federal abstinence-only funding or limit how the money was spent.[16] Additionally, under President Obama, there was a sharp reduction of federal emphasis on abstinence-only sex education, although abstinence federal funding for states remains available under Title V.[17]

However, a policy shift at the federal level does not mean the demise of abstinence-only sex education because curricular decisions generally are a state or local matter. Many state and local school boards still endorse abstinence-only sex education and forbid comprehensive sex education in the classroom.

Sexuality, Health, and Health Burdens in Adolescence

The sexual development of children to adulthood includes biological, psychological, cultural, and developmental passages.[18] Even before sexual maturity, children engage in sexual play and are sexually curious.[19] The process of sexual maturation, known as "puberty," takes approximately 4.5 years. In American boys, the process begins at around eleven years of age, and spermarche, the release of sperm in the ejaculate and the beginning of fertility, begins between thirteen and fourteen years of age. American girls enter puberty in the ninth or tenth year of life and typically begin menstruation at around twelve years.

Sexual activity during adolescence is undeniable even though it is not regarded as desirable by larger society. According to the Centers for Disease Control (CDC), roughly one-third of youth between fifteen and seventeen have engaged in sexual intercourse, and that number increases to two-thirds between the ages of eighteen to twenty. Other sexual behaviors occur with more frequency. For example, among those fifteen to seventeen years of age, 42% of females and 44% of males have engaged in oral sex.[20]

Teens engage in some particularly risky sexual behaviors, including failure to use condoms and other forms of contraception, having multiple sex partners, and engaging in oral and anal sex without protection as substitutes for intercourse.[21] Long-term consequences of improvident sex affect teens over their lifetime. For example, there is evidence that oral cancers due to exposure to the human papillomavirus (HPV) is increasing as a consequence of unprotected oral sex.[22] The CDC warns that "many young persons in the United States engage in [risky sexual] behavior and experience negative reproductive health outcomes" as a result.[23]

The lifelong consequences of early unprotected sex are undeniable. Unintended pregnancy, sexually transmitted diseases (STDs), and HIV/AIDS carry lifelong health and socioeconomic consequences.[24] These burdens are particularly more severe for females. Differences in physiology between men and women mean that STDs do more damage to female internal organs and are more destructive to a woman's health. In addition, unplanned teenage pregnancies have much greater negative health and economic consequences on females than males, including lost educational and economic opportunities.[25] Children born to young mothers also face negative consequences, such as lower birth weights, risk of vertically (from mother to newborn) transmitted STDs, higher mortality rates, and more developmental delays than other infants.[26]

Sexual Health Concerns among Minorities

The CDC also finds that, for whatever reason, health disparities by race and ethnicity are substantial when it comes to the negative outcomes of early sex.[27] Cultural values and socioeconomic circumstances offer some explanation why differences exist.[28] The CDC reports that "noticeable disparities" include higher rates of early pregnancy and incidence of AIDS and STDs in non-white youth populations.[29] Thus, the reduced socioeconomic opportunities and the negative health outcomes that result from early sex experiences fall disproportionately on minority youth.

Sexual minority youth also suffer disproportionate health burdens. Lesbian, gay, bisexual, and transgender (LGBT) youth are a particularly vulnerable and underserved population with unique health risks. Feelings of attraction to the same sex may begin as young as nine or ten, and, increasingly, LGBT youth are "coming out" during adolescence, often while still living at home and attending school. Because of this, providing sex information to LGBT youth should not be postponed until adulthood.[30] Moreover, LGBT teens are less able to obtain information through the "usual" channels of parents, physicians, and other adults.[31] Sexual minority youth often encounter ambivalent or negative family reactions to their sexuality, foreclosing the parental avenue for advice about sex.[32] Often pediatricians lack sufficient training to meet the medical needs of LGBT youth; in fact, less than half report any formal training in treating them.[33] Studies have shown that physicians find it difficult to discuss sexuality with their LGBT patients.[34] While schools have an opportunity to bridge these gaps in resources, they more often are regarded as inhospitable to LGBT students.[35]

Generally, LGBT youth have greater sexual health risks than other youth for a variety of reasons. For example, homosexual male youth "report earlier sexual debuts, higher rates of sexual abuse, more high-risk behaviors, more lifetime sexual partners, less consistent use of contraceptives, and a greater number of episodes of running away from home than their heterosexual peers."[36] In fact, negative social and family reactions lead to LGBT youth being overrepresented in homeless and runaway youth populations, where they are exposed to greater health risks.[37] Further, homosexual adolescent males engage more frequently in prostitution than other youth populations.[38] Unfortunately, even though the health risks of LGBT youth are high, social stigma "make[s] it difficult for them to engage in health protective behaviors, such as consistent condom use and immunizations for hepatitis B."[39]

Adolescents Are Medically Underserved

All in all, American adolescents are an underserved medical population, and this exacerbates the negative health consequences associated with early sex. Because it is more difficult for youth to acquire health information through the traditional doctor-patient relationship, sex education in schools is that much more important. Studies show that "[e]arly, middle, and late adolescents all underutilize physician offices relative to their population proportion"; in fact, "[e]arly adolescents have the lowest rate of [physician] office visits than any age group across the lifespan."[40] When seeking health care, adolescents often do not confide about matters of sexual health because they fear parental notification.[41] Interestingly, studies show that the threat of parental notification has insidious effects; researchers have demonstrated that when teens fear parental notification by health providers they limit their utilization of health care but do not reduce sexual activity.[42]

In sum, early sexual conduct takes a preventable toll on America's youth, and it is hoped that sex education can mitigate those harms. Formulating sex education policies based on sound public health strategies to reduce health risks places children first. However, determining what the *content* of sex education should be has proven to be a contentious political debate about American core values.

The Debate about Sex Education and Values Education

Control of the public school curriculum has always been regarded as a political prize well worth the fight because the winner gets to define America's core values, indoctrinate youth to those values, and thus shape the future. Kenneth Karst observes:

> The "common school," as the American public school was called, has been expected from the beginning to inculcate common values. For one social group after another, that expectation has translated into a desire, and often a legislative program, to make the public schools express the group's moral values as the true national values. When Our group wins a battle in the schools, we see ourselves as capturing part of a huge expressive apparatus that we can point toward a dual purpose. First, we expect the schools to acculturate children to Our authoritative meanings. . . . Second, we hope to capture the schools in order to reassure ourselves of Our group's status dominance as the true Americans.[43]

Predictably, the content of school subjects that touch upon hot-button issues in the social and poltical arenas are often the most controversial.[44]

The sex education curriculum in America's schools has long been regarded as one of those key battleground issues in American politics.[45] It is hardly surprising that sex education is politically charged as it necessarily touches upon social topics that have dominated American political discourse, such as abortion, homosexuality, traditional marriage, and the gender roles of men and women. Thus, the fight over sex education is emblematic of the deep divide between liberal and conservative values that cuts a wide swath across America's social identity.[46]

Abstinence-Only versus Comprehensive Sex Education

In the recent debate over sex education, distinctions have not been sharply drawn between what factual information should be imparted and what values should be inculcated. Owing to the concern that providing comprehensive information will convey permissiveness, proponents of abstinence-only sex education reject a factually comprehensive curriculum. Abstinence-only programs focus exclusively on the dangers of having sex outside of a traditional monogamous marriage in order to instill fear about teen sex. The curricula's singular approach ignores the needs of youth who are engaging in sexual activity and need more information about human sexuality and instruction on measures to prevent disease and pregnancy.[47]

Abstinence-only sex education is extraordinarily narrow in focus, specifically limiting sex instruction to teaching the benefits of abstinence until marriage, a commitment to sex only within traditional marriage, the possibility of avoiding disease and unwanted pregnancy through abstinence only, and the psychological and physical harm of sex outside of marriage.[48] By definition, abstinence-only sex education rejects the idea of teaching alternative disease and pregnancy prevention methods, of providing comprehensive sex education, and of acknowledging sexual lifestyles outside of traditional marriage. Studies show that faith-based abstinence programs also reinforce negative stereotypes about men and women, such as "men need sex from their wives and women need financial support from their husbands."[49] Further, because racial and ethnic minorities,[50] LGBT persons,[51] and females[52] carry a greater sexual health burden than teens as a whole, there is a concern that, in failing to provide a curriculum that prepares these populations for sexual activity, they suffer greater harm from an abstinence-only focus that youth as a whole.

Even in schools that provide comprehensive sex education, a minor still may not have access to sex education. Some minors are denied access because parental opt-out/opt-in provisions in school sex education policies allow parents to remove their children from sex education classes.[53] Most states have adopted these provisions in order to avoid state-parent conflicts and to accommodate parental preferences.[54] These provisions allow schools to acquiesce to parents' wishes, but opt-out provisions do not require schools or parents to recognize any right of the child to that information.

Researchers studying the effectiveness of various sex education curricula have found that abstinence-only education is not effective. Notably, abstinence-only sex education deliberately avoids providing sexually active teens with information about how to maintain their health—including how to prevent pregnancy, STDs, and HIV/AIDs—while sexually active. Thus, by design, the curricula do not serve the educational needs of sexually active youth. Unless the curricula are 100% effective at achieving absolute abstinence, these curricula, by definition, fail every student who is sexually active.

Public health research has shown that abstinence-only education does not delay the initiation of sex or equip students to manage sexual activity. Several large studies have concluded that "abstinence-only programs [have] no significant effect in delaying the initiation of sexual activity or in reducing the risk for teen pregnancy and STDs."[55] Worse than merely failing, some researchers warn that abstinence-only curricula actually place teens in peril because "the focus on failure rates of contraceptives and the manipulation of data undermines desirable health practices among sexually active teens."[56] Thus, the data suggest that, at best, abstinence-only sex education has simply not achieved its aims; at worst, abstinence-only sex education has exposed teens to negative health impacts that could otherwise have been avoided. [57]

The narrow focus of abstinence-only sex education is not the curricula's only problem. They have been found in many instances to be factually false and inaccurate. A 2004 congressional study, commissioned by Representative Henry Waxman, found "serious and pervasive" problems of deceptive and inaccurate information in nearly all of the curricula studied.[58] It found, for example, that the curricula misstated the failure rate of condoms, the risks associated with abortion, and the effectiveness of methods available to prevent pregnancy and STDs.

Further, the values messages in the curricula have been criticized as imbedded with discriminatory and outmoded gender-role stereotyping. "The abstinence-only approach is permeated with stereotyped messages and sex-based double standards about acceptable male and female sexual behavior and appropriate social roles."[59] Those critical of the message about female sexuality assert that reinforcing discriminatory stereotypes in public school teaching "undermines the shared sense of agency and responsibility that young people need to avoid coerced or unwanted sex, unplanned and unprotected sex, and unwanted pregnancy."[60]

A Child's Right to Sex Information

Critics of abstinence-only sex education have argued that minors, as sexual beings, need and deserve comprehensive sex education. At the very least, if the government funds sex education, then the information provided should be factually accurate, inclusive toward all citizens, and nondiscriminatory. The federal emphasis on abstinence-only education over the last thirty years prompted an increasing number of influential professional health organizations to adopt public positions opposing federal policy and calling it misguided and inadequate.[61] Even though many in public health and education roundly criticized abstinence-only sex education, the search for an adequate legal framework on which to rest a minor's right to information has not been altogether satisfactory.

Barbara Bennett Woodhouse has observed that, in the child-parent-state triad, "we are so accustomed to the notion that parents have 'rights' while children have mere 'interests' that we hardly notice the yawning hole in our jurisprudence of rights."[62] Children's rights advocates have complained that challenges in the educational context that pit the rights of parents against the interests of the state subordinate the child when, instead, the child's rights should be the centerpiece of the dispute.[63]

Conceptualizing a minor's right to accurate and comprehensive sex education is challenging because "the prevailing interpretation of U.S. constitutional law is largely ambivalent with respect to protecting minors' individual rights."[64] Problematically, although education has been recognized as the cornerstone of a free and democratic nation, the U.S. Supreme Court has not recognized that citizens have a right to education, let alone established a constitutional test of its quality.[65] Given our impoverished view of children's rights, generally, and "without constitutional protection for a minor's right to education, it is difficult to see how a U.S. court would be willing to recognize that minors have an affirmative right under the Constitution to a particular educational content."[66] Nevertheless, scholars who argue that an adolescent's right to sex information deserves special treatment in the law are advancing some novel arguments.

One obstacle to creating a minor's right to sex information that must first be acknowledged is the general rule that the government enjoys wide latitude to choose and advance its own message, even if the message it promotes is unsound. It is well established that "a government entity is entitled to say what it wishes . . . and to select the views that it wants to express."[67] In the educational realm, pedagogical decisions are largely vested within the sound discretion of the schools.[68] Thus, while it might seem axiomatic that what schools teach should be truthful and pedagogically effective, schools may deliberately fall short.

There are some restraints on governmental speech; for example, the government's own speech must not advance religion under Establishment Clause,[69] or burden the individual's exercise of a fundamental right or speech,[70] or amount to discrimination.[71] Child-centered legal arguments against abstinence-only sex education have focused on those traditional limits on government speech and on the exposure to harm children face from the curricula. These arguments draw from principles embodied in international human rights,[72] equal protection and equality,[73] the First Amendment,[74] and the due process autonomy and privacy rights in health and reproduction[75] to establish that minors have a fundamental right to accurate, nondiscriminatory, and comprehensive sex education.

Sex Information Safeguards Autonomy and Privacy Rights

Sex education stands close to the sphere of privacy and autonomy rights that surrounds the medical and reproductive decision-making rights of mature minors, and this kinship invites analogies. In medical treatment, the obligation to obtain "informed consent" protects a bedrock principle that a patient possesses an essential "right to determine what shall be done with his own body" and that "true" consent can only be achieved when one has "an opportunity to evaluate knowledgeably the options available and the risks attendant upon each."[76] Informed consent is not merely a medical tort principle; it protects both state interests and the patient's autonomy and privacy interests rooted in constitutional law.[77] As a matter of common law, mature minors enjoy some extended rights to make medical decisions separate from their parents.[78] When a minor exercises those rights, the benefits of informed consent inure to the minor. In the reproductive rights cases, the Supreme Court has acknowledged the decisional rights of minors, stating that "the right to privacy in connection with decisions affecting procreation extends to minors as well as adults," and is limited only to the extent of "any significant state interest . . . that is not present in the case of an adult."[79]

To the extent that abstinence-only sex education conveys inaccurate and misleading information about condom use, abortion, and prevention of STDs, certain analogies can be drawn to reproductive rights cases. In these cases, the U.S. Supreme Court has allowed the government latitude to convey its own message and promote its desired policies. However, the Court has stopped short of endorsing a governmental prerogative to convey false and misleading speech designed to limit a woman's reproductive choice. For example, in *Planned Parenthood of Southeast Pennsylvania v. Casey*, the Court found that a state's informed consent statute that required giving truthful, non-misleading information about the nature of abortion and its risks was constitutional even though it was aimed at discouraging abortion.[80] The implication that one can certainly draw is that a state would not be allowed to systematically provide misleading and inaccurate information in order to burden a woman's choice to have an abortion.

Admittedly, drawing analogies between sex education and medical and reproductive liberties is not entirely satisfactory. Sex education is not quite the same as health information—sex education is broader, and it lacks the immediacy of informed consent. Yet sex education is also not quite like any other course that schools teach. Sex education stands on a different footing than other curricular offerings because providing sex information affects how youth make constitutionally protected choices about their sexuality and their health. Catherine Ross suggests that the autonomy and privacy interests minors possess necessarily encompass a right to information. From this, it follows that adolescents possess a First Amendment right to obtain sex information. Ross observes,

> The right to receive information is integrally related to any effort to achieve the individual self-realization that is essential to the structure of the First Amendment. In that sense, the right to receive information is reinforced when it is combined with other autonomy claims protected under the Constitution.[81]

In this sense, it is only by providing minors with accurate sex information that can they be empowered to realize the recognized rights of privacy and autonomy that they possess.

A Right to Non-discriminatory Educational Content

When the government promotes values through sex education, it cannot promote a discriminatory and regressive message through harmful stereotyping. Critics of abstinence-only sex education have examined the curricula and found, for example, that the

> overt teachings and the pervasive subtext of abstinence-only curricula reflect the expectation that women should and will become mothers, rely on their husbands for financial support, care about their relationships with males more than the males do, have a greater stake in and identification with chastity than men, and do not value the importance of sexual release as highly as men do.[82]

Such curricula perpetuate harmful stereotypes that conflict with equality principles rooted in the constitution. This leads some to argue that "[t]he abstinence only approach is permeated with stereotyped messages and sex-based double standards about acceptable male and female sexual behavior and appropriate social roles. Public school teaching of gender stereotypes violates the constitutional bar against sex stereotyping and is vulnerable to equal protection challenge."[83]

Invoking equality principles as a check the government's right to control its own message elevates and protects the child's present and future right to self-actualization. Equality serves as a scaffold to support a child's right to be free from instruction designed to limit a child's aspirations and erode civil rights. Under a construct that demands a non-discriminatory message, schools remain generally free to inculcate social values but not to advance values that are contrary to the democratic principle of equality. "If it is contrary to equal protection to make even formally neutral governmental decisions based on sex stereotypes, it would seem, a fortiori, unconstitutional to teach those same views in public schools."[84] In other words, logic suggests that if the state must not act in a discriminatory manner toward certain citizens, it follows that state-sponsored teaching must not be embedded with a discriminatory message. "By promulgating sexual double standards, those curricula foster a world view and behavior at odds with our equal protection law."[85]

Lesbian, gay, bisexual, and transgender youth experience another form of discrimination in some school-sponsored sex education. In some sex education curricula, LGBT youth are "invisible," as their sexual health needs are ignored altogether. "These abstinence-only programs are public health interventions, designed at their core to be ineffective for gay and lesbian adolescents."[86] The exclusion of matters related to the health of sexual minorities from school sex education curricula altogether sends a chilling discriminatory message to sexual minority youth that reinforces a closeted existence.

Abstinence-only sex education extols the virtues of sex within traditional marriage and focuses on teaching teen heterosexuals delaying tactics. This singular focus on heterosexuality and traditional marriage sends a discriminatory and harmful state-sponsored message that denies the sexuality of LGBT youth and suggests that their sexuality will not now or ever be condoned. Lesbian, gay, bisexual, and transgender youth are effectively "disenfranchised and erased from the nation's public culture" through state educational programs that ignore their sexuality altogether.[87] Our law has progressed beyond the viewpoint that government can punish homosexuality as immoral, and there has been increasing recognition of due-process protections to same-sex relationships.[88] Sex education that excludes LGBT youth ignores the civil rights gains sexual minorities have made.

> It may not be that gay and lesbian students have a constitutional right to education that nourishes their self-confidence and hopes for future happiness in life. However, they undoubtedly have a right to an education that does not purposely denigrate that vision by singling them out as a group that is unworthy of equal treatment in society. Abstinence-only education's impact on gay and lesbian students, and particularly from communities of color, goes beyond mere indifference to their sense of personhood and violates the Equal Protection Clause in ways likely to cause severe psychological harm to these students.[89]

A child's right to be free from discrimination thus serves as a limitation on the government's right to establish the content of sex education curricula.

Sex Education and International Human Rights

The case for a minor's right to accurate and comprehensive sex information can also draw from the wellspring of international human rights law for support, although the most powerful of these, the United Nations Convention on the Rights of the Child (CRC), is merely of aspirational importance to U.S. domestic policies.[90] Sex education policies that respond to a political or social agenda that are disconnected from a child's needs are out of step with international human rights norms.[91]

Important human rights treaties and conventions, particularly the CRC, strongly support a minor's right to health access, health information, and to comprehensive sex education.[92] Notably, the Committee on the Rights of the Child has reminded countries of their

> obligations to provide adolescents with access to information, stating that countries must ensure that adolescents have access to "sexual and reproductive information, including on family planning and contraceptives, the dangers of early pregnancy, the prevention of HIV/AIDS and the prevention and treatment of sexually transmitted diseases (STDs)."[93]

Although the United States was instrumental in drafting the CRC, it has yet to ratify the convention.[94] It is not coincidence that, in the United States, the two most powerful objections to the ratification of the CRC are that it conflicts with the sovereignty rights of the states and it interferes with the right of parents to raise the child as protected by the U.S. Constitution.[95] The force of these arguments against the CRC, a convention that seeks to elevate the rights of the child, demonstrates again how difficult it is to shift the debate in the United States from the conflict between parents and the state toward a discussion of what children need.

Yet, even short of ratification of the CRC, to the extent that the United States aspires to lead in the context of human rights, its domestic policies can be positively influenced by such international norms. As one commentator observed, "[T]he principles enshrined in international human rights law counsel the United States to ensure that its own legal system provides adequate protections for minors, which necessarily include respecting and nurturing their ability to make informed decisions about their sexual health."[96]

Protecting Children by Empowering Children

Comprehensive sex education empowers children to make independent judgments about sex. However, its proponents must also respond to the claim that the narrow focus and conservative message of abstinence-only curricula protects children by shielding them from harms that attend sexual permissiveness. Abstinence-only sex education versus comprehensive sex education implicates two strands of children's rights, one based on the child's liberty and autonomy rights, and the other based on the child's right to protection and dependency.

If abstinence-only sex education actually protects children from the social and health burdens of early sex, then one must balance that protection against the toll abstinence programs exacts with regard to equality, liberty, and autonomy. However, systematic evaluation of abstinence-only programs shows that these curricula prefer ignorance to empowerment without any corresponding benefit to youth. Abstinence-only instruction does not result in a delay in initiating sex, reducing the number of partners, or reducing the incidence of STDs, pregnancy, or HIV/AIDS. Simply put, without evidence of any protective benefits, there is no justification for abstinence-only education.

Conclusion

For over three decades, the United States implemented a policy of public funding for abstinence-only sex education at the federal level. Many schools continue to teach abstinence-only, even though the federal emphasis on abstinence-only sex education has recently waned. The curricula have been criticized by various national organizations of educators, health care professionals, and school counselors. Public health researchers labeled the curricula as misleading, ineffective, and discriminatory. Despite the widespread criticism of the curricula's narrow and ineffective approach, no altogether-convincing legal theory exists that compels the conclusion that children, as a matter of right, are entitled to information about sex that they need to mature into healthy and adjusted sexual beings. Drawing on principles of equality, privacy, autonomy, and looking to international norms for guidance, we can develop a more robust child-centered approach that both protects and respects children.

A child's need for information about sexuality compels recognition of a corresponding right to that information.[97] Recognizing a child's right to be, and to become, a self-actualized sexual being requires that we also recognize a concomitant right to information about sex that permits intelligent choices. This chapter provides a construction of a "right to sexual information" that honors the autonomy, self-identity, and privacy rights that we regard as fundamental to all individuals in a free society.

NOTES

1. *See, e.g.*, Wisconsin v. Yoder, 406 U.S. 205 (1972) (parental challenge to compulsory education on First and Fourteenth Amendment grounds); Pierce v. Society of Sisters, 268 U.S. 510, 534 (1925) (challenging state's right to compel public education); Meyer v. Nebraska, 262 U.S. 390 (1923) (challenging state's right to prohibit foreign language instruction until eighth grade); Selman v. Cobb County Sch. Dist., 449 F.3d 1320 (11th Cir. 2006) (challenging state's right to place a sticker on biology texts stating that evolution is only a theory on grounds violates the Establishment Clause); Kitzmiller v. Dover Area Sch. Dist., 400 F. Supp. 2d 707 (M.D. Pa. 2005) (challenging state's right to teach intelligent design). As part of the right to control the message, states also exclude access as well. *See, e.g.*, Child Evangelism Fellowship of New Jersey Inc. v. Stafford Tp. Sch. Dist., 386 F.3d 514 (3d Cir. 2004) (whether religious organization can distribute materials in public elementary school in public fora).

2. For example, many states allow parents to "opt out" of sex education on behalf of their child, even though not constitutionally required. See Keith Brough, *Sex Education Left at the Threshold of the School Door: Stricter Requirements for Parental Opt-Out Provisions*, 46 Fam. Ct. Rev. 409 (2008).

3. Steven Mintz, *Placing Children's Rights in Historical Perspective*, 44 Crim. L. Bull. 313 (2008).

4. Hazel G. Beh & Milton Diamond, *The Failure of Abstinence-Only Education: Minors Have a Right to Honest Talk about Sex*, 15 Colum. J. Gender & L. 12, 17–18 (2006).

5. *Jeffrey P. Moran, Teaching Sex: The Shaping of Adolescence in the 20th Century* (Harv. Univ. Press 2000), 15.

6. *Id.*
7. *Id.*
8. *Id.*
9. Beh & Diamond, *Failure of Abstinence-Only Education, supra* note 4, at 18–20.
10. *Id.* at 19.
11. *Id.* at 20.
12. *Id.*

13. Samuel J. Philhower, *A Moral and Political Roadblock to Viable Sex Education: How Abstinence Education Has Established Itself at the Center of Public Policy*, 31 Women's Rts. L. Rep. 147 (2009) (tracing funding and legislation from the 1990's onward); Catherine Carroll, *Children's Lives as a Political Battleground: The Plague of Abstinence Only Education*, 3 DePaul J. Soc. Just. 41, 50–63 (2009) (tracing increasing funding for abstinence sex education through presidential terms).

14. The programs were the Adolescent Family Life Act, 42 U.S.C. § 300z (2005); Personal Responsibility Act of 1996, 42 U.S.C.S. § 719 (2005) (also known as Section 510 of Title V of the Social Security Act); and Special Projects of Regional and National Significance—Community Based Abstinence Education. The latter was initially known as SPRANS-CBAE and later as CBAE.

15. Beh & Diamond, *Failure of Abstinence-Only Education*, supra note 4, at 30.

16. Carroll, *Children's Lives as a Political Battleground*, supra note 13, at 62–63.

17. SIECUS (Sexuality Information and Education Council of the United States), *State by State Decisions: The Personal Responsibility Education Program and Title V Abstinence-Only Program*, www.siecus.org/index.cfm?fuseaction=Page.ViewPage&PageID=1272 (discussing federal funding for both comprehensive sex education through the Patient Protection and Affordable Care Act as well as reauthorization of Title V abstinence-only grants to state) (last visited June 18, 2014).

18. Vern L. Bullough, *Children and Adolescents as Sexual Beings: A Historical Overview*, 13(3) Child & Adolescent Psychiatric Clinics N. Am. 447 (2004).

19. Jose A. Nieto, *Children and Adolescents as Sexual Beings: Cross-Cultural Perspectives*, 13(3) Child & Adolescent Psychiatric Clinics N. Am. 461 (2004).

20. *See* Centers for Disease Control, *Sexual and Reproductive Health of Persons Aged 10–24 Years—United States, 2002–2007*, 58 Morbidity and Mortality Weekly Report, Surveillance Summaries (July 17, 2009), www.cdc.gov/mmWR/PDF/ss/ss5806.pdf (last visited June 18, 2014).

21. *Id.* at 7 and tables 2 & 3.

22. Micah Globerson, *Gardasil a Year Later: Cervical Cancer as a Model for Inequality of Access to Health Services*, 15 Cardozo J.L. & Gender 247, 250 (2009).

23. Centers for Disease Control, *Sexual and Reproductive Health of Persons Aged 10–24 Years—United States, 2002–2007*, supra note 20, at 1.

24. Beh & Diamond, *The Failure of Abstinence-Only Education*, supra note 4, at 21–15.

25. *Id.* at 23–24.

26. *Id.* at 25.

27. Centers for Disease Control, *Sexual and Reproductive Health of Persons Aged 10–24 Years—United States, 2002–2007*, supra note 20, at 9–10.

28. Sarah Smith Kuehnel, *Abstinence-Only Education Fails African American Youth*, 86 Wash. U. L. Rev. 1241, 1244–1247 (2009).

29. Centers for Disease Control, *Sexual and Reproductive Health of Persons Aged 10–24 Years—United States, 2002–2007*, supra note 20, at 1.

30. Caitlin Ryan, *Families of Lesbian, Gay, and Bisexual Adolescents*, in *Gay and Lesbian Issues in Pediatric Health Care*, 34(10) *Current Probs. Pediatric Adolescent Health Care* 369 (2004); Ritch C. Savin-Williams, *Growing Up with Same-Sex Attraction*, in *Gay and Lesbian Issues in Pediatric Health Care*, 34(10) *Current Probs. Pediatric Adolescent Health Care* 369 (2004).

31. Barbara L. Frankowski, *Sexual Orientation and Adolescents*, 113 *Am. Acad. Pediatrics* 1827 (2004).

32. One study described the range of parental reactions: "[M]any parents reacted to learning about their child's lesbian or gay identity with a great deal of ambivalence. Few were initially accepting and some were openly rejected and even reacted with violence and hostility. Some youth were ejected from their homes after their parents learned about their sexual orientation." Ryan, *Families of Lesbian, Gay and Bisexual Adolescents*, supra note 30, at 370.

33. Jeffrey A. East & Fadya El Rayess, *Pediatricians' Approach to the Health Care of Lesbian, Gay, and Bisexual Youth*, 23 *J. Adolescent Health* 192 (1998).

34. *Id.*

35. Les B. Whitbeck et al., *Mental Disorder, Subsistence Strategies, and Victimization among Gay, Lesbian, and Bisexual Homeless and Runaway Adolescents*, 41 *J. Sex Res.* 330 (Nov. 2004).

36. Lynn Rew et al., *Sexual Health Risks and Protective Resources in Gay, Lesbian, Bisexual, and Heterosexual Homeless Youth*, 10 *J. Specialists Pediatric Nursing* 11, 12 (2005).

37. Whitbeck et al., *Mental Disorder, Subsistence Strategies, and Victimization*, supra note 35, at 330 (observing that "about [20%] of homeless and runaway adolescents are gay, lesbian, or bisexual in larger magnet cities (e.g., Los Angeles, San Francisco, Seattle) with perhaps a slightly lower proportion in smaller, non-magnet cities"); Rew et al., *Sexual Health Risks and Protective Resources*, supra note 36, at 11 (discussing previous study finding 40% of gay and bisexual adolescents have had episodes of running away from home). *See* Chapter 9, in this volume.

38. Whitbeck et al., *Mental Disorder, Subsistence Strategies, and Victimization*, supra note 35, at 330.

39. Rew et al., *Sexual Health Risks and Protective Resources*, supra note 36, at 12.

40. Amitai Ziv et al., *Utilization of Physician Offices by Adolescents in the United States*, 104 *Pediatrics* 40 (1999).

41. Linda Hock-Long et al., *Access to Adolescent Reproductive Health Services: Financial and Structural Barriers to Care*, 35 *Persp. Sex.& Reprod. Health* 144 (2003); Diane M. Reddy, *Effect of Mandatory Parental Notification on Adolescent Girls' Use of Sexual Health Care Services*, 288 *J. Am. Med. Ass'n* 712 (2002); Rachel K. Jones et al., *Adolescents' Report of Parental Knowledge of Adolescents' Use of Sexual Health Services and Their Reactions to Mandated Parental Notification for Prescription Contraception*, 293 *J. Am. Med. Ass'n* 340 (2005).

42. Jones et al., *Adolescents' Report of Parental Knowledge of Adolescents' Use of Sexual Health Services*, supra note 41, at 347.

43. Kenneth L. Karst, *Law, Cultural Conflict, and the Socialization of Children*, 91 Cal. L. Rev. 967, 992–993 (2003).

44. *See, e.g.*, Epperson v. Ark., 393 U.S. 97 (1968) (creationism and science); Loewen v. Turnipseed, 488 F. Supp. 1138, 1154 (N.D. Miss. 1980) (racial discrimination in text selection); Chiras v. Miller, 432 F.3d 606 (5th Cir. 2005) (dispute over textbook's characterization of causes of environmental problems).

45. Beh & Diamond, *The Failure of Abstinence-Only Education, supra* note 4, 26.

46. "As the pendulum swings back and forth between sexual liberalism and social conservatives, the debate over sex education has seemed to become less a dispute over the curriculum than a ritual dance to signify a broader range of social and sexual attitudes." Moran, *Teaching Sex, supra* note 5, at 15.

47. Beh & Diamond, *The Failure of Abstinence-Only Education, supra* note 4, at 28–29.

48. The working definition presented in 42 U.S.C. § 710 (2005) applies to both CBAE and Section 510. The statute provides:

> (2) For purposes of this section, the term "abstinence education" means an educational or motivational program which—
> (A) has as its exclusive purpose, teaching the social, psychological, and health gains to be realized by abstaining from sexual activity;
> (B) teaches abstinence from sexual activity outside marriage as the expected standard for all school age children;
> (C) teaches that abstinence from sexual activity is the only certain way to avoid out-of-wedlock pregnancy, sexually transmitted diseases, and other associated health problems;
> (D) teaches that a mutually faithful monogamous relationship in context of marriage is the expected standard of human sexual activity;
> (E) teaches that sexual activity outside of the context of marriage is likely to have harmful psychological and physical effects;
> (F) teaches that bearing children out-of-wedlock is likely to have harmful consequences for the child, the child's parents, and society;
> (G) teaches young people how to reject sexual advances and how alcohol and drug use increases vulnerability to sexual advances; and
> (H) teaches the importance of attaining self-sufficiency before engaging in sexual activity.

Under the law, preventive health behaviors other than abstinence are not discussed, as "[a]bstinence-only programs are based on a simple premise: give adolescents a clear and consistent message to wait until marriage to have sex. If birth control is mentioned, the message says that no birth control is 100% effective at preventing pregnancy and avoiding sexually transmitted diseases." Jerrold E. Barnett & Cynthia S. Hurst, *Abstinence Education for Rural Youth: An Evaluation of the Life's Walk Program*, 73 J. Sch. Health 264 (2003).

49. *See* Jennifer S. Hendricks & Dawn Marie Howerton, *Teaching Values, Teaching Stereotypes: Sex Education and Indoctrination in Public Schools*, 13 U. Pa. J. Const. L. 587 (2011).

50. *See* Risha K. Foulkes, *Abstinence-Only Education and Minority Teenagers: The Importance of Race in a Question of Constitutionality*, 10 Berkeley J. Afr.-Am. L. & Pol'y 3 (2008); Kuehnel, *Abstinence-Only Education Fails African American Youth, supra* note 28, at 1241.

51. James McGrath, *Abstinence-Only Adolescent Education: Ineffective, Unpopular, and Unconstitutional*, 38 U.S.F. L. Rev. 684 (2004).

52. Beh & Diamond, *The Failure of Abstinence-Only Education, supra* note 4, 23.

53. SIECUS (Sex Information and Education Council of the United States) tracks state policies related to sex education, including parental opt-out/in provisions. SIECUS, *SIECUS State Profiles: Sexuality and HIV/STD Education Policies*, www.siecus.org/_data/global/images/10%20Sexuality%20and%20HIV-STD%20Education%20Policies%20Chart.pdf (hereinafter SIECUS, *State Profiles*) (last visited June 18, 2014).

54. Eric A. DeGroff, *Sex Education in the Public Schools and the Accommodation of Familial Rights*, 26 Child. Legal Rts. J. 27 (2006) (quoting Troxel v. Granville, 530 U.S. 57, 91 (2000) (Scalia, J. dissenting)). Emily J. Brown, *When Insiders Become Outsiders: Parental Objections to Public School Sex Education Programs*, 59 Duke L.J. 109 (2009) (contending that parents are entitled to opt-out as a matter of constitutional law).

55. Pamela K. Kohler et al., *Abstinence-Only and Comprehensive Sex Education and the Initiation of Sexual Activity and Teen Pregnancy*, 42 J. Adolescent Health 349 (2008); Matthew Hogben et al., *Sexuality Education Policies and Sexually Transmitted Disease Rates in the United States*, 21 Int'l J. STDs & AIDs 293 (2010); Michele M. Isley, *Sex Education and Contraceptive Use at Coital Debut in the United States: Results from Cycle 6 of the National Survey of Family Growth*, 82 Contraception 236 (2010).

56. Hazel G. Beh, *Recognizing Sexual Rights of Minors in the Abstinence-Only Sex Education Debate*, 26 Child. Legal Rts. J. 8 (2006).

57. Hogben et al., *Sexuality Education Policies and Sexually Transmitted Disease Rates in the United States, supra* note 55, at 293.

58. Minority Staff Special Investigations Division, Committee on Government Reform, U.S. House of Representatives, *The Content of Federally Funded Abstinence-Only Education Programs* (Dec. 2004), www.apha.org/apha/PDFs/HIV/The_Waxman_Report.pdf (last visited June 18, 2014).

59. Cornelia T. L. Pillard, *Our Reproductive Choices: Sexuality in Sex Education, Contraceptive Access, and Work-Family Policy*, 56 Emory L.J. 941 (2007); Jennifer Greenblatt, *"If You Don't Aim to Please, Don't Dress to Tease" and Other Public School Sex Education Lessons Subsidized by You, the Federal Taxpayer*, 14 Tex. J. C.L. & C.R. 1 (2008).

60. Pillard, *Our Reproductive Choices, supra* note 59, at 948.

61. Beh & Diamond, *The Failure of Abstinence-Only Education, supra* note 4, at 43–44. Professional organizations, including, among many others, the American Medical Association, the American Academy of Pediatrics, the American Public Health Association, the American College of Obstetricians and Gynecologists, the American Psychological Association, the Society for Adolescent Medicine, the National Education Association, the American School Health Association, and the

American Association of University Women, have official policies supporting comprehensive sexuality education and opposing state and federal mandates of abstinence-only education that censor information about condoms and contraception for the prevention of pregnancy, HIV, and other STDs. *Id.*

62. Barbara Bennett Woodhouse, *Speaking Truth to Power: Challenging the Power of Parents to Control the Education of Their Own*, 11 Cornell J. L. & Pub. Pol'y 485 (2002).

63. Beh & Diamond, *The Failure of Abstinence-Only Education, supra* note 4, at 50–51.

64. Leah J. Tulin, *Can International Human Rights Law Countenance Federal Funding of Abstinence-Only Education?* 95 Geo. L.J. 1994 (2007).

65. San Antonio Ind. Sch. Dist. v. Rodriquez, 411 U.S. 1 (1973).

66. Tulin, *Can International Human Rights Law Countenance Federal Funding of Abstinence-Only Education? supra* note 64, at 1994.

67. Pleasant Grove City Utah v. Summum, 555 U.S. 460 (2009) (quoting Rosenberger v. Rector and Visitors of Univ. of Va., 515 U.S. 819, 833 (1995) and Rust v. Sullivan, 500 U.S. 173 (1991)).

68. *See, e.g.*, Bd. Of Educ. Island Trees Union Free Sch. Dist. No. 26 v. Pico, 457 U.S. 853, 869 (1982) (generally a school has "discretion in matters of curriculum" based upon its "duty to inculcate community values").

69. *Pleasant Grove*, 555 U.S. 460 (2009).

70. Rust v. Sullivan, 500 U.S. at 201 (government's limitations on abortion counseling did not "impermissibly burden" a fundamental right to choose under Fifth Amendment).

71. Loewen v. Turnipseed, 488 F. Supp. 1138 (D.C. Miss. 1980) (textbook selection process evidenced a discriminatory purpose in violation of law). *See also* Helen Norton, *Constraining Public Employee Speech: Government's Control of Its Workers' Speech to Protect Its Own Expression*, 59 Duke L.J. 23 (2009) (government speech "that furthers race, national origin, or gender discrimination may violate the Equal Protection Clause").

72. *See* Cynthia Soohoo & Suzanne Stolz, *Bringing Theories of Human Rights Change Home*, 77 Fordham L. Rev. 459, (2008); Tulin, *Can International Human Rights Law Countenance Federal Funding of Abstinence-Only Education? supra* note 64, at 1979.

73. Pillard, *Our Reproductive Choices, supra* note 59, at 941; Greenblatt, *"If You Don't Aim to Please, Don't Dress to Tease," supra* note 59, at 14; Foulkes, *Abstinence-Only Education and Minority Teenagers, supra* note 50, at 3.

74. Hendricks & Howerton, *Teaching Values, Teaching Stereotypes, supra* note 49, at 587.

75. Beh & Diamond, *The Failure of Abstinence-Only Education, supra* note 4, at 12; Pillard, *Our Reproductive Choices, supra* note 59, at 941.

76. *See* Canterbury v. Spence, 464 F.2d 772, 780 (D.C. 1972) (rejecting a "physician-oriented standard and adopting the "patient-oriented" standard for informed consent in medical treatment).

77. *See, e.g.*, Planned Parenthood of Southeastern Pennsylvania v. Casey, 505 U.S. 833 (1992).

78. *See*, e.g., Cardwell v. Bechtol, 724 S.W.2d 739 (Tenn. 1987); Belcher v. Charleston Area Medical Center, 422 S.E.2d 827 (W. Va. 1992).

79. Carey v. Population Servs. Int'l, 431 U.S. 678, 693 (1977).

80. Planned Parenthood of Southeastern Pennsylvania v. Casey, 505 U.S. 833 (1992). In attempting to ensure that a woman apprehends the full consequences of her decision, the State furthers the legitimate purpose of reducing the risk that a woman may elect to have an abortion only to discover later, with devastating psychological consequences, that her decision was not fully informed. If the information the State requires to be made available to the woman is truthful and not misleading, the requirement may be permissible. *Id. See also* Rust v. Sullivan, 500 U.S. 173, 200 (1991) (in upholding limits on counseling abortion under Title X, the Court specifically observed that the limits on the physician "cannot be reasonably thought to mislead").

81. Catherine J. Ross, *An Emerging Right for Mature Minors to Receive Information*, 2 U. Pa. J. Cons. L. 250 (1999).

82. Pillard, *Our Reproductive Choices, supra* note 59, at 956.

83. *Id*. at 948.

84. *Id*. at 956.

85. *Id*.

86. McGrath, *Abstinence-Only Adolescent Education, supra* note 51, at 684.

87. William N. Eskridge, Jr., *Law and the Construction of the Close: American Regulation of Same-Sex Intimacy, 1880–1946*, 82 Iowa L. Rev. 1109 (1997).

88. 539 U.S. 558 (2003).

89. Foulkes, *Abstinence-Only Education and Minority Teenagers, supra* note 50, at 38–39.

90. Lanie Rutkow & Joshua T. Lozman, *Suffer the Children? A Call for United States Ratification of the United Nations Convention on the Rights of the Child*, 19(1) Harv. Hum. Rts. J. 166 (2006).

91. Soohoo & Stolz, *Bringing Theories of Human Rights Change Home, supra* note 72, at 479–783.

92. *United Nations Convention on the Rights of the Child*, G.A. Res. 44/25, art. 24 (2) (e), Nov. 20, 1989. Although the United States played a substantial role in drafting the Convention and signed it—thereby signaling an intent to ratify it—in the decades since, it has not ratified the Convention.

93. Soohoo & Stolz, *Bringing Theories of Human Rights Home, supra* note 72, at 481.

94. Rutkow & Lozman, *Suffer the Children? supra* note 90, at 166–172.

95. *Id.* at 174–181.

96. Tulin, *Can International Human Rights Law Countenance Federal Funding of Abstinence-Only Education? supra* note 64, at 2015.

97. *See* Barbara Bennett Woodhouse, *"Out of Children's Needs, Children's Rights": The Child's Voice in Defining the Family*, 8 BYU J. Pub. L. 321 (1994).

8

Policing Gender on the Playground

Interests, Needs, and Rights of Transgender and Gender Non-conforming Youth

SACHA M. COUPET

Sex, gender identity, and gender role usually develop in accordance with one another and within the fairly clear boundaries that define what is traditionally "male" and traditionally "female." However, this is not always the case. There are some whose natal sex differs from their gender identity and those whose gender role or gender expression is not confined to the traditional male-female binary, lying instead somewhere in between. Such discordance and variance exists not only in adults but in children as well. This chapter explores the ways in which children's gender identity is addressed in the various spaces in which children reside, particularly when their affirmed gender identity differs from that assigned to them at birth or when they find themselves somewhere along the gender spectrum rather than rooted at either end. While the focus of this text is on children in the broad scope of sex and sexuality, this chapter departs somewhat in its particular focus on the ways in which the social construction of sex also matters to children. This chapter explores the challenges facing transgender and gender-variant children and the ways in which they and their families are, in turn, challenging both social norms and the systems in which children's gender expression is made visible.[1]

"Sex as the Hardware, Gender as the Software": Who Are Transgender and Gender Non-conforming Children?

Any attempt to define transgender and gender non-conforming youth must begin with a contextualization of those terms within the broader scope of children's gender identity development.² As a basic matter, we might first ask, What exactly is gender identity, and how do children conceive of their own and other people's gender identity?

Historically, sex and gender have been recognized as distinct operative concepts and terms, both of which aim to get at the difference between biological markers and social constructs—or, more playfully, as some note—the hardware and the software. In the most general sense, "sex" is defined as "the biological characteristics which define humans as female or male."³ Said biological characteristics are anatomical ones, largely because "[s]ex is [understood to be] a system of classification that divides body types based on presumed reproductive capacity as determined typically by visual examination of the external genitalia."⁴ Indeed, at birth, in place of any genetic or chromosomal testing to determine sex, one is assigned a birth sex based on visual inspection of external genitalia. It is as simple as that, at least when the hardware is unambiguous.⁵

Gender identity, in contrast, is a much more complex concept. "Whereas biological sex is determined by genetic and anatomical characteristics, gender is an acquired identity that is learned, changes over time, and varies widely within and across cultures."⁶ To borrow again from the analogy above, gender identity is the software that enables us to understand ourselves as male or female.⁷ It has been variously defined as either "knowing that one is a member of one sex rather than the other," "the degree to which one perceives the self as conforming to cultural stereotypes for one's gender," or "a fundamental sense of acceptance of, and belonging to, one's gender."⁸ In 2007, a panel of experts in international human rights law and on sexual orientation and gender identity published the following comprehensive definition of gender identity: "each person's deeply felt internal and individual experience of [a gendered self], which may or may not correspond with the sex assigned at birth, including the personal sense of the body (which may involve, if freely chosen, modification of bodily appearance or function by medical, surgical or other means) and other expressions of gender, including dress, speech and mannerisms."⁹

Gender identities are believed to function on two levels—the individual, in reference to one's own perceived gender and the collective, in reference to perceiving oneself as a member of a gender group.¹⁰

Breaking down this broader concept into a multidimensional model, gender researchers have proposed five major components that capture the underlying cognitive dimensions of gender identity: "(a) membership knowledge (knowledge of membership in a gender category); (b) gender typicality (the degree to which one feels one is a typical member of one's gender category); (c) gender contentedness (the degree to which one is happy with one's gender assignment); (d) felt pressure for gender conformity (the degree to which one feels pressured from parents, peers, and self for conformity to gender stereotypes); and (e) intergroup bias (the extent to which one believes one's own sex is superior to the other)."[11] Gender identity is, at the very least, a complex cognitive process that unfolds over time and one upon which we place tremendous value in our human interactions, beginning even in infancy.

One example of our fascination with gender identity and the important role it plays in shaping our expectations is the notoriety gained over the past few years by those children around the globe whose parents have made an affirmative choice *not* to make public the assigned birth sex of their children.[12] Although small in number, such children are the subject of much international media scrutiny following their parents' refusal to divulge any information about birth sex, a decision with political undertones that has sparked a mix of scorn and praise from the public. Said the Canadian parents of one such child, Storm Stocker, in a January 2011 birth announcement e-mail: "We decided not to share Storm's sex for now—a tribute to freedom and choice in place of limitation, a standup to what the world could become in Storm's lifetime."[13] In June 2011, Egalia Preschool in Sweden made headlines across the globe when it announced that it would no longer use the gendered pronouns "he," "she," him," or "her" in an attempt to create a gender-neutral learning environment in which the message of gender equality is reinforced.[14] Not surprisingly, both of these unconventional choices were met with a mix of derision, admiration, and curiosity from across the globe. Such experiments with gender are rare, however, and "genderless" babies, as Storm is known,[15] and gender-neutral preschools, like Egalia, remain the exception. The uproar created by such experiments speaks to the strength of gender as an organizing factor in our interactions with one another. As we've come to learn, not only do the adults in children's lives use gender identity based on natal sex to categorize children, but children themselves—from as young as two and a half years old—also experience and act upon a definite sense of their gendered selves.

* * *

Much of what we know about how an understanding of gender develops early in life has been learned from research in the area of cognitive development. The ways in which children form a concept of gender identity is highly contextual in relation to their cognitive development and is, therefore, shaped by children's emerging cognitive capacities about self and membership in a gendered group. "Understanding social categories, and that one belongs to one or more of these categories, is a major transition in children's lives. Moreover, categorizing others and the self in terms of gender starts early and quickly. Habituation studies with babies as young as 9 months old reveals that they are able to visually discriminate between male and female faces."[16] "Converging evidence suggests that a more precise gender identity may emerge between eighteen and twenty-four months based on tacit preverbal measures of gender knowledge, such as gender-typed visual preferences, recognition of labels associated with faces, and metaphoric associations with gender. Between the ages of twenty-seven and thirty months, most children can accurately label their sex and place a picture of themselves among those of other same-sex children, but many children attain basic gender identity even earlier."[17] By age three, children use gender labels of "he" or "she" when referring to males and females. "By age five children spontaneously categorize people by gender."[18] Researchers who have observed the development of children's gender identity note that, in addition to recognition of gender membership, children play "gender police" at young ages, calling attention to perceived transgressions of gender norms. Even among preschool children there is a strong felt pressure for gender conformity, and, even at this early age, children "tend to regard gender stereotypes as moral imperatives."[19] In addition to self-awareness of one's gender conformity and that of one's peers, preschool children are also capable of experiencing gender contentedness or dissatisfaction. "For most children, gender contentedness is high . . . [h]owever, some preschoolers are gender dysphoric," which, in extreme cases, may result in a diagnosis of Gender Identity Disorder (GID), discussed in greater detail both below and again later in this chapter.[20]

The term "transgender" is used to describe individuals whose gender identity is incongruent with their anatomical or assigned gender based on natal sex. "Transgender" is also thought of more broadly as an umbrella term referring to "individuals whose gender self-identification or expression transgresses established gender norms."[21] Given the breadth of operative definitions and the stigma associated with it, it is quite difficult to assess the prevalence of transgender persons. Obtaining accurate data is particularly challenging, as many people who experience incongruity between natal sex and gender identity often do not disclose and are able to obscure from public view any perceived incongruity. For many decades, estimates of the prevalence of transgenderism have been based on the number of persons seeking sex-reassignment surgery, which, for obvious reasons, would likely result in an underreporting of the actual prevalence in the general population. In 2007, researchers exploring the issue of prevalence reported to the World Professional Association for Transgender Health (WPATH) that prevalence data should be adjusted to reflect rates in the range of 1:2,000 to 1:4,500 for males and 1:5,500 to 1:8,000 for females, which is nearly two orders of magnitude greater than the old figures of 1:30,000 and 1:100,000. The authors of the 2007 study observe that "[t]he number of people falling under the larger transgender umbrella is by most accounts and definitions at least an order of magnitude greater than the prevalence of [male to female] transsexualism . . . [and] appears likely to be on the order of at least 1:100 (i.e., 1%) or more."[22]

Gender identity issues in children were first diagnosed in 1980, with the publication of the *Diagnostic and Statistical Manual of Mental Disorders*, 3rd ed. (*DSM-III*), which covers all mental health disorders for children and adults, and with the entry of Gender Identity Disorder of Childhood into the *DSM* nosological system. The term "transgender" as applied to children, however, typically encompasses a broader range of behaviors, including both the gender incongruency evident when some children express that they are "born in the wrong body"—those likely to be diagnosed with GID—as well as those children whose gender expression falls far outside of the stereotypical boundaries, a category referred to in this chapter as "gender non-conforming children." The fourth edition of the *Diagnostic and Statistical Manual of Mental Disorders* (*DSM-IV*) defines Gender Identity Disorder of Childhood as a "strong and persistent cross-gender identification" that is distinguished from simple nonconformity to stereotypical sex-role behavior by the extent and pervasiveness of the cross-gender wishes, interests, and activities.[23] In addition to the cross-gender identification, the *DSM-IV* diagnosis also requires that there be a persistent discomfort with his or her sex or sense of inappropriateness in the gender role of one's assigned sex. The *International Statistical Classification of Diseases and Related Health Problems* (*ICD-10*) defines Gender Identity Disorder of Childhood as "[a] disorder, usually first manifest during early childhood (and always well before puberty), characterized by a persistent and intense distress about assigned sex, together with a desire to be (or insistence that one is) of the other sex. There is a persistent preoccupation with the dress and activities of the opposite sex and repudiation of the individual's own sex. The diagnosis requires a profound disturbance of the normal gender identity; mere tomboyishness in girls or girlish behaviour in boys is not sufficient."[24] This diagnosis does not refer to children who have reached or are entering puberty, regardless of age, who are instead, in the *ICD-10*, regarded as suffering from Sexual Maturation Disorder—characterized by uncertainty about his or her gender identity, which, in turn, causes anxiety or depression.[25]

It is important to note that neither of these diagnoses includes elements pertaining to sexual attraction or sexual orientation. Simply put, "gender identity" refers to one's self-concept, while "sexual orientation" refers to one's sexual and romantic attraction to another. Nonetheless, as it is frequently in the context of adults, transgenderism and homosexuality are conflated when we discuss children, even pre-pubescent ones who have yet to develop or act upon sexual attraction to others.[26] However, because gender identity and gender expression are often conflated with sexual orientation, the recognition of transgenderism in children—and even the diagnosis of GID itself—is haunted by the specter of homophobia. In that vein, transgender children are sometimes taken to be "*pre*-homosexuals," still capable of "correction" before they enter puberty, presumably the time at which both their gender identity and sexual orientation would become fixed. What this flawed logic ignores is that, although both may be marked in early childhood by gender noncomformity, and although it is indeed possible for one to be both transgender *and* homosexual, these are separate and distinct labels, experiences, and identities. Says the noted female-to-male transgender advocate Jamison Green on the subject of transgender children,

> [i]t is easy to read a transgender childhood as a lesbian childhood (or a gay one, as the case may be), but there is an important difference. First, I use the term transgender to mean "breaking or going across gender boundaries," and I define a transgender childhood as one in which the child unconsciously (at first, and perhaps consciously later) expresses gender characteristics or behaviors that are typically associated with those of the opposite sex to the point of making other people uncomfortable or otherwise acutely aware of the dissonance. It is important to note, too, that some children may have these feelings acutely, without manifesting them in any way. Just because transness is invisible in some people, that does not mean it doesn't exist or that their experience of it is any less valid.[27]

The conflation of sexual orientation and gender identity is also observed by the author Phyllis Burke,[28] who describes cases of children as young as age three who have been treated with a diagnosis of GID for widely varying gender nonconformity, most likely developing from a fear that the child might grow up to become homosexual. She presents evidence of increasing use of a GID diagnosis for children suspected of being "*pre*-homosexual" and not necessarily transgender. Diagnosis and treatment is often at the insistence of non-accepting parents with the intent of changing a perceived homosexual orientation, as interpreted through a child's gender non-conforming behaviors.

Gender identity clinics, the first one of which was established in 1965 at Johns Hopkins University,[29] have long focused on the treatment and support of transgender adults. Although the number of such clinics continued to grow rapidly through the 1970s and beyond, there are to date only a handful of clinics in major cities, including Los Angeles, Boston, and, most recently, Chicago, that focus specifically on children and adolescents. Gender identity clinics specialize in the psychological and medical care and treatment of individuals who identify as lesbian, gay, bisexual, or transgender, as well as those questioning their sexual orientation or gender identity. Those clinics treating transgender or gender non-conforming youth provide consultation and support for children and their families and, where appropriate, medical intervention to assist in the transition process to bring the physical bodies of transgender youth into closer alignment with their internal gender identity.

While transgenderism remains fairly uncommon, especially among children, we are undeniably in an era in which a new generation—perhaps the first—is openly exploring and declaring their sexual orientation, gender identity, and gender non-conformity at increasingly younger ages.[30] "Like heterosexual youth, lesbian, gay, and bisexual youth become aware of their sexual orientation based on their thoughts and emotions often long before they have their first sexual encounter. In fact, many youth report awareness of their sexual orientation by age five."[31] Similarly, as it relates to gender identity and gender expression, children are becoming increasingly vocal about perceived gender incongruity and gender fluidity and are articulating their needs and interests at younger and younger ages. Although in past generations gender non-conformance—so-called "sissy boys" and "tomboy girls"—was met solely with societal stigma and shame, based on the belief that such behavior was the product of dysfunction within the individual, parents, or the home, today it prompts a myriad of questions regarding the ways in which the environments in which such children exist can be better adapted to promote their well-being through acceptance and accommodation.[32] Indeed, a growing awareness of gender variance in children has prompted the systems within which children interact to respond quite differently to gender incongruity and for parent and other supportive adults to serve as advocates for and allies with transgender and gender non-conforming children.

Transgender and Gender Non-conforming Children as Portrayed in the Media, Literature, and Entertainment

While transgenderism in adults has been explored in science, art, literature, and popular press dating back to as early as 1910,[33] any discussion of the occurrence of transgenderism in children has only recently been brought to the fore. Within the last decade, exploration of the topic has grown exponentially. Entering the term "transgender children" into a Google search yields just over sixty-seven million hits, a staggering figure that reflects the wide interest in this topic.[34] Indeed, those who have not actually met a transgendered child need only explore the Internet, television, social media, literature, film, and other fora of popular culture to learn of their existence and the unique challenges that they face.

Not surprisingly, as more media attention has been shed on transgender children and gender non-conformance, the topic is making its way into young adult and children's literature. The 2004 young adult book, *Luna*, by Julie Anne Peters, was the first to introduce young adult readers to the struggles faced by transgender youth who encounter many obstacles in their attempt to express their true identities. Met with a mix of praise and criticism, *Luna* ushered in a wave of similar texts since published, including the 2007 young adult novel *Parrotfish* by Ellen Wittlinger, which explores a transgendered young adult's social transition, and the 2011 novel *I am J*, by Cris Beam, which became the first book with a transgender theme to make it to the California Department of Education's recommended reading list in March 2013.[35] Advocates, who see the inclusion of books on tolerance and acceptance as beneficial to children, hail these publications, while critics decry the exposure of children to issues of gender identity as a form of harmful social engineering.

Although less directly focused on transgenderism itself, a growing number of texts exploring gender non-conformance are aimed at an even younger audience. The 2008 book *10,000 Dresses* by Marcus Ewert explores gender non-conformity through a boy (referred to in the book as both "he" *and* "she") named Bailey, who dreams each night about "magical dresses: dresses made of crystals and rainbows, dresses made of flowers, [and] dresses made of windows." The story follows Bailey's struggle for acceptance as a boy who likes dresses in the face of tremendous societal pressure to conform. Although Bailey's imagination and courage become the focal point of the book, the story reflects the pressure, rejection, and threats of violence directed toward gender nonconforming children. Author and mother Cheryl Kilodavis was similarly inspired by her five-year-old son's love of pink, sparkly dresses when she wrote the book, *My Princess Boy*. Marketed as a children's book addressing the broad theme of acceptance, *My Princess Boy* tells the tale of a four-year-old boy who "happily expresses his authentic self by enjoying 'traditional' girl things like jewelry, sparkles or anything pink,"[36] even in the face of taunts and teasing by his peers. The most recent children's picture book to join the shelves is Eileen Kiernan-Johnson's 2013 book *Roland Humphrey Is Wearing a What?* which tells the story of a little boy whose interest in pink dresses festooned with sparkles is frowned upon.[37] In his "quest to be his authentic self," Roland challenges the narrow and rigid rules of gender expression, particularly the "color rules" for boys that leave less room for self-expression than those afforded for girls.[38] Although the message that these children's authors try to convey is one of love and acceptance, all of these books have drawn criticism both for the controversial subject of gender variance itself and for the authors' attempts to tackle very complex concepts like gender identity and expression in overly simplistic ways.

Young adult and children's literature are not the only fora in which the deeply painful lived experiences of gender-variant children are reflected, and increasingly, other forms of media—television, social media, film, and broadcast news—have been used to depict the stigma, distress, and uniquely complicated nature of childhood transgenderism. Films like *Ma Vie en Rose* (1997), the first cinematic exploration of child transgenderism, and *Boys Don't Cry* (1999), which portrayed the murder of an eighteen-year-old transgender male, as well as an increasing number of news stories profiling the varied struggles that children and their families confront when crossing this "final frontier," continue to teach that gender incongruity in children, as it is with adults, is accompanied by, among other things, a tremendous degree of judgment, scorn, and ostracism. With increasingly frequent regularity, we are presented with talk shows, news articles, television specials, blog posts, and other probing portrayals of these children and their families. Indeed, "on the Internet, Tumblrs and Listservs and thousands of YouTube videos chronicle the gender transitions of teen-agers [that] variously resemble diaries, instruction manuals, music videos, and manifestos."[39] As public and social media facilitate connections within this growing community of children, parents, and allies, it also exposes those unfamiliar with transgenderism in children to the unique struggles that they face. Not surprisingly, the literature and media coverage of the issue and its principle focus on boys' transgression of gender norms mirrors the heightened value placed on boys' fidelity to a rigid gender stereotype and how much more room is offered to girls perceived as having masculine traits, interests, and preferences. All but one of the young adult and children's books on the issue address the experiences of boys who either identify as girls or with stereotypical girl interests.

Perceptions and Treatment of Transgender Children

Although literature, film, news, and social media portray anecdotal stories about the challenges facing transgender and gender non-conforming children with ever increasing frequency, only limited scientific research exists on this population. Research is limited, in part, because the condition itself is often unacknowledged by parents and pediatricians, and discussion of the topic as it relates to children is muddied by the persistent conflation of gender identity and sexual orientation, the latter of which pre-pubertal children are presumed not to possess. The small-scale studies that have been done suggest that transgender children are at high risk of serious psychosocial maladjustment owing to related internal and external stressors.

Researchers posit that these children may suffer from discomfort, even despair, when they evaluate themselves on a spectrum of gender typicality and find themselves to be noticeably atypical. "Various bases for the expected link between gender typicality and psychological well-being have been suggested. Children who appraise themselves to be gender atypical may fear ostracism, denial of privileges, or a loss of protection by the group. They may also experience a loss of self-esteem, negative sanctions, or simply a sense of being inadequate as group members."[40] There is, however, a perilous interactive effect at play here that must be carefully examined, as the internal conflicts that such children experience are both related *to* and exacerbated *by* social stigma and pressure for gender conformity that is imposed upon them. Gender atypicality itself may not cause internal distress; rather, the societal reaction to a child's gender non-conformance may be the key precipitating factor. Gender non-conforming children, and particularly transgender children, suffer from high rates of depression and social maladjustment in part because of the quite negative social reactions that their gender variance provokes in *others*.[41] Gender identity researchers note that "children who wish[ed] they were the other sex or who desire[d] to engage in cross-sex activities [were] distressed mainly when they perceive[d] their social environment to be telling them that they cannot be whom they wish to be."⁴² Indeed, Carver et al. report that, under sustained pressure to conform, "children with low sense of gender typicality were significantly more likely to experience internalized distress [including anxiety, sadness, social withdrawal, and self-deprecation] and perhaps more likely to be victimized by peers."⁴³

Not surprisingly, this same social stigma is believed to intensify the underlying distress and anxiety that may be inherent to perceptions of gender incongruity, as researchers have observed that "[t]he feeling of being at home or not at home in one's body is almost certain to affect satisfaction with the self."⁴⁴ Transgender youth often suffer from depression as a result of having to "cope with adverse consequences of living with a self-concept that is never socially acknowledged or reinforced." Their internal sense of not having a gender that meets with societal expectations and their resulting experience of social exclusion contributes to severe psychological problems, including substantially increased risks of suicidality. A 2007 study surveying fifty-five self-identified transgender youth between the ages of fifteen and twenty-one found that almost half (45%) of the subject sample reported serious thoughts of suicide, while a quarter (26%) reported a history of life-threatening behaviors, including actual suicide attempts.⁴⁵ This figure is nearly fifteen times the 1.6% suicide rate reported for the general U.S. population. From self-reports and interviews, researchers in this same study learned that differences between transgender youth who attempt suicide and those who do not include the existence of parental abuse and the degree of body satisfaction. Transgender youth who attempted suicide reported significantly higher rates of parental verbal and physical abuse and more dissatisfaction with their bodies.⁴⁶ A recent 2012 study conducted at the Gender Management Service Clinic at Boston Children's Hospital—the first study of a U.S. cohort of children and adolescents with gender identity disorder—confirmed these earlier findings. A significant proportion (44%) of the ninety-seven patients presented with significant psychiatric histories, with 20% reporting self-mutilation at least once and 9% reporting at least one suicide attempt.⁴⁷ In addition to self-harm, transgender youth are at high risk for substance abuse, victimization, homelessness, rejection and discrimination at home, high rates of dropping out of high school, and so on.⁴⁸

The internalized distress experienced by transgender youth is likely influenced by a heightened antipathy directed toward transgender persons as a whole. Indeed, research reveals that attitudes toward transgender persons, including children and adolescents, tend to be more negative than those towards lesbians, gays, or bisexuals. This negativity may be rooted, in part, in the threat posed by persons who cross over from one gender to another or who cannot easily be categorized as either sex. Transgender persons "evoke negative reactions because they violate the widespread assumption that sex and gender are 'naturally' dichotomous."[49] Researchers found that men and women alike expressed more negative attitudes toward transgender people to the extent that they also endorsed a binary conception of sex.[50] Gender non-conforming youth may, therefore, draw such intense ire because they challenge long-held notions of traditional boyhood and girlhood, existing in that "middle space" that has, until now, hardly been acknowledged, let alone openly expressed or supported. Said one mother of a gender non-conforming son on her blog, "Pink Is for Boys," "It might make your world more tidy to have two neat and separate gender possibilities, but when you squish out the space between, you do not accurately represent lived reality. More than that, you're trying to 'squish out' my kid."[51]

Gender Identity as a "Disorder": Understanding Gender Identity within the Scope of Individual Disability and Societal Stigma

Both within the psychological community and among advocates for transgender persons, a prolonged debate continues on the appropriateness of the diagnostic category of Gender Identity Disorder in Childhood and the application of a disability lens through which to understand this phenomenon. At the heart of the broader conceptual debate is the fact that labeling Gender Identity Disorder as a mental disorder or form of mental illness, which is what categorization within the *Diagnostic Statistical Manual of Mental Disorders* has done, focuses on an internalized individual pathology rather than societal stigma and harm inflicted upon an individual as a result of his or her gender non-conformity. To many, this framing of the trans experience inappropriately lays the blame upon the victim. They argue that it is wrong to label as inherently disordered those who do not fit cultural expectations of what it means to be traditional male or female because the distress captured in the diagnostic criteria is better understood as a product of societal prejudice and discrimination directed toward transgender persons rather than any inherently internalized pathology.[52] As one critic put it: "If an 8-year-old girl has a really hard time in school because of her short hair and boyish clothes, and is bullied for that, that's not *her* pathology—it's the *world's*."[53]

* * *

Although the current version of the *Diagnostic and Statistical Manual of Mental Disorders* reflects the conceptual shift away from a disability and disease model, earlier versions clearly frame the trans experience as inherently pathological, which is evident in the criteria for GID as outlined in the *Diagnostic and Statistical Manual of Mental Disorders*, 4th ed., *Text Revision* (*DSM-IV-TR*). They are as follows:

> A. A strong and persistent cross-gender identification (not merely a desire for any perceived cultural advantages of being the other sex.)
>
> In children, the disturbance is manifested by four (or more) of the following:
> 1. repeatedly stated desire to be, or insistence that he or she is, the other sex.
> 2. in boys, preference for cross-dressing or simulating female attire; in girls, insistence on wearing only stereotypical masculine clothing.
> 3. strong and persistent preferences for cross-sex roles in make-believe play or persistent fantasies about being the other sex.
> 4. intense desire to participate in stereotypical games and pastimes of the other sex.
> 5. strong preferences for playmates of the other sex.
>
> In adolescents and adults, the disturbance is manifested by symptoms such as stated desire to be the other sex, frequent passing as the other sex, desire to live or be treated as the other sex, or the conviction that he or she has the typical feelings and reactions of the other sex.
>
> B. Persistent discomfort with his or her sex or a sense of inappropriateness of the gender role of that sex.

In children, the disturbance is manifested by any of the following: in boys, an assertion that his penis or testes are disgusting or will disappear or assertion that it would be better not to have a penis, or aversion toward rough-and-tumble play and rejection of male stereotypical toys, games, and activities; in girls, rejection of urinating in a sitting position, assertion that she has or will grow a penis, or assertion that she does not want to grow breasts or menstruate, or marked aversion toward normative feminine clothing.

In adolescents and adults, the disturbance is manifested by symptoms such as preoccupation with getting rid of primary and secondary sex characteristics (e.g. request for hormones, surgery, or other procedures to physically alter sexual characteristics to simulate the other sex) or belief that he or she was born the wrong sex.

C. The disturbance is not concurrent with physical intersex condition.

D. The disturbance causes clinically significant distress or impairment in social, occupational, or other important areas of functioning.[54]

The fifth edition of the *Diagnostic and Statistical Manual of Mental Disorders* (*DSM-5*), which was published in May 2013, has reconfigured its approach to the subject of gender identity in children, focusing less on gender identity itself and more on the distress—or dysphoria—young people may feel as a result of it.[55] In addition to amending the diagnosis itself to now read Gender Dysphoria, rather than Gender Identity Disorder in Children, the updated *DSM-5* lists the diagnosis on its own—rather than as it is listed in *DSM-IV-TR*—as a sexual disorder alongside other paraphilias that include voyeurism, exhibitionism, and pedophilia.[56] Although the amendment is linguistically subtle, the change in the diagnosis from one focusing on identity to one addressing the emotional response to gender identity incongruence is likely to have a tremendous impact on the way in which transgender individuals are both perceived and treated.

The updated *DSM-5* describes Gender Dysphoria as follows:

A. A marked incongruence between one's experienced/expressed gender and assigned gender, of at least 6 months duration, as manifested by at least 6 of the following indicators (including A1):

1. a strong desire to be of the other gender or an insistence that he or she is the other gender
2. in boys, a strong preference for cross-dressing or simulating female attire; in girls, a strong preference for wearing only typical masculine clothing and a strong resistance to the wearing of typical feminine clothing
3. a strong preference for cross-gender roles in make-believe or fantasy play
4. a strong preference for the toys, games, or activities typical of the other gender
5. a strong preference for playmates of the other gender
6. in boys, a strong rejection of typically masculine toys, games, and activities and a strong avoidance of rough-and-tumble play; in girls, a strong rejection of typically feminine toys, games, and activities.
7. a strong dislike of one's sexual anatomy
8. a strong desire for the primary and/or secondary sex characteristics that match one's experienced gender

B. The condition is associated with clinically significant distress or impairment in social, school, or other important areas of functioning.[57]

The pronounced focus on the affective experience of gender identity or incongruity is not surprising given that "[a] child's acquisition of gender identity is [understood to be] more than a cognitive milestone; it is also surrounded by affective significance."[58] According to Kenneth Zucker, the psychiatrist appointed to chair the American Psychiatric Association's *DSM-5* Committee on Gender Identity Disorders, although child developmentalists have paid scant attention to the affective component of gender identity and gender incongruity, it has always been the hallmark of clinicians thinking on this issue.[59] It is not uncommon that both children who experience gender incongruity and those experiencing gender atypicality suffer some distress related to both conditions. Not surprisingly, it is perhaps this distress, more than any other feature of the transgender child, with which it seems easiest for others to identify and empathize. Such empathy for the psychological distress suffered by transgender children was evident in a 2004 Australian case *In re Alex*, in which the court authorized the commencement of puberty-blocking hormones by a thirteen-year-old female-to-male transgender child. The distress the child was experiencing may have, indeed, been the strongest persuasive factor prompting the court's support of Alex's expressed needs. Said the judge in his opinion:

> Anatomically, and in the eyes of the law, Alex is a girl. However, Alex has been diagnosed as having what some of the experts define medically as a gender identity disorder and has a profound and longstanding wish to undergo a transition to become male in appearance. I think it questionable whether this condition is properly described as a disorder. I prefer the expression *"dysphoria"* which I think is a more accurate description and will use the terminology throughout the remainder of this judgment.[60]

While the experience of psychological distress and/or dysphoria is a critical defining feature captured in the psychological and medical diagnoses attached to gender identity in children, the challenge still lies in identifying the root cause of the distress. It could be related to, among other things, the binary nature and rigid categorization of gender as well as bigotry and prejudice toward those who transgress established gender norms. Indeed, regardless of how one hypothesizes about the cause or nature of the disorder itself, the distress related to gender identity disorder and its resulting impact on child well-being has already and will likely continue to shape the response to transgender and gender nonconforming children.

A Spectrum of Choices for Transgender and Gender Nonconforming Children

There are many choices faced by parents and guardians of transgender and gender non-conforming youth concerning the way in which they will intervene, if at all, in matters concerning their children's gender self-expression and gender identity and the degree to which children themselves can exercise agency in making such decisions. Traditional therapies, which were popular until the mid-twentieth century, encouraged parents to steer their children toward gender-stereotypical dress, toys, and activities and advised parents to prohibit any cross-gender behaviors. Since then, there has been a growing cadre of clinicians who advise precisely the opposite. Rather than trying to extinguish cross-gender identification, clinicians who oppose traditional therapies focus on teaching children to deal with intolerance.[61] It is unknown how many elect this supportive treatment over traditional corrective methods, but "challenges to the conventional model have become increasingly popular in the United States and Europe, in medical publications and among professionals and parents themselves."[62] This supportive approach, unlike its predecessor, makes room for a range of gender-affirming responses while also raising the question of just how far along the spectrum of transitioning young people should be supported in progressing while still minors.

Social Transitioning

While "the growing awareness of transgenderism and its early manifestation [in children as young as pre-schoolers] has meant that some families now support their children through the first steps of a transition, it has also made those steps more frightening, as parents realize sooner where the path is headed."[63] The first step along the spectrum of transitioning is called "social transitioning" and includes all of the accommodations that can be made in dress, name, hairstyle, and so forth, for children to live life in their affirmed gender or outside of the traditional boundaries of stereotypical gender. For many children, social transitioning allows them to live more comfortably in their affirmed gender, as they appear to the outside world in nearly all respects as a child of the opposite sex. Transitioning at this phase along the spectrum has a rather interactive dimension, as the child also requires the environment at large (at home, school, play, etc.) to be affirming of the gender in which he or she presents, not the gender that was assigned at birth. In many respects, parents perhaps take an even more active role in social transitioning than children themselves. Parents are charged with negotiating the spaces in which their children will be present, which includes talking to schools, family, and friends in order to maintain a safe environment for their children. For some transgender children, social transitioning is the extent of the transition process, as they do not move further to pursue medical interventions.

Sometimes, however, social transitioning is insufficient in helping children cope with the fundamental underlying mismatch that they perceive between their affirmed gender and their biological birth sex. Although they are permitted to present in their affirmed gender, many children retain a persistent and significant dislike of their bodies and anxiety about impending bodily changes that accompany puberty. "They may shower with their clothes on so they don't have to see themselves. Or demand to know when their penises will grow in. Or, in extreme cases, try to cut their penises off."[64] Interventions beyond social transitioning are, therefore, usually considered when the looming specter of puberty and all of the accompanying physical changes that accompany it appear to exacerbate a child's distress.

Medical and Surgical Transitioning

The next steps beyond social transitioning involve medical interventions that run the spectrum from fully reversible to irreversible. These interventions are described, and their use prescribed, by the World Professional Association for Transgender Health, an international multidisciplinary professional association whose mission is the promotion of health standards for transsexual, transgender, and gender nonconforming persons. The WPATH standards of care (WPATH-SOC), the 7th edition of which was published in 2011,[65] outline the three categories of medical intervention. They include

(1) Fully reversible medical interventions such as hormone treatments to suppress physical changes related to puberty. Adolescents are eligible for puberty suppressing hormones as soon as the first signs of puberty emerge, specifically when an adolescent reaches Tanner Stage 2.[66]
(2) Partially reversible medical interventions include administration of cross-hormones aimed at masculinizing or feminizing the body. Reversal of this intervention may require surgical intervention. Adolescents are eligible for partially reversible treatment as early as age 16, with parental consent.
(3) Irreversible medical interventions include sex reassignment surgery, a procedure that is not recommended until adulthood.

Fully reversible medical interventions include hormone-suppression treatment, which delays and/or prevents children from experiencing the development of secondary sex characteristics of their natal sex. For example, girls taking hormone-suppressing medications will not develop breasts or start menstruating. Likewise, boys who identify as girls can take puberty blockers to avoid developing broad shoulders, a deep voice, or facial and pubic hair. The WPATH identifies two goals that they assert justify the use of puberty-suppression medication. First, it affords young pre- or early pubertal adolescents more time to explore their identity, and, second, it may greatly facilitate later transition by preventing the development of sex characteristics that are difficult or impossible to reverse if the adolescent progresses later in adulthood to sex reassignment. Because the age of onset of puberty varies greatly, it is difficult, if not impossible, to dictate a precise age at which it is recommended to start hormone blockers. This particular treatment is regarded as reversible because, as soon as the child stops taking the hormone, puberty commences.

Most prevalent among the partially reversible medical interventions are cross-hormones—testosterone for female-to-male transboys (FTMs) and estrogen and progesterone for male-to-female transgirls (MTFs)—that are recommended for minors only over the age of sixteen. Unlike suppression treatment, this step—sometimes called the "medical transition"—begins the process of actually reshaping the body chemically. Because the use of cross-hormones is, however, partially irreversible, it has prompted the WPATH to advise that decisions regarding their use should be made with the adolescent, the family, and the treatment team. Because the WPATH makes no similar explicit mention of inclusive decision making with respect to those interventions that are medically reversible, it can be inferred that minor decision-making autonomy is subordinated in relation to the degree of permanence of the proposed medical intervention. Not surprisingly, therefore, the WPATH draws a line with respect to a minor's autonomy in the realm of medical decision making at the most permanent of medical interventions, surgical transitioning, which creates the most obvious outward signs of the "target" gender by removing or creating breasts and genitals. The WPATH recommends that such interventions be withheld until a child reaches eighteen or is otherwise an adult of legal age.

With respect to the efficacy of medical interventions, one study reports that candidates treated with GnRH (a growth hormone) analogs between 2000 and 2008 showed improved psychological functioning. None opted to discontinue pubertal suppression, and all eventually began cross-sex hormone treatment. More recently, the same researchers found that adolescents with GID who underwent pubertal suppression had improved behavioral, emotional, and depressive symptoms with psychometric testing.[67]

The risks and benefits of intervening early in the lives of young children experiencing gender dysphoria raises the question of how much and exactly when such interventions should take place, and, more importantly, who gets to decide. Should transgender and gender nonconforming children who have had a careful and protracted evaluation by a skilled gender specialist be compelled to complete puberty *before* being offered the same therapy used for adults? Are children as young as twelve or thirteen, when many begin puberty, mature enough to make decisions about medical treatment that is only partially reversible? And at what age can children make decisions about medical interventions that are permanently irreversible? Although the WPATH has published recommendations, no national or international protocols of practice exist, and there are opposing views on how to proceed. One side argues that interventions should be tailored to a child's stage of development and that most interventions should be delayed until *after* puberty, ostensibly when children are more mature in their decision making and presumably because teenagers are more likely than adults to change their minds about their gender identity. The opposing view, however, argues for early medical intervention to prevent the severe depression that accompanies the onset of an unwanted puberty and to avoid the physically and psychologically painful procedures required to reverse puberty's physical manifestations.[68]

Person-Environment "Fit": Using the Law to Make Room for the Needs of Transgender and Gender Non-conforming Youth

Tension over the choices facing children and parents regarding social and medical transitioning mirrors, in many respects, the underlying debate about the diagnosis of GID in children itself. Much like the tension revolving around the diagnosis, in which it is debated whether the pathology resides with the child or with the environment, the question now becomes whether the locus of the accommodation should be with the child or the environment in which the child resides. Do children and/or their parents have a right to accommodation, so to speak, corresponding with a child's gender identity or gender self-expression? If so, what kind of accommodations must be made in recognition of this right? These questions invariably touch upon the issue of person-environment "fit"—exploring how an environment might be altered to accommodate the person and, vice versa. Relatedly, issues around accommodation point our attention to advocacy for transgender youth, who, under the broad "disability" of youth, are presumed to be too young to advocate on their own behalf. Such advocacy would include aspects of social and medical transitioning such as what name to be called, what restroom to use, and when to begin hormone suppression or cross-hormone treatment.

Unlike transgender adults whose autonomous decision-making regarding many aspects of transitioning, including gender self-expression, is protected by the expansive scope of privacy rights, transgender and gender non-conforming children must often defer to the decisions of their parents or guardians, if not in reference to gender identity, at least in reference to gender expression. This deference is consistent with our understanding of parental authority over children. Rights granted to parents regarding the care, custody, and control of their children are understood to include a child's name as well as the child's dress and other outward manifestations of expressed gender identity, all of which make up the process of social transitioning. Even those wholly supportive of transgender children acknowledge the primacy of parental decision making regarding matters of transitioning. For example, the transgender advocate Jamison Green defers to parents with respect to transitioning decisions, even though he considers it inhumane to deny social and early hormonal transition to children "in cases where family stability is demonstrated and clear, consistent signals about the child's gender identity indicate that the stress of living in the wrong gender could be alleviated with treatment." Such deference to parental choice and control is evident in Green's conclusion that, "when *parents* are clearly aware and accepting of their child's gender identity, and *agree* with the child's wish to have her or his sex align with his or her gender, this should be honored" (emphasis mine).[69]

As some observe, however, agreement between parents and transgender children on the matter of transitioning cannot always be assumed, which raises the question of whether transgender children and adolescents can advocate on their *own* behalf on matters of social transitioning and medical treatment, particularly in the face of parental opposition.[70] In some states, transgender youth may be able to advocate on their own behalf by invoking the mature minor doctrine, which allows physicians to provide medical services without parental consent to adolescents deemed mature "enough" to make medical decisions. The limited availability of the doctrine, particularly as it relates to hormone treatment and other more permanent medical interventions, guarantees that not all transgender youth will be able to exercise personal autonomy and choice as it concerns their treatment options.[71] At the core of the rich and complex debate regarding parental and child decision making in this context is the overarching tension between the parents' "right" to raise their child as they choose and the child's "right" to self-expression, including as it relates to matters of gender identity. Owing to the constraints of this book chapter, however, I defer for another place and time a lengthier and more probing discussion about the subordination of transgender and gender non-conforming children's decision making.

Putting aside the potential conflict of interests between parents and children about what should be done to accommodate the needs of transgender children, even when alignment exists on decisions about social and/or medical transitioning, other person-environment fit conflicts may arise. These are particularly likely to occur in the context of schools and other settings in which a child's gender expression is made visible beyond the privacy of the family home.[72] These settings have typically included schools, as well as other custodial contexts—for example, child welfare and juvenile justice—in which the state, under its *parens patriae* powers, assumes the role of legal parent.

Transgender Children in Schools

Not surprisingly, since it is the environment in which children spend the majority of their time, schools have become the site of conflicts regarding issues of person-environment fit. The central question concerns whether and how schools are required to make accommodations to support transgender children. Accommodations for transgender youth in schools include such matters as personal privacy, bathroom and locker room accessibility, gender-segregated activities, dress codes, and discrimination and harassment.[73]

Schools range in their responses to the needs of transgender youth, although survey research reveals that transgender students face a myriad of problems, sometimes at the hands of bullying peers and, at other times, as a result from teachers and administrators. Research shows that transgender students often face unsafe school environments, including verbal harassment, physical harassment and physical assault, to a greater extent even than do their lesbian, gay, and bisexual peers.[74] The 2011 National School Climate Survey found that an overwhelming majority of transgender students experienced verbal harassment at school because of their sexual orientation and gender expression, more than half experienced physical harassment because of their sexual orientation and gender expression, and more than a quarter experienced physical assault because of their sexual orientation and gender expression. These levels of victimization were significantly higher than those faced by their non-transgender peers and even higher than the other lesbian, gay, and bisexual students who participated in the survey.[75] Most distressing is that although the victimization appears fairly widespread, only a small fraction of transgender students said they were aware of their school's anti-harassment policy and that it included specific protections based on sexual orientation, gender identity, and gender expression.[76] The lack of awareness, both by students and school personnel, may contribute to the increased risk of victimization faced by transgender and gender non-conforming students.

In some cases, public schools have been obliged, through state and federal legislation with broader reach than the school setting, to include gender identity in the scope of available protections. These protections, in turn, have compelled subsequent accommodation.[77] For example, in 2008, Oregon enacted the Oregon Equality Act (OEA), which provided a definition of gender identity to include "what a person believes his or her gender to be, including how the person chooses to express his or her gender."[78] Under the act, "[g]ender identity protection also encompasses any behavior that differs from what may be traditionally associated with the person's sex at birth. The law protects people who identify as transgender as well as people who do not fit into stereotypes of how a man or woman should look or act."[79] Because the law extends to children, school officials were compelled to develop policies and guidelines, including those related to bullying, in compliance with the act. In 2009, one year after the OEA was enacted, the Oregon Safe Schools Act was signed into law and included gender identity in the definition of a protected class as defined by the anti-bullying legislation. Among the recommended guidelines of the latter legislation, students have the right to be addressed by the name and pronoun corresponding to their gender identity and to have access to the restroom that corresponds to their gender identity.[80] Other progressive states like Oregon have enacted protections for transgender youth, some of which serve as model policy. In 2009, for example, the California Safe Schools Coalition released a model policy for transgender and gender non-conforming students that included a range of protections concerning privacy, naming, and restroom accessibility, among others.[81] This model policy became law in 2013 when California adopted a bill requiring that students "be permitted to participate in sex-segregated school programs and activities, including athletic teams and competitions, and use facilities consistent with his or her gender identity," irrespective of natal sex.[82] While California became the first state to enact statewide legislation specifically aimed at K–12 public school students, Massachusetts had earlier enacted a gender identity statute prohibiting discrimination on the basis of gender identity. The broadened student anti-discrimination statute prompted revision of elementary and secondary school regulations in 2012 to ensure a safe and supportive school environment for transgender and gender non-conforming students.[83]

Accommodation, however, remains a controversial issue in some states where it is unclear whether transgender students may utilize restrooms corresponding with their gender expression or whether a separate restroom is a sufficient accommodation. For example, in a decision overturning a ruling by the Maine Human Rights Commission in favor of a transgender child denied the right to use the gender-appropriate restroom at her public school, a Maine state court held that a school district superintendent was not required to make such accommodations. The case involved a transgender fifth-grade girl, Nicole Maines, who, although biologically male, identified as female from a very young age. Despite her parents' working with the school to develop a "reasonable accommodation" plan, Nicole was denied access to the girls' bathroom when the grandfather and legal guardian of a male student objected to her presence. In their lawsuit against the school district, the family claimed that the school's failure to accommodate their daughter forced them to leave the district to find a more supportive school environment. In April 2011, the court found that "[n]either the language of the [Maine Human Rights Act], the language of the [Maine Human Rights Commission's] own internal regulations, nor prevailing case law interpreting the Civil Rights Act requires this [specific] type of accommodation."[84] In holding that Maine's law did not prohibit denial of access to public accommodations based on "sexual orientation," the court added: "Nor is the Court aware of any precedent—federal or state—implementing a rule that requires a place of public accommodation to reasonably accommodate a transgender person by specifically allowing that person to access and use the restroom facility of his or her 'gender identity' or expression."[85] The school's decision to bar Nicole from using the girls' restroom was again upheld in a November 2012 decision by the Penobscot County Superior Court wherein the judge held that the school acted within the bounds of Maine's public accommodation law by providing her with access to the staff bathroom.[86] A fairly similar case unfolded in Colorado, where a first-grade transgender girl, Coy Mathis, was barred from using the girls' restroom in her public school.[87] Although Coy had been using the girls' restroom through kindergarten, her parents were informed that the school's concern about the future impact upon others of a boy with male genitals using the girls' restroom left them no option but to limit Coy to either the boys' bathroom, the nurse's bathroom, or a gender-neutral faculty bathroom. When Coy's parents' attempt to come to a resolution with the school district failed, they brought a suit against the Fountain Fort-Carson School District under Colorado's Anti-Discrimination Act. In June 2013, the Colorado Civil Rights Division ruled in favor of Coy Mathis, whose case was the first to challenge a restroom restriction under the Colorado statute.[88]

Dress codes are another aspect of school policy in which conflict between schools and transgender children has arisen, as, not surprisingly, students' desires to dress in ways that convey their identity may conflict with conventional gender stereotypes and norms and, more precisely, with gender-specific school dress-code policy. It has long been accepted that schools may lawfully prohibit students from wearing to school anything that is obscene, threatening, lewd, or vulgar and that schools can ban clothing that could be either disruptive or distracting to the educational process or that could affect the safety of students. Supreme Court jurisprudence establishes that such bans do not violate a student's First Amendment rights.[89] However, the question of whether a student who dresses in a manner consistent with his or her gender expression poses such a disruption remains unclear and highly subjective. In the *Yunits* case, in 2000, a transgender middle-school student in Brockton, Massachusetts, sued her school after she was repeatedly disciplined for wearing female clothes, makeup, and fashion accessories to school. The student, described in the court opinion as having "the soul of a female in the body of a male," sought injunctive relief allowing her to wear clothing to school that was consistent with her affirmed gender, as well as damages for the school's earlier refusal to permit her to attend while wearing such clothing. The court denied, in part, the school's motion to dismiss, finding that the student fit within the generic definition of a "qualified handicapped individual" or one with a recognized disability. Moreover, the court ruled that the student had a free-speech right to express her gender identity through the manner in which she dressed, as long as it was not disruptive.[90]

Although many other school districts have taken heed from the landmark ruling in *Yunits*, the issue of dress codes continues to make headline news. In 2009, nearly a decade after *Yunits*, the *Atlanta Journal Constitution* reported that a sixteen-year-old male student, Jonathan Escobar, withdrew from North Cobb High School only three days after commencing classes because school officials said he would have to start dressing "more like a boy" or consider home schooling.[91] Although neither Jonathan nor school officials claim that he is transgender, his conflict with the school over cross-gender clothing is analogous to those claims raised by transgender students. The dress code of which Jonathan was accused of violating states, like the one in *Yunits*, that students should "refrain from any mode of dress which proves to contribute to any disruption of school functions." A fight broke out in school when a friend of Jonathan's defended him from verbal teasing.

Transgender Children in the Child Welfare System

School conflicts typically involve parental and child interests that are aligned. Indeed, in most school-related cases, it is parents who request accommodations to be made on behalf of their transgender children. This alignment of interests removes from the discussion any exploration of how transgender children's interests are made subordinate to those of their presumably fit parents. Two custodial settings in which questions of deference to parental authority are absent with respect to social and medical decision making are the child welfare and the juvenile justice systems. In both contexts, the state acts as guardian, substituting its decision making for that of parents. The state, acting under its *parens patriae* powers, does not enjoy the same assumptions about deference to decision making that legal parents do, which raises the possibility of transgender youth and the state having distinct and separate interests. In 2003, a transgender female successfully brought an action barring New York's child welfare system, the Administration for Children's Services (ACS), from preventing the minor from wearing female clothing at an all-male foster care residential facility. The minor's treatment plan called for her to dress in a manner corresponding to her affirmed gender identity. The court held that the minor's diagnosis of GID was a disability within the meaning of the New York State Human Rights Law, that ACS did not discriminate against the youth, but that ACS failed to make reasonable accommodation to the minor's disability.[92] A few years later, also in New York, a transgender female named Mariah, in the care of ACS, was denied provision of medical services recommended by her physicians and therapists, including hormone treatment and sex reassignment surgery. Based on ACS's statutory duty to provide Mariah with "medically necessary care," the New York Family Court ordered ACS to arrange and pay for Mariah's surgery.[93] This decision was later reversed by the Appellate Division, which ruled that, while ACS must provide necessary medical and surgical care to all children in its care, the Family Court did not have the authority to rule that ACS provide particular care, including surgery for Mariah.

Transgender Children in the Juvenile Justice System

The issues facing transgender youth in the juvenile justice system are similar to those of children in state custody in foster care and typically involve conflicts regarding accommodation. Because the focus of the juvenile justice system is rehabilitation of the subject youth, usually in a secure detention facility, conflicts between conditions of detention and the interests of transgender youth arise. Findings from an Equity Project study suggest that it is not uncommon for transgender youth to face backlash from juvenile justice personnel for gender non-conforming mannerisms, behavior, and dress. "Professionals often mistakenly believe that these youth are acting out or seeking attention, rather than expressing a fundamental aspect of their identity."[94] The study observed an additional burden for transgender youth in detention who are often placed in sex-segregated facilities according to their birth sex, rather than their gender identity, a practice that places transgender girls in particular at great risk of sexual and other abuse by both residents and staff.[95]

Some juvenile justice systems have developed policies analogous to those in place within schools. For example, in August 2006, the King County (Washington State) Adult-Juvenile Detention Policies were amended to reflect the treatment of transgender inmates to define gender as "encompassing all relational aspects of social identity, psychological identity, and human behavior." The policy also notes that gender identity "is someone's sense of their own gender, which is communicated to others by their gender expression." The policy advises staff to, among other things, use last names when referring to inmates and refrain from punishing inmates who respectfully clarify a name or pronoun. Most significantly, the policy provides that "*as long as it does not disrupt the safe and secure functioning of the facility*, transgender . . . inmates shall be permitted to wear the same items as anyone else of their adopted gender."[96] Although the development of policy addressing the needs of transgender youth is a mark of progress, juvenile detention facilities are far from meeting their requirement to provide adequate nutrition, health care, clothing, shelter, and education to all youth detained in their physical custody pending adjudication or awaiting placement.

One common feature shared by the school, child welfare, and juvenile justice settings is the way in which reasonable accommodations are grounded in claims of disability. Indeed, in the face of a limited gender-rights paradigm, transgender children and their families are compelled to seek protection under the scope of disability rights in order to access accommodations that allow transgender and gender non-conforming children to live out their lives consistent with the gender with which they identify. The disability label has both positive and negative consequences for transgender youth who may be further stigmatized and, at the same time, assisted by it.

Gender Identity Rights for Children as Human Rights

In exploring the challenges facing transgender and gender non-conforming youth, it is clear that, at present, their rights are not coextensive with those of transgender adults. Because broadly defined rights related to gender expression that are generally accorded to adults tend to be protected by privacy interests that children lack, it remains unclear where exactly children's rights to gender identity and gender expression are grounded. Children not only lack as deeply developed a privacy interest in matters related to sexuality, gender identity, and gender expression, they are generally not conceived of as rights holders within the scope of sex and gender. In developing a rights-based rubric for transgender youth, advocates may instead have to look to international human rights standards for guidance.

Understanding transgender rights as human rights is not novel. In 2006, in response to well-documented global patterns of violence directed at those who transgress gender norms, international human rights experts meeting in Yogyakarta, Indonesia, outlined a set of international principles relating to sexual orientation and gender identity. The resulting Yogyakarta Principles address a broad range of international human rights standards, applying them specifically to issues of sexual orientation and gender identity. They include, among others, the right to enjoyment of all human rights, the right to equality and non-discrimination, and the right to freedom of opinion and expression. While the Principles address "persons" without specifically referencing children, the Preamble calls for the application of the best-interests standard in all actions concerning children. In addition, children who are "capable of forming personal views" are regarded as having the right to express those views freely, relative to their age and maturity.

The right to expression reflected in the Principles mirrors those in the United Nations Convention on the Rights of the Child (UNCRC)—the first legally binding international instrument to incorporate the full range of human rights—civil, cultural, economic, political, and social rights—for children.[97] Among the most relevant provisions for those seeking to frame children's gender identity rights as human rights are Articles 12 and 13 of the UNCRC, which, read together, impose upon states the responsibility of assuring children's participation in all matters affecting them and the right of the child to freedom of expression. Although human-rights-based claims have yet to play a role in advocacy for transgender and gender non-conforming children, both the Yogyakarta Principles and the UNCRC offer a valuable rights-based framework for advancing their interests.

Speaking even more directly to the unique challenges faced by transgender and gender non-conforming children is the Transgender Children's Bill of Human Rights, a human rights draft document recognizing children's right to gender identity and gender expression. Among the rights contemplated by the draft document are the right to be called by a name children recognize as their own and to have the personal pronoun (he/she) that they prefer used to describe them, the right to be accepted by everyone as the gender they prefer, the right to appear on the outside the way they feel on the inside, and the right to be supported by all adults working with them in school and in other support services.[98]

Conclusion

One of the principle challenges facing transgender and gender non-conforming youth is that they come into an awareness of their gender identity long before they have been traditionally vested with the scope of rights and privileges upon which the exercise of autonomy or choice in this area is typically based. Unlike transgender adults, children are dependent upon their parents or legal guardians to assist them in their attempts to align their natal sex with their affirmed gender identities, including social transitioning or medical interventions. Parents may, within the scope of their right to care, custody, and control of their child, withhold approval of such interventions, and it remains unclear how, or if, the state would intervene in support of a transgender child in such circumstances. Intrafamilial tension aside, even when parents and transgender children agree about what should be done, the various spaces in which children's gender identity is made visible may not be accommodating. Legal challenges have only recently begun to clarify the burden of accommodation that school, child welfare, and juvenile justice authorities bear in relation to transgender youth, and, undoubtedly, more challenges will follow as transgender children and adolescents become both more visible and vocal in our society. Perhaps more meaningful, however, than the legal victories concerning access to bathrooms, for example, is the way in which society is being pushed to confront the ways in which we use gender to organize children's lives and why binary gender categories matter so much to us. It is unclear whether transgender youth will ever benefit from the panoply of rights and protections currently afforded to transgender adults; however, once they are over the threshold of minority, the road ahead for them is looking much brighter than it has in years past.

NOTES

1. Note that this chapter does not explore the topic of *intersex* children, an admittedly related issue, but one with unique concerns that might be more appropriately addressed elsewhere.

2. The title of this section is from *Jamison Green, Becoming a Visible Man* 7 (Vanderbilt Univ. Press 2004).

3. Note that the UN International Research and Training Institute for the Advancement of Women (INSTRAW) definition of "sex" also includes a broader spectrum than the dichotomous "male" and "female," noting that "[t]hese sets of biological characteristics are not mutually exclusive as there are individuals who possess both, but these characteristics tend to differentiate humans as males and females." INSTRAW, *Glossary of Gender-Related Terms and Concepts*, www.un-instraw.org (last visited June 2, 2013).

4. *Green, supra* note 2, at 4.

5. Some explanation of intersex conditions is warranted. We may like to think of binary categories of genitalia, but the evidence suggests otherwise.

6. INSTRAW, *Glossary of Gender-Related Terms and Concepts, supra* note 3.

7. This dichotomous or binary definition of gender is introduced as the "traditional" model. The concept of gender as a continuous variable, or a spectrum, however, is gaining wider acceptance and forms part of the definition of gender nonconformance—gender understood as existing between and beyond these binary categories.

8. Priscilla R. Carver, Jennifer L. Yunger, & David G. Perry, *Gender Identity and Adjustment in Middle Childhood*, 49 Sex Roles 95 (2003), http://link.springer.com/article/10.1023%2FA%3A1024423012063 (last visited June 19, 2014).

9. International Commission of Jurists, *Yogyakarta Principles—Principles on the Application of International Human Rights Law in Relation to Sexual Orientation and Gender Identity* (March 2007), www.refworld.org/docid/48244e602.html (last visited June 19, 2014).

10. May L. Halim & Diane Ruble, *Gender Identity and Stereotyping in Early and Middle Childhood*, in Handbook of Gender Research in Psychology 496 (J.C. Chrisler & D.R. McCreary eds. 2010).

11. Carver *et al.*, *Gender Identity and Adjustment in Middle Childhood*, supra note 8, at 95.

12. So scorned were the parents of one such child that their decision not to announce their youngest child's sex ended up being featured in a Huffington Post article describing the "worst" parenting failures of 2011. Lisa Belkin, *Worst Parenting Fails? A Year of Explosive Parenting Fails*, Huffington Post, Dec. 6, 2011, 1:51 P.M., www.huffingtonpost.com/2011/12/06/worst-parenting-fails_n_1129372.html (last visited June 19, 2014).

13. Associated Press, *Couple's Gender Secret for Baby Storm Touches Off Debate* (May 27, 2011), www.silive.com/news/index.ssf/2011/05/couples_gender_secret_for_baby.html (last visited June 19, 2014).

14. Jenny Soffel, *Gender Bias Fought at Egalia Preschool in Stockholm, Sweden*, Huffington Post, June 26, 2011, 8:01 P.M., www.huffingtonpost.com/2011/06/26/gender-bias-egalia-preschool_n_884866.html (last visited June 19, 2014).

15. Note that Storm's mother, Kathy Witterick, claims that the child is not being raised *without* a gender but instead *with* an opportunity to explore his or her identity without the imposition of gender stereotypes.

16. Peggy T. Cohne-Kettenis & Freidemann Pfäfflin, *Transgenderism and Intersexuality in Childhood and Adolescence: Making Choices* 7 (Sage Publ'ns 2003).

17. Halim & Ruble, *Gender Identity and Stereotyping in Early and Middle Childhood*, supra note 10, at 496.

18. *Id.*

19. Carver *et al.*, *Gender Identity and Adjustment in Middle Childhood*, supra note 8, at 96.

20. Gender Identity Disorder (GID) will be described in detail later in this chapter.

21. Johanna Olson, Catherine Forbes, & Marvin Belzer, *Management of the Transgender Adolescent*, 165 Archives Pediatric & Adolescent Med. 171 (2011). Note also that some describe transgender as a category within the broader subset of transsexualism, defined by the World Health Organization as "a desire to live and be accepted as a member of the opposite sex, usually accompanied by a sense of discomfort with, or inappropriateness of, one's anatomic sex, and a wish to have surgery and hormonal treatment to make one's body as congruent as possible with one's preferred sex." *International Statistical Classification of Diseases and Related Health Problems*, 10th rev.,

ver. 2010 (hereinafter cited as *ICD-10*), F64.0, *Transsexualism*, http://apps.who.int/classifications/icd10/browse/2010/en#/F64.0 (last visited June 19, 2014).

22. Femke Olyslager & Lynn Conway, On the Calculation of the Prevalence of Transsexualism (Sept. 6, 2007) (unpublished paper presented at the World Professional Association for Transgender Health [WPATH] Twentieth International Symposium), http://ai.eecs.umich.edu/people/conway/TS/Prevalence/Reports/Prevalence%20of%20 Transsexualism.pdf (last visited June 19, 2014).

23. Am. Psychiatric Ass'n, Diagnotstic and Statistical Manual of Mental Disorders (4th ed. 1994) (*DSM-IV*).

24. *ICD-10, supra* note 21, at F64.2, *Gender Identity Disorder of Childhood*, http://apps.who.int/classifications/icd10/browse/2010/en#/F64.0 (last visited June 19, 2014).

25. *Id.* at F.66.0.

26. The *other* definition of "sex" of course is in reference to sexual conduct. In thinking through the conflation of gender identity and sexual orientation, it is important to reflect on how we regard transgender children who have not yet developed a sexual identity. Since young children are regarded as "sexless" and therefore incapable of forming some kind of sexual identity, those who regard transgender children as expressing a *sexual*, rather than *gender*, preference, believe any such labeling is premature. Arguably, the way in which transgender children are currently understood does strip them of a sexual orientation—neutering them, so to speak (both figuratively and literally through the use of hormones to suspend puberty).

27. *Green, Becoming a Visible Man, supra* note 2, at 12–13.

28. *Phyllis Burke, Gender Shock: Exploding the Myths of Male and Female* (Anchor Books 1996).

29. *Cohne-Kettenis & Freidemann Pfäfflin, Transgenderism and Intersexuality in Childhood and Adolescence, supra* note 16, at 159–160.

30. Benoit Denizet-Lewis, *Coming Out in Middle School*, N.Y. Times Mag., Sept. 27, 2009, at MM36.

31. *Katayoon Majd, Jody Marksamer, & Carolyn Reyes, Hidden Injustice: Lesbian, Gay, Bisexual, and Transgender Youth in Juvenile Courts* 45 (2009).

32. Take, for example, the 1977 account from psychiatrist George Rekers, who advocated for treatment for the social maladjustment of a cross-gender identified boy (also described as "gender-disturbed" to prevent the possibility of adult homosexual deviance). Rekers regarded supporting the cross-gender identified boy in his chosen gender as "ethically unacceptable" and "professionally irresponsible." George A. Rekers, *Atypical Gender Development and Psychosocial Adjustment*, 10 J. Applied Behav. Analysis 559 (1977), www.ncbi.nlm.nih.gov/pmc/articles/PMC1311226/pdf/jaba00114–0187.pdf (last visited June 19, 2014).

33. *Magnus Hirschfeld, Transvestites: The Erotic Drive to Cross-Dress* (Prometheus Books 1991) (1910).

34. "In the United States, children have been openly transitioning genders for probably less than a decade," says Jack Drescher, a New York psychiatrist who is a leader in the field of gender orientation. Petula Dvorak, *Transgender at Five*, Wash.

Post, May 19, 2012, www.washingtonpost.com/local/transgender-at-five/2012/05/19/gIQABfFkbU_story_1.html (last visited June 19, 2014).

35. *Julie Anne Peters, Luna: A Novel* (Little, Brown 2004); *Ellen Wittlinger, Parrotfish* (Simon & Schuster Books for Young Readers 2007); *Cris Beam, I am J* (Little, Brown 2011); Adolfo Guzman-Lopez, *First Book with Transgender Theme Makes It on CA Schools Reading List*, Mar. 22, 2013, www.scpr.org/blogs/education/2013/03/22/13033/first-book-with-transgender-theme-makes-it-on-ca-s (last visited June 19, 2014).

36. *Marcus Ewert, 1,000 Dresses* (Seven Stories Press 2011). *Cheryl Kilodavis, My Princess Boy: A Mom's Story about a Young Boy Who Loves to Dress Up* (Aladdin 2011); quotation from the *My Princess Boy* website, http://myprincessboy.com (last visited Aug. 8, 2014). *See also* Guzman-Lopez, *First Book with Transgender Theme Makes It on CA Schools Reading List*.

37. Eileen Kiernan-Johnson, *Roland Humphrey Is Wearing a WHAT?* (Huntley Rahara Press 2012); also see *Roland Humphrey Is Wearing a WHAT? Picture Books Review* (2012), www.picturebooksreview.com/2013/05/roland-humphrey-is-wearing-what-2012.html (last visited Aug. 7, 2014).

38. See *Roland Humphrey Is Wearing a WHAT? Goodreads*, www.goodreads.com/book/show/17541951-roland-humphrey-is-wearing-a-what (last visited Aug. 7, 2014). Stephanie Riesco, *Because I Like Them: Local Woman's Son Inspires Book on Boys Who Wear Dresses and Challenge Gender Norms, Boulder Weekly*, Feb. 28, 2013, http://npaper-wehaa.com/boulder-weekly/2013/02/28/?g=print#?article=1827833 (last visited June 19, 2014).

39. Margaret Talbot, *About a Boy, New Yorker*, Mar. 18, 2013.

40. Carver et al., *Gender Identity and Adjustment in Middle Childhood, supra* note 8, at 98.

41. *Id.* at 99.

42. *Id.*

43. *Id.* at 98.

44. *Id.* at 99.

45. Arnold H. Grossman & Anthony R. D'Augelli, *Transgender Youth and Life-Threatening Behaviors*, 37 Suicide and Life-Threatening Behav. 527 (2007).

46. *Id.* at 535.

47. Normal P. Spack et al., *Children and Adolescents with Gender Identity Disorder Referred to a Pediatric Medical Center*, 129 Pediatrics 418 (2012).

48. Bryan N. Cochran et al., *Challenges Faced by Homeless Sexual Minorities: Comparison of Gay, Lesbian, Bisexual, and Transgender Adolescents with Their Heterosexual Counterparts*, 92 Am. J. Pub. Health 773 (2002). *See also* Ctr. for Am. Progress, *Gay and Transgender Youth Homelessness by the Numbers*, www.americanprogress.org/issues/2010/06/homelessness_numbers.html (last visited Mar. 20, 2013).

49. Aaron T. Norton & Gregory M. Herek, *Heterosexuals' Attitudes toward Transgender People: Findings from a National Probability Sample of U.S. Adults*, 68 Sex Roles 738 (June 2013).

50. *Id.*

51. *Pink Is for Boys,* http://pinkisforboys.wordpress.com (last visited Mar. 20, 2013).

52. *World Prof'l Ass'n for Transgender Health, Standards of Care for the Health of Transsexual, Transgender, and Gender Nonconforming People* (7th ver. 2011), http://www.wpath.org/uploaded_files/140/files/IJT%20SOC,%20V7.pdf (last visited June 19, 2014).

53. Jesse Green, *S/He: Parents of Transgender Children Are Faced with a Difficult Decision, and It's One They Have to Make Sooner than They Ever Imagined,* N.Y. Mag., May 27, 2012, http://nymag.com/news/features/transgender-children-2012-6 (last visited June 19, 2014).

54. *Am. Psychiatric Ass'n, Diagnostic and Statistical Manual of Mental Disorders Text Revision* 581 (4th ed. 2000) (*DSM-IV-TR*).

55. *Am. Psychiatric Ass'n, DSM-5 Development,* www.dsm5.org/Pages/Default.aspx (last visited Mar. 20, 2013); *Nicholas M. Teich, Transgender 101: A Simple Guide to a Complex Issue* (Colum. Univ. Press 2012); J. Bryan Lowder, *Being Transgender Is No Longer a Disorder, Slate,* Dec. 3, 2012, www.slate.com/articles/health_and_science/medical_examiner/2012/12/dsm_revision_and_sexual_identity_gender_identity_disorder_replaced_by_gender.html (last visited June 19, 2014).

56. *Teich, Transgender 101, supra* note 53.

57. *Am. Psychiatric Ass'n, DSM-5 Development, supra* note 55, at 452.

58. *Kenneth J. Zucker & Susan J. Bradley, Gender Identity Disorder and Psychosexual Problems in Children and Adolescents* 3 (Guilford Press 1995).

59. *Id.*

60. Eithne Mills, *Re Alex: Adolescent Gender Identity Disorder and the Family Court of Australia,* 9 Deakin L. Rev. 365 (2004).

61. Ruth Padawer, *BoyGirl: Raising a Boy Who Prefers to Look and Act Like a Girl Tests Even the Most Progressive Parents,* N.Y. Times Mag., Aug. 12, 2012, at 21.

62. *Id.*

63. Green, *S/He: Parents of Transgender Children Are Faced with a Difficult Decision, supra* note 53.

64. Dvorak, *supra* note 34.

65. *World Prof'l Ass'n for Transgender Health, Standards of Care for the Health of Transsexual, Transgender, and Gender Nonconforming People* 176–177 (7th ver.), *supra* note 52.

66. The Tanner Stages, also referred to as Tanner Scale, are predictable sequences of puberty that are scaled for children, adolescents, and adults. The scale, first identified by the British pediatrician James Tanner, defines physical measurements of development based on external primary and secondary sex characteristics, such as the size of the breasts, genitalia, and development of pubic hair. *See also* Child Growth Found., *Puberty and the Tanner Stages,* www.childgrowthfoundation.org/CMS/FILES/Puberty_and_the_Tanner_Stages.pdf (last visited June 19, 2014).

67. Spack *et al., Children and Adolescents with Gender Identity Disorder Referred to a Pediatric Medical Center, supra* note 47.

68. Norman Spack, *Transgenderism,* Lahey Clinic Med. Ethics J. 1 (Fall 2005), www.imatyfa.org/permanent_files/spack-article.pdf (last visited June 19, 2014).

69. Green, *Becoming a Visible Man*, supra note 2, at 131.

70. "Rather than providing a refuge from this mistreatment, the home often represents an additional site of harassment and violence: Parental abuse of transgender youth is widespread." Maureen Carroll, *Transgender Youth, Adolescent Decisionmaking and Roper v. Simmons*, 56 UCLA L. Rev. 725, 733 (2009).

71. *Id.* at 735.

72. Parental support of transgender children may open the door to state supervision of parental decision making, an issue explored at length in an article critiquing the removal by state child protective services of a transgender child. *See* Noa Ben-Asher, *Paradoxes of Health and Equality: When a Boy Becomes a Girl*, 16 Yale J.L. & Feminism 275 (2004).

73. "On a day-to-day level, restrooms are one of the most important and pressing concerns for transgender students. Indeed, a transgender focus group conducted by the Gay Straight Alliance Network found that among participants the lack of safe bathrooms was the biggest problem that gender non-conforming students face." *Gender Spectrum, School Policies and Law*, www.genderspectrum.org/education/school-policies-law (last visited June 19, 2014).

74. Joseph Kosciw et al., *The 2011 National School Climate Survey: The Experiences of Lesbian, Gay, Bisexual and Transgender Youth in Our Nation's Schools*, Gay, Lesbian and Straight Educ. Network (2011), http://glsen.org/sites/default/files/2011%20National%20School%20Climate%20Survey%20Full%20Report.pdf (last visited June 19, 2014).

75. *Id.* at 89.

76. Emily Greytak, Joseph Kosciw, & Elizabeth Diaz, *Understanding School Safety for Transgender Students*, Cal. Safe Sch. Coal., Safe Schools Res. Brief 13, www.casafe-schools.org/CSSC_Research_Brief_13.pdf (last visited June 19, 2014).

77. Title IX of the Education Amendment Acts of 1972 prohibits discrimination based on sex in education programs and activities receiving federal financial assistance. One of the forms of prohibited conduct under Title IX is discrimination on the basis of gender non-conformity. If, for example, a boy is bullied because he is perceived to be effeminate, the school's failure to take steps to stop that harassment may violate Title IX. *See, e.g.*, Montgomery v. Independent Sch. Dist. No. 709, 109 F. Supp. 2d 1081 (D. Minn. 2000).

78. Lambda Legal, *The Oregon Equality Act: Protection for Lesbian, Gay, Bisexual and Transgender People* (2007), http://data.lambdalegal.org/pdf/fs_oregon-equality-act.pdf (last visited June 2, 2013).

79. *Id.*

80. TransActive, *Oregon Equality Act + Safe Schools Act: A How-To Guide for Oregon Public & Charter Schools*, www.transactiveonline.org/community_education/documents/TransActive%20OEA-SSA%20Brochure-Color%20Cover.pdf (June 2, 2013).

81. Cal. Safe Sch. Coal., *Model School District Policy Regarding Transgender and Gender Nonconforming Students*, www.genderspectrum.org/images/stories/csscmodelpolicy1209.pdf (last visited June 19, 2014).

82. California Assembly Bill No.1266, Chapter 85, http://leginfo.legislature.ca.gov/faces/billNavClient.xhtml?bill_id=201320140AB1266 (last visited June 19, 2014).

83. *Mass. Dep't of Elementary & Secondary Educ., Guidance for Massachusetts Public Schools: Creating a Safe and Supportive School Environment* (2013), www.doe.mass.edu/ssce/GenderIdentity.pdf (last visited June 19, 2014).

84. Judy Harrison, *Suit over Transgender Students' Bathroom Rights to Go Forward, Judge Says*, Bangor Daily News, Apr. 20, 2011, http://bangordailynews.com/2011/04/20/news/bangor/lawsuit-over-use-of-girls%E2%80%99-bathroom-at-orono-school-may-go-forward-judge-says (last visited June 19, 2014); *see also* Kathleen Hirsman, *LGBT Issues in the Public Schools: A Legal Perspective*, 32 Child. Legal Rts. J. 1, 24 (2012).

85. Doe v. Clenchy, No. 09–201 (Me. Super. Ct. Apr. 1, 2011) (order denying in part and granting in part Defendant's motion to dismiss), http://statecasefiles.justia.com/documents/maine/superior-court/PENcv-09–201.pdf?ts=1385514753 (last visited Aug. 7, 2014).

86. Judy Harrison, *Judge Finds in Favor of Orono Schools over Transgender Girl's Use of Bathroom*, Bangor Daily News, Nov. 20, 2012, http://bangordailynews.com/2012/11/20/news/bangor/judge-finds-in-favor-of-orono-schools-over-transgender-girls-use-of-bathroom (last visited June 19, 2014).

87. Josh Levs, Ed Payne & Ashley Fantz, *School's Transgender Ruling: Fairness or Discrimination? CNN.com*, Mar. 1, 2013, www.cnn.com/2013/02/28/us/colorado-transgender-girl-school (last visited June 19, 2014).

88. Joey Bunch, *Coy Mathis, Colorado Transgender First-Grader, Wins Civil Rights Case*, Denver Post, June 23, 2013, www.denverpost.com/ci_23523502/colorado-transgender-coy-mathis-wins-civil-rights-case (last visited June 19, 2014).

89. Tinker v. Des Moines Indep. Cmty. Sch. Dist., 393 U.S. 503 (1969).

90. Doe ex rel. Doe v. Yunits, No. 001060A, 2000 WL 33162199 (Mass. Super. Ct. 2000).

91. Alexis Stevens, *Cobb Teen Told He Can't Dress Like a Female at School*, Atlanta Journal-Constitution, Oct. 7, 2009, www.ajc.com/news/news/local/cobb-teen-told-he-cant-dress-like-a-female-at-scho/nQX6z (last visited June 19, 2014).

92. Doe v. Bell, 754 N.Y.S.2d 846 (2003).

93. In re Brian (a/k/a Mariah) L. v. Administration for Children's Services, No. K-1154/96 (N.Y. Fam. Ct. Feb. 21, 2007).

94. Majd et al., Hidden Injustice, *supra* note 31.

95. *Id.*

96. King County (Washington State), Dep't Adult & Juvenile Detention, *Adult Divisions General Policy Manual*, ch. 6, *Inmate Classification and Discipline, 6.03007 Transgender Inmates* (2006), www.aclu.org/files/images/asset_upload_file70_27801.pdf (last visited Aug. 7, 2014). The policy is also noted in Lornet Turnbull, *Transition to Fairness*, Seattle Times, Dec. 18, 2006, http://seattletimes.com/html/local-news/2003482879_transpolicy18m.html (last visited Aug. 7, 2014).

97. UNICEF, *Convention on the Rights of the Child* (Nov. 29, 2005), www.unicef.org/crc.

98. Transkids, *Draft Transgender Children's Bill of Human Rights*, http://transkids.synthasite.com/transgendered-childrens-bill-of-rights.php (last visited Mar. 21, 2013).

9

Gender at the Crossroads

LGBT Youth in the Child Welfare and Juvenile Justice Systems

BARBARA FEDDERS

Each year, approximately five million young people become involved in the child welfare and juvenile justice systems.[1] These youth are overwhelmingly poor.[2] They are disproportionately likely to have disabilities, which negatively affect their academic performance.[3] They are disproportionately youth of color.[4] And, if the estimates of the general youth population serve as a guide, up to 13% of them engage in same-sex sexual behaviors or experience same-sex romantic desires, are actively questioning their sexual orientation and gender identity, and/or identify as lesbian, gay, bisexual, transgender, or queer.[5]

The child welfare and juvenile justice systems are charged, respectively, with caring for youth whose parents the state deems unfit[6] and with rehabilitating youth charged with committing so-called "status offenses" (truancy, running away, being out of the control of their parents) or with breaking criminal laws.[7] When a state agency removes children from their homes and places them state custody, or leaves them in the community but imposes significant liberty restrictions, that agency must in fact act according to the caretaking and rehabilitative missions. It should take care to provide youth the conditions they need to thrive: the opportunity to make certain decisions independently,[8] support and understanding when they make mistakes out of immaturity,[9] the experience of some amount of privacy,[10] information about their bodies and comprehensive sex education,[11] and the ability to explore and express their sexual orientation and gender identity unencumbered by bias and discrimination, with access to supportive adults.[12]

Instead, youth in these systems must contend with heightened scrutiny, unrealistic expectations from adults, and insufficient system resources to meet their multiple needs. When they are housed in group homes, detained, and incarcerated, they may be subject to physical violence and verbal abuse from other youth and from staff. It is wrong that youth experience as dangerous and hostile the systems mandated to care for them after their own families have abdicated, or been stripped of, the responsibility to do so. Those at the most risk for mistreatment are the most disenfranchised—poor youth of color who are, or are perceived to be, lesbian, gay, bisexual, or transgender (LGBT).[13]

Over the last twenty years, advocates for LGBT youth have won important legal and policy victories establishing the obligation of juvenile justice and child welfare facilities not to discriminate and to keep these youth safe. We now must move into a second stage of advocacy and organizing in which we acknowledge the multiple sites of oppression visited on LGBT youth. We ought to strive not only to protect LGBT youth but also to interrogate and to change the conditions that allow anti-gay behaviors and statements to flourish. More broadly, we need to seek more fundamental change in the conditions that lead young people into these systems in the first place. It is not enough to work for a fairer and more equitable child welfare and juvenile justice systems, though to do so is surely important. We must also find other ways of addressing the complex social problems currently addressed through the one-dimensional, overly crude mechanisms of child removal and prosecution. Our vision needs to be broader, our advocacy more intersectional, and our agenda more radical.[14]

The Systems Defined

The "child welfare system" is the constellation of government agencies, private agencies that contract with them, and family courts charged with responding to and adjudicating allegations of maltreatment, providing services to families believed to be at risk of committing abuse or neglect, and taking custody of children found to have been seriously neglected or physically or sexually abused by parents or primary caregivers.[15] In 2008, an estimated total of 3.7 million children were investigated or assessed for maltreatment—the highest number in five years.[16]

Most investigations stem from reports not of abuse but of neglect.[17] While federal law requires that removal from the home be a last resort, only after in-home services are attempted, in fact children are removed from their parents and placed in foster care simply because of the poverty of their parents.[18] When a family cannot afford safe and habitable housing, for example, or when parents must work but cannot find or afford child care, they risk the removal of their children.[19]

An estimated 312,000 children are removed annually from their homes.[20] Most children who are removed are placed with a relative or in a foster home, but some are placed in congregate facilities, or "group homes."[21] Out-of-home placements are expensive—they can cost more than $19,000 per child per year.[22] What is more, removing a child from her home, community, and school—often with little explanation to the child regarding the reasons or the long-term plan—is traumatizing.[23] Once a child is removed, a child's safety ceases to be the polar star determining placement. A child's reunification with her parents becomes subject to the idiosyncratic whims of judges and caseworkers, who demand that parents measure up to idealized and often unrealistic standards.[24]

Anti-poverty measures—such as universal or even more accessible health care, subsidized child care, or a living wage—would constitute a better and certainly a cheaper response for many of a family's poverty-related problems that are currently handled in the nation's family courts, foster homes, and child welfare offices.[25] Yet these do not appear to be political priorities. Likely this is because, while children of all classes and races are of course abused and neglected, those most affected by the child welfare systems are poor people who are disproportionately people of color—a politically weak constituency. Supreme Court precedent makes clear that parents are entitled to raise their children as they wish, absent clear demonstrations of lack of fitness.[26] Yet for poor people whose children have been removed, this precedent seems not to apply.[27]

Youth become subject to the jurisdiction of the juvenile delinquency courts when they are under eighteen and are charged with one of two types of offenses—either a so-called status offense[28] or a violation of the state's criminal law. The former category is composed of infractions that are unlawful only for minors, such as truancy, running away, and incorrigibility.[29] Juvenile courts typically process around two million cases annually.[30] Most cases are resolved with a disposition of probation and supervision while the child remains in the home, but more serious or repeated (even if not serious) violations can land a young person in a locked facility.[31] Nearly one hundred thousand youth each year spend time in detention pending resolution of their cases.[32]

While young people of all classes and races commit crimes, the juvenile justice system disproportionately ensnares poor youth and youth of color.[33] Youth of color receive harsher treatment than white youth at nearly every stage of the process. They are confined and sentenced for longer periods and are less likely to receive probation. This is true controlling for criminal record and seriousness of the offense. Nationwide, 39% of U.S. youth population was made up of youth of color, yet these youth constituted 65% of the secure detention population.[34]

The treatment of youth charged with crimes has changed dramatically over the last century. The juvenile court was founded in the late nineteenth century and has its roots in the social welfare movement of that time. Led by Jane Addams and other women from Chicago's Hull House, activists sought to create a rehabilitation-oriented alternative to the criminal court that would separate children from adults and focus on reform rather than only punishment.[35] Proponents envisioned the juvenile court judge as a "kind and just parent."[36]

In the panic of the late 1980s and early 1990s over an imagined onslaught of juvenile "superpredators," however, each state amended its laws to make it easier to try youth as adults.[37] Over the same period, legislatures changed the purpose of state juvenile courts to include more traditional retributive goals, such as offender accountability and public safety, such that juvenile court itself became more punitive. Delinquency adjudications now trigger a host of collateral consequences. They can imperil an immigrant's prospects of naturalization, keep a child on a sex-offender registry for multiple years or even—in some instances—for life, prevent a child from enlisting in the military, keep her from being accepted by a college or university or hinder her chances at obtaining financial aid, disqualify her family from obtaining public housing, and prevent a child from eventually obtaining employment in law enforcement.[38] Additionally, a delinquency adjudication enhances adult sentences in all fifty states in one form or another.[39] In nearly half of all states, delinquency adjudications make a child eligible for transfer to adult criminal court.[40] Despite the punitive legislative trends of the last twenty years, statutes defining the purposes of juvenile court in nearly every state retain at least some rehabilitative aims.[41]

LGBT Youth: Promise and Peril
Descriptions and Definitions

Before analyzing LGBT youths' pathways into the child welfare and juvenile justice systems, and the experiences they have once inside, I first more precisely define the youth being here considered, and then I briefly consider trends for LGBT youth outside the systems. Attempts at definition engender multiple questions. What, precisely, do we mean when we say someone is lesbian, gay, bisexual, or transgender? Theorists, activists, researchers, and medical professionals debate whether these terms must be reserved only for those who claim them as a matter of self-identification or may properly be applied to an individual based on her sexual behaviors and desires as well as her gender expression.[42] Activists argue over whether "coming out" is required to be able to claim these identities and, if so, whether any degree of closeted-ness is ever acceptable.[43] Where are the boundary markers best drawn? Is there a "distinct population of persons who 'really are' gay," or is sexuality more fluid, such that same-sex desire resides even within "apparently heterosexual people?"[44] Another area of dispute is causation. Is "being gay" something that is inborn and immutable? Or is it subject to influence by sociocultural forces?[45] "Transgender" describes individuals whose gender identity or expression differs from the gender associated with the sex they were assigned at birth. Is this only a clinical category, or can it also be an act of self-affirmation, a political act?[46] Are sexual orientation and gender identity separate and discrete categories, or are they related?[47] Finally, can a shared gay, lesbian, bisexual, or transgender identity unify people across diverse race, class, and gender backgrounds? Feminists and critical race theorists have argued powerfully that class, race, and gender privilege create power differentials within LGBT populations that have historically been unacknowledged by wealthy, white gay men, and, as a result, arguments for "gay rights" have too often reflected the agendas of this relatively small subset of people affected by heterosexism and homophobia rather than those of the most disempowered.[48]

While these questions cannot possibly be definitively resolved here, it is important to tease out some of their implications for youth in the child welfare and juvenile justice systems. For one, a somewhat common response when issues regarding sexual minority youth are raised is to minimize their numbers, if not to deny their existence altogether.[49] Some of the explanation for this response lies with the belief of many adults that any variation from heterosexual, gender non-conforming norm must necessarily represent only a developmental phase, out of which the young person will soon grow. Furthermore, adults seem to believe that young people who do not self-identify and come out are not, in fact, lesbian, gay, bisexual, or transgender, and that, therefore, no specific changes to any policies or programs that serve youth need to be made without the obvious presence of a self-identified, out LGBT youth. Yet this attitude fails to account for the variety of sexual experiences and desires—as well as for the particularities of being young.

When asked about their experiences or feelings, for example, the numbers of young people reporting some interest in same-sex coupling is always higher than when asked about self-identification.[50] This discrepancy is consistent with adult reporting; in a 2008 national survey, only one-third of adults who had had same-sex sexual experiences identified as either lesbian, gay, or bisexual.[51] Anti-gay bias surely must help explain the discrepancy. The demographer Gary Gates, who analyzed the survey, argues: "Given that nearly half of Americans still believe that homosexual relationships are morally wrong, it is not surprising to find ambiguity between how people behave sexually and how they identify their sexual orientation."[52] Gates's views find support in two parallel trends; namely, the increasingly early age at which youth are coming out, as well as the regional variations in self-reporting on identity. First, the average age at which people become both aware of same-sex attraction and who then go on to self-identify as gay, lesbian, or bisexual has been steadily dropping. According to a 2005 study, the average age at which young people became aware of same-sex attraction is ten; the average age of self-identification as gay or lesbian is thirteen. Those are significantly lower ages from what youth reported when asked the same question ten years earlier.[53] This drop has occurred amidst increased visibility of LGBT images and advances in rights and legal protections for LGBT individuals.

Similarly, youth rates of self-identification as lesbian, gay, or bisexual are higher in coastal, traditionally liberal areas of the country than in the middle of the country. Given that sexual orientation appears to be evenly distributed throughout the U.S. adult population, the most probable explanations for the differences in self-reported identity would seem to be regional differences in attitudes of acceptance of sexual minorities.[54] Both of these sets of findings point to a dialectical relationship between culture and self-identification—the more open and tolerant the environment, the more likely one is to put a name on a set of feelings and experiences.

But, for youth, there would appear to be something additional afoot. For some adolescents—regardless of sexual orientation—sexuality simply is not a core part of their identity.[55] One researcher argues that young women relative to young men are less likely to accord their sexuality special significance.[56] Other adolescents question their sexual orientation and gender identity. Lesbian, gay, bisexual, and transgender organizations, particularly those involving youth, have appended "queer"[57] and/or "questioning" to their acronyms. Perhaps this incorporation is due to recognition that adolescent identity is always in flux, and questioning one's sexuality and gender can be part of an unremarkable developmental trajectory.[58]

Questions surrounding causation have also had particular salience with respect to youth. Over the years, the belief that sexual orientation is amenable to change by outside interventions has motivated parents to enroll their children in so-called reparative or conversion therapy and to have them committed to psychiatric hospitals.[59] Proponents of these "treatments" believe that gay people can be converted to straight sexual orientation and that all individuals can (and should) learn to behave in accordance with gender norms associated with their birth-assigned sex. Attempts to change sexual orientation historically have included "treatments" such as education on "dating skills" and "assertiveness training," as well as harsher and painful techniques such as strip-searching, isolation, electroshock treatment, and penile plethysmography. In some states, adolescents may refuse to consent to such treatment; however, parents can avoid this barrier by sending their children to private, faith-based programs not subject to state regulation.[60]

By now, every major medical and mental health organization has condemned reparative therapy,[61] with research showing that attempts to change a young person's sexual orientation result in much higher rates of suicidal ideation as well as a host of other mental health problems.[62] These "interventions" are ineffective, for one, but they also problematically rest on an assumption that homosexuality is "a developmental arrest, a severe form of psychopathology, or some combination of both."[63]

A similar quandary exists in the debates over how a young person's gender identity and expression does and should develop. Initially, gender was thought to flow from biological, birth-assigned sex. When a girl didn't act like a "girl," she was teased, verbally abused, or worse, and when her behaviors continued into womanhood, she could be legally discriminated against. Over time, medical explanations have evolved for behavior that diverges from strict, stereotypical gender norms.[64] People whose sense of their own gender identity varies from the gender that others ascribe to them may be diagnosed with "gender identity disorder" ("GID"). This diagnosis—created after the removal of homosexuality from the *Diagnostic and Statistical Manual of Mental Disorders* in 1973—is to be given by psychiatrists to those children and adolescents who experience "a strong and persistent cross-gender identification . . . persistent discomfort with [their] sex or sense of inappropriateness in the gender role of that sex . . . [and] clinically significant distress or impairment in social, occupational, or other important areas of functioning."[65]

The diagnosis of GID has allowed some transgender people to obtain important benefits. Attorneys for transgender youth diagnosed with GID have relied on the diagnosis to win for their clients the right to wear the clothes of their choice when state actors had prevented them from doing so. In *Doe v. Bell*, for example, a New York trial court ruled that the Administration for Children's Services (the state's child-welfare agency) could not lawfully prohibit a seventeen-year-old in a residential facility designated for males from wearing skirts or dresses.[66] The plaintiff had been designated a boy at birth but identified as a girl and had been diagnosed with GID. Two doctors qualified as experts in transgender issues testified that the plaintiff's treatment plan was consistent with being allowed to dress in "feminine" attire. The court ruled that because GID is a disability, allowing Doe to dress in "girls'" clothes was a reasonable accommodation mandated by the state's disability anti-discrimination statute.[67]

Notwithstanding these important legal victories, the medical explanation for gender non-conformity is limited, limiting, and cuts against the goal of self-determination in important ways. When GID is a necessary prerequisite for the attainment of legal rights and sensitive medical care for transgender people, those individuals who identify as transgender but who do not experience "clinically significant" impairment or distress will face the dilemma of having to either misrepresent their experiences or may find themselves without recourse in their quest for equality and proper medical treatment. Medical sanctioning of the notion that deviation from extremely narrow gender roles is a sickness can ultimately reify those narrow roles. What is more, the use of the diagnosis suggests that a person is subject to and affected by forces outside of her control.[68] Gender identity disorder seems not to allow for the possibility that one might choose not to behave in ways associated with one's biological sex simply as a matter of expression and personal preference.

Lesbian, gay, bisexual, and transgender youth have been belittled in the debates around marriage equality and parenting and custody rights for lesbian, gay, and bisexual adults. Opponents of marriage equality and parenting rights argue that a child raised by gay or lesbian parents will herself grow up to be gay or lesbian.[69] One response, of course, could be, So what?[70] Yet proponents of marriage equality and parenting rights have largely chosen to respond to these accusations by downplaying the impact of gay and lesbian parenting on a child's own sexual development and arguing that gays and lesbians are as likely to raise heterosexuals as anyone else.[71]

During Iowa legislative hearings on same-sex marriage, for example, a YouTube video featuring a handsome, seemingly straight, white young man proudly testifying that the sexual orientation of his lesbian mothers "made no difference" to his development went viral.[72] Would an effeminate, earrings-wearing boy, or a tattooed and leather-wearing girl have been seen as the appropriate messenger for marriage equality?[73] What is the message sent when seemingly straight youth are deployed to act as spokespersons for the rights of gay parents to marry? Must same-sex marriage rights depend on the ability of lesbian and gay parents to raise straight children? For gay men and lesbians struggling to gain or hold on to parenting and custody rights in conservative family courts, the only way to persuade a homophobic judge may well be to marshal the evidence that sexual orientation is inborn and not subject to change by external forces.[74] While these arguments are clearly necessary in homophobic family courts, they do play into the biased notion that a gay identity is something best to be avoided, if at all possible.[75]

The Real World: Trends for LGBT Youth

What is life like, then, for young people who have come out as lesbian, gay, bisexual, or transgender? Who engage in same-sex sexual behaviors and experience same-sex sexual desires, but don't identify as LGBT? Who are gender non-conforming? In key ways, it is better than it was in the past. Momentous advances have been made for LGBT adults: the invalidation of a part of the Defense of Marriage Act in *United States v. Windsor*, the recently won right to marry for same-sex couples in nineteen states and the District of Columbia,[76] and the repeal of the "Don't Ask, Don't Tell" military policy, for example.[77] And so young people can look toward a future in which discrimination is no longer to be expected as a fact of life in all areas.

For most LGBT youth, though, the present can be difficult.[78] Sixteen states and the District of Columbia have enacted legislation designed to protect LGBT youth in schools, and over four thousand school-based "gay-straight alliances" are now registered.[79] Yet harassment and bias persists. Over 80% of LGBT youth are verbally harassed, almost half physically harassed, and nearly 20% physically assaulted at school because of their sexual orientation. Even larger percentages report harassment and assault because of gender expression. Nearly three-quarters hear homophobic remarks, such as "faggot" or "dyke," frequently at school. About a third of LGBT students miss class because of safety concerns—more than a third more than students in a national sample of secondary school students. Youth in many parts of the country attend schools in which key components of their identities are officially invisible. In some states, schools are banned from discussing LGBT identities and experiences in any part of the curriculum, including the sex education programs.[80] Schools with "abstinence-only" sex education curricula are likely to ignore lesbian and gay issues.[81] A few states actually require that sex education curricula in the schools include *anti*-gay materials.[82] The last two years have seen several high-profile suicides by gay and lesbian adolescents and young adults, who killed themselves after ongoing harassment.[83]

In short, it is a time of progress and promise, but many youth live in peril, and none more so than those who become involved in the child welfare and juvenile justice systems.

At the Crossroads: Sexual Orientation, Gender Identity, and the Child Welfare and Juvenile Justice Systems

Pathways In

Among the group of young people most likely to become involved in these systems—poor youth and youth of color—certain factors make youth who engage in same-sex sexual behaviors and who are out as lesbian, gay, bisexual, or transgender uniquely vulnerable to system involvement and, as well, render them more likely to be hurt by the systems once they enter them.

First, family conflict based on a young person's actual or perceived sexual orientation or gender identity can lead a child to one or both of the two systems, sometimes directly and sometimes more circuitously. Consider a parent who is troubled over a child's gender non-conforming clothes, same-sex girlfriend or boyfriend, or LGBT friends. Such a parent can petition a juvenile court to initiate an "ungovernability" or "incorrigibility" status-offense action against a child, the aim of which is to obtain a judicial order to force a child to comply with parental rules.[84]

Courts have a variety of options for handling status offenders—they can order individual counseling for the child, family counseling, or removal of custody from the parents.[85] Some judges are equipped to filter out the parents' bias and recognize that at the root of the child's "misbehavior" is resistance to unsupportive and damaging parental overreaching. They take the opportunity afforded by a status-offense petition to interrupt the cycle of parental disapproval and punishment. In jurisdictions with such resources, a judge could order the parents and child to participate in appropriate, home-based services designed to address family conflict over a child's sexual orientation or gender identity.

Yet these sorts of responses by judges are not typical.[86] In New Orleans, for example, a judge took an eleven-year-old youth into his chambers without counsel to discuss the youth's sexual orientation. Partly in response to his mother's request, the judge detained the youth on charges of ungovernability, solely, according to advocates, because the youth was gay.[87] Against a backdrop of near-complete deference to the right of parents to inculcate their values in their children,[88] and in the wake of cuts to community-based services in the more recent past, courts are more likely to simply issue orders restricting the child's liberty without confronting the parent about her bigotry-based and damaging actions toward the child. Courts can, of course, remove a child from the home when a parent's phobias and fears result in abuse that threatens the child's safety. But a legal process that terminates in a child having to leave the home is likely to result in the child's feeling that her LGBT identity is the problem—rather than her parents' bias.

Even when parents do not initiate court action, their rejection of a child can lead that child into the systems. One study found that over 30% of gay men and lesbians reported suffering physical violence at the hands of a family member as a result of disclosure or discovery of their sexual orientation.[89] Young people hurt in this way may be removed by child protective services and placed in foster care. Another study found that 26% of adolescents were forced to leave home after disclosing their sexual orientation.[90] Multiple sources indicate that the youth homeless population is disproportionately composed of LGBT people.[91] On the street, a youth has minimal, and poor, options for supporting herself. Youth often must engage for their survival in activities that expose them to risk for arrest and prosecution, such as sex work, theft, and selling drugs.[92]

LGBT youth—whether homeless or not—are at heightened risk for criminal and sexual victimization, as well as arrest.[93] A 2005 study by Amnesty International found that police officers target transgender youth and LGBT youth of color for selective enforcement of "quality of life" offenses and "morals" regulations. [94]

Second, youth who engage in same-sex sexual behavior are uniquely vulnerable to prosecution under and stigmatization by sex offense laws. So-called crimes against nature statutes invalidated by the Supreme Court in *Lawrence v. Texas* continue to be enforced against minors in North Carolina and Georgia.[95] This prosecution is possible because of language in *Lawrence* that state courts have interpreted to mean that *Lawrence*'s holding is confined to adults.[96] While, theoretically, all youth are eligible for prosecution for engaging in oral and anal sex, crimes against nature or sodomy laws historically have targeted gay men and lesbians.[97]

Additionally, youth engaging in same-sex sexual behavior also appear to be disproportionately prosecuted for alleged violations of age-of-consent laws.[98] These laws criminalize sex with individuals below a particular age, whether or not the under-age individual was a willing party; they reflect a legislative determination that young people under some prescribed age do not have the capacity to consent.[99] In some states, age-of-consent laws deem all sexual activity with a person under the age of consent a felony, no matter the age of the "perpetrator."[100] However, likely out of recognition that sexual experimentation between same-age adolescents is common[101]—if not normative—many states have carved out exceptions when both individuals are close in age yet one individual is below the age of consent. These "Romeo and Juliet" provisions either mitigate punishment or completely exculpate the above-age party; they also relieve the above-age individual from having to register as a sex offender.[102] While in most states, Romeo and Juliet provisions apply to both same-sex and opposite-sex encounters, Texas[103] and Alabama[104] each restrict the exemption to opposite-sex sexual couplings.

What is more, when *both* individuals are younger than the prescribed age and eligible for prosecution, district attorneys must decide whether and whom to charge with violation of the applicable age-of-consent laws. In part because it seems illogical and perhaps morally unappealing to prosecute an under-age individual when that individual is among the class the statute was designed to protect,[105] most consensual sex between under-age youth goes unprosecuted. When it is prosecuted, however, bias and stereotypes can influence the decision about whom to charge.[106] Young men are more likely to be prosecuted than young women,[107] and same-sex sexual activity appears disproportionately to trigger prosecutorial attention as well.

Problems within the Systems

Recent studies have demonstrated that, for all youth, the child welfare and juvenile justice systems can fail to ameliorate underlying causal conditions and may in some cases exacerbate those conditions.[108] This seems particularly true for youth who identify as, or are perceived to be, LGBT, as well as those whose behaviors indicate that they are questioning their sexual orientation or gender identity.

The extent of the harm that may follow depends in part on the length of time a youth spends in the systems and the depth of her involvement once within them. Those factors are, in turn, informed by the class and race of a youth. An eleven-year-old whose employed mother is briefly investigated by a state social services agency after a neighbor reports that she left the child at home one evening is unlikely to experience the same effects as an eight-year-old whose single mother is poor, experiencing chronic homelessness, and addicted to drugs.[109] Similarly, a middle-class suburban adolescent who shoplifts from Bloomingdale's will experience the system differently from a low-income, urban youth who commits the same crime. The former will likely have his case diverted; the latter is much more likely to be prosecuted.

Youth who are placed out of their homes, particularly when detained or incarcerated, are at particular risk. For one, youth may well be placed with a foster family or in a group home in which the adults are as homophobic or transphobic as in their families of origin. State policies regarding qualifications for foster parents work to discourage LGBT adults from becoming foster parents. For example, several states prohibit unmarried cohabiting individuals from becoming foster parents—which amounts to a de facto ban on lesbian and gay couples fostering youth.[110] In Alabama, the department of social services has the discretion to determine whether a prospective foster parent is suitable by assessing the applicant's "moral character," which functions to screen out openly gay or lesbian individuals, particularly those who are cohabiting.[111] Further, states require foster parents to respect their foster children's religion and culture, for example, but make no specific similar requirements regarding sexual orientation and gender identity.[112] Additionally, even in states with no similar bars, child welfare professionals have sometimes failed to consider such a youth's need for supportive foster parents, placing youth with homophobic or transphobic foster parents.[113] There has also been at least one case of a youth's attorney disrupting an apparently appropriate placement with a lesbian couple because of the *attorney's* belief that this placement was improper because the boy should not be "subjected" to the women's "immoral" lifestyle.[114]

The point here is not that all LGBTQ youth need to be housed with LGBTQ parents to receive fair treatment. However, given the overwhelming social pressures on youth to conform to heterosexual and gender-conforming norms, out LGBTQ foster parents could provide much needed, happy, healthy counterexamples to the not-so-subtle messages youth daily receive that being straight not only is easier but is a morally superior way to live.[115]

Once a youth is in the juvenile justice system—even when she is charged with a minor offense—conflict in a youth's family or problems at school stemming from actual or perceived sexual orientation or gender identity can drive her to deeper involvement in the system, sometimes leading to detention. For example, a young person who receives a term of probation as the result of a delinquency adjudication will be required to follow a curfew and attend school daily. When a parent's demands that a young person "act straight" make being at home difficult, the youth can have her probation revoked and be sentenced to a secure facility—even though the problem lies with the parent and would be more appropriately handled through family counseling or education of the parent. Similarly, a young person who faces bullying or harassment at school may find it impossible to safely attend school regularly. If she skips, she will also find her probation violated, and secure confinement can follow.

An LGBT identity, expressions of same-sex desire, or even just the perceptions of other youth that a young person is LGBT can expose youth sentenced to secure facilities to disproportionately harsh treatment in juvenile justice facilities. At one "boot camp" program for young offenders, a seventeen-year-old girl believed to be a lesbian exhibited what her probation officer had termed "sexually predatory" behavior. The offense was that she had talked with some of the boys in the program about the breasts of one of the other girls. The probation officer sought to have her placed in a residential treatment program for female sex offenders. None of the boys involved in this incident were punished in any way.[116] Additionally, in Louisiana, one child was subjected to secure detention for wearing his hair in what facility officials believed to be a "feminine" way.[117]

Even more troubling, studies reveal that youth in detention who identify as, or are perceived to be, LGBT are disproportionately sexually assaulted.[118] These findings are consistent with the experience of men in prison, who also are much more likely to be raped and assaulted if they are, or are perceived to be, gay or transgender.[119] Prisons operate according to strict gender norms and promote a "hypermasculinity."[120] Variations from these norms are not tolerated. Men anxious to prove their own heterosexuality seek out weaker inmates on whom to vent aggression and establish their dominance; rape and other forms of unwanted sex serve as useful mechanisms for establishing hierarchies within prison.[121] Extensive ethnographic research is available documenting this phenomenon in adult facilities;[122] considerably less is available for juvenile facilities. It is therefore unclear precisely to what extent boys and girls mimic the patterns seen in adult male facilities. However, the higher rates of reported assault of LGBTQ youth suggest disturbing similarities in the populations of confined adult and juvenile youth.

Transgender and gender non-conforming youth are at particular risk for discrimination, abuse, and violence.[123] They may be prohibited from dressing according to norms they view as associated with their identified gender; staff may refuse to call them by their chosen name or with their desired pronouns. They will likely be forced to receive health care from by medical staff unfamiliar with the particular health care needs of transgender youth. They may be placed in housing units without regard to their vulnerability to hostility and abuse from other youth in close proximity. Staff may sexualize these young people or improperly try to persuade or coerce them into behaving in accordance with their birth-assigned sex.[124]

From Awareness to Advocacy

While these problems are dire, progress has been made. Only in the last thirty years or so have adults acknowledged the reality of LGBT youth. Since that time, youth and their advocates have achieved some important successes with respect to the child welfare and juvenile justice system. A few examples of advocacy, litigation, and education are important to mention specifically:

* At least five studies have been published, three of them of national scope, of the experiences of lesbian, gay, bisexual, and/or transgender youth within the child welfare and juvenile justice systems, with specific "best practices" recommendations.[125]
* In several jurisdictions, advocates have lobbied for and won the creation of specialized group homes for LGBT youth.[126]
* Anti-discrimination laws and policies pertaining to LGBT youth have been

passed. California passed a state law—the first of its kind in the country—prohibiting discrimination in the foster care system on the basis of sexual orientation and gender identity.[127] The Illinois Department of Children and Families Services promulgated a model policy guide improving coordination of services for LGBT youth.[128] In 2008, in response to a lawsuit by a transgender young woman denied hormones by state-run facilities,[129] the New York State Office of Children and Family Services promulgated a set of guidelines designed to protect LGBTQ youth in out-of-home care.[130] The rules allow transgender youth to have input into their housing placements, wear clothing and hairstyles that conform to their gender identity, shower privately, and be called by their chosen name rather than their legal name. The agency also included transgender youth in its anti-discrimination policy—a first for any New York state agency.[131]

*The rights of LGBT youth in a Hawai'i juvenile incarcerative facility were protected by a preliminary injunction in federal court.[132] In *R. G. v. Koller*, the federal district court judge made findings that the youth would likely prevail at trial on their claims that the state had deliberately violated their constitutional rights. Specifically, the court found that the defendants had been deliberately indifferent to the health and safety of the plaintiffs by failing to have (1) policies and staff training necessary to protect LGBT youth, (2) adequate staffing and supervision, (3) a functioning grievance system, and (4) a classification system to protect vulnerable youth. The court also found that the facility's practice of isolating LGBT youth, purportedly to protect them from abuse, violated Hawai'i Youth Correctional Facility's legal obligations to the youth. The case eventually settled, and the state agreed to a financial settlement with the plaintiffs. It also agreed to hire a court-appointed consultant to train all staff and to adopt official policies and procedures protecting LGBT youth from harm.[133]

The outcome in *R. G. v. Koller* should serve to help shape policy in all child welfare and juvenile justice bureaucracies. All youth have a right to safety when in the custody of the state, which means that child welfare and juvenile justice professionals must take care to ensure the physical and psychological well-being of all the youth in their care.[134] State officials must ensure the provision of appropriate medical care to youth, including transition-related medical care to transgender youth.[135] Child welfare and juvenile justice professionals may not ridicule or demean a youth based on the youth's actual or perceived sexual orientation or gender identity. They may not attempt to persuade a young person that she is or ought to be straight or gender conforming.[136] Rather than trying to change a gay or lesbian young person, responsible adults instead ought to work to change societal attitudes of ignorance, bias, and hostility toward gay and lesbian youth.[137] All agencies and offices involved in both systems should develop and enforce policies that explicitly prohibit discrimination and mistreatment of youth on the basis of actual or perceived sexual orientation and gender identity at all stages of the juvenile justice process, from initial arrest through case closure.[138]

Professionals in both systems must take care to respect a youth's privacy and never disclose a youth's sexual orientation or gender identity without a youth's explicit permission.[139] Youth may be out to some individuals but not to others, including family members. Adults in these systems must not assume they have permission to make disclosures.

Additionally, in most facilities, placement policies are made according to gender; boys on one floor, girls on another. With respect to transgender youth, placement decisions must be made with greater care. For youth whose birth-assigned sex is male but now identify as female, correctional experts recommend housing with females. Otherwise, transgender girls are unnecessarily at elevated risk for abuse from other confined individuals. Female-to-male transgender boys present a tougher case, but most believe that they too ought to be housed with girls for their safety.[140] In general, experts suggest, placement decisions should be made with maximum consultation with the involved youth.

A Way Forward

"I don't really have anything to say about gay youth in my courtroom. I don't think there have been any that I am aware of."[141]

So said a juvenile court judge when surveyed as part of a national study on the LGBT youth in the juvenile justice system. Likely he thinks he knows what a "gay youth" is—someone who claims the identity and declares it to his lawyer and to probation officers or, perhaps, someone who displays effeminate characteristics stereotypically associated with gay men. However, as already discussed, young people may be questioning their sexuality, engaging in same-sex sexual behaviors without identifying as lesbian or gay, or identifying as LGBT but suppressing these identities when they enter the alien and intimidating world of the child welfare and juvenile justice systems.[142]

Insofar as we confine our advocacy to protection and rights enforcement for "LGBT youth," we run the risk of suggesting that there is an essentialized and coherent category that any of us can see if we simply know what we are looking for. What is more, we must move beyond pushing for adoption of policies and laws to protect this category of youth. While states that adopt and promulgate such policies do provide remedies to youth who are suffering and, as well, perform the important expressive function of signaling disapproval of official expressions of homophobia and transphobia, they do little by themselves to change the heterosexist, patriarchal culture through which anti-gay and gender-policing behavior emerges.

Moving forward, we must fashion advocacy strategies that do not assume that youth will self-identify or come out as LGBT. We also should aim at making these systems safe for anyone to be, *or to become*, lesbian, gay, bisexual, transgender, queer. Specialized placements designed for LGBT youth are crucial. Yet many youth would not feel comfortable requesting such a placement, as to do so would constitute an identification that may feel wrong. So, the goal must be to create living environments in which all youth can live without fear of harassment. Toward that end, facilities must adopt policies that teach youth about multiple cultures and encourage respect for diversity. More than that, they must express a value that *there is nothing wrong with being lesbian, gay, bisexual, or transgender*. We must move beyond mere tolerance and promotion of safety and toward genuine acceptance.

Facilities must also include programming in which boys and young men, and girls and young women, are engaged in activities not associated with traditional gender norms. Boys should be taught cooking and sewing; girls should be taught carpentry.[143] Staff should, wherever possible without compromising the safety of other residents, engage youth in collaborative activities within the facility rather than relying only on security and order-maintenance policies. Punishment as a means of encouraging respect for difference has had decidedly limited effectiveness.

Ultimately, however, efforts must be expended to keep all young people out of both the child welfare and juvenile justice systems.[144] These are systems that serve in many ways as high-cost dumping grounds for young people who are victims of larger societal forces such as poverty, racism, and heterosexism. Research has demonstrated that other alternatives are more effective—or at least no less ineffective—at reducing crime, rehabilitating offenders, and ensuring adequate parenting than our current systems. Because we can never know for sure which young people may be LGBT, our efforts on their behalf are ultimately best served by working to keep *all* youth from being pushed into these two systems.

NOTES

1. Children's Bureau, Admin. for Children & Families, U.S. Dep't of Health & Human Servs., *Child Maltreatment 2008*, www.acf.hhs.gov/programs/cb/resource/child-maltreatment-2008 (estimating that 3.7 million children were investigated or assessed by state child welfare agency in 2008) (last visited June 22, 2014); M. Sickmund, A. Sladky, & W. Kang, *Easy Access to Juvenile Court Statistics: 1985–2011* (2014), www.ojjdp.gov/ojstatbb/ezajcs/asp/process.asp (last visited June 22, 2014); C. Puzzanchera & W. Kang, *Easy Access to Juvenile Court Statistics: 1985–2008*, www.ojjdp.gov/ojstatbb (1,653,300 delinquency cases processed in 2008) (last visited June 22, 2014).

2. *See, e.g.*, Annette Appell, *The Myth of Separation* , 6 NW J. L. & Soc. Pol'y 291 (2011) (child welfare); and Tamar Birckhead, *Delinquent by Reason of Poverty*, 38 J. Law & Pol'y 53 (2012) (juvenile justice).

3. Joseph B. Tulman & Douglas M. Weck, *Shutting Off the School-to-Prison Pipeline for Status Offenders with Education-Related Disabilities*, 54 N.Y.L. Sch. L. Rev. 875, 882 (citing Mary Quinn et al., *Youth with Disabilities in Juvenile Corrections: A National Survey*, 71 Exceptional Child 339 (2005).

4. *See* Bruce A. Boyer & Amy E. Halbrook, *Advocating for Children in Care in a Climate of Economic Recession: The Relationship between Poverty and Child Maltreatment*, 6 NW J. L. & Soc. Pol'y 300, 303–304 (2011) (child welfare); Jeff Armour & Sarah Hammond, *Minority Youth in the Juvenile Justice System: Disproportionate Minority Contact* (Nat'l Conference of State Legislatures 2009) (juvenile justice), www.ncsl.org/print/cj/minoritiesinjj.pdf (last visited June 22, 2014).

5. *Katayoon Majd, Jody Marksamer, & Carolyn Reyes; Hidden Injustice: Lesbian, Gay, Bisexual, and Transgender Youth in Juvenile Courts* 44 (Equity Project 2009) (citation omitted).

6. *See* Stanley v. Illinois, 405 U.S. 645 (1972) (holding that a child may not be deemed a ward of the state absent a finding that the parent is unfit); *see also* 42 U.S.C. § 671(a)(16) and (5)(A) (requiring states to develop for all children in state custody via child

welfare system a plan to assure "safe and proper care consistent with the child's best interest and special needs").

7. *See, e.g.*, Kent v. U.S., 383 U.S. 541, 554 (1966) (explaining that juvenile justice systems exist to provide guidance and rehabilitation, not to fix criminal responsibility or guilt).

8. Emily Buss, *Allocating Developmental Control among Parent, Child and the State*, in *The Law and Child Development* 62 (Emily Buss and Mavis Maclean eds. 2010) (discussing maturing child's interest in "making decisions regarding how she is educated, with whom she spends time, which activities she pursues, and other matters with important developmental effects").

9. In two recent cases, the Supreme Court has found that young people have deficiencies in decision-making capacity that render them less culpable and thus deserving of heightened protection under the Eighth Amendment. *See* Roper v. Simmons, 543 U.S. 551, 569 (2005) (outlawing capital punishment for people who commit capital murder while under the age of eighteen); and Graham v. Florida, 130 S. Ct. 2011, 2030 (2010) (banning life without parole for individuals who commit non-homicide crimes while under eighteen).

10. Skyler T. Hawk et. al., *Adolescents' Perceptions of Privacy Invasion in Reaction to Parental Solicitation and Control*, 28 J. Early Adolescence 583 (2008), http://jea.sagepub.com/content/28/4/583.full.pdf+htm (last visited June 22, 2014).

11. *See, e.g.*, Amy Schwartz, Note, *Comprehensive Sex Education: Why America's Youth Deserve the Truth about Sex*, 29 Hamline J. Pub. L. & Pol'y 115 (2007) (arguing for comprehensive sex education); Marla E. Eisenberg, Debra H. Bernat, Linda H. Bearinger, & Michael D. Resnick, *Support for Comprehensive Sexuality Education: Perspectives from Parents of School-Age Youth*, 42 J. Adolescent Health 352 (2008) (noting that comprehensive sex education is more effective than abstinence-only sex education and supported by parents).

12. Caitlin Ryan et al., *Family Acceptance in Adolescence and the Health of LGBT Young Adults*, 23 J. Child & Adolescent Psychiatric Nursing 205 (2010) (reporting on findings from study of LGBT young adults in which researchers found "lasting, dramatically protective influence of specific family accepting behaviors related to an adolescent's LGBT identity").

13. This chapter discusses the problems that result from including all youth who engage in same-sex behaviors, experience same-sex desire, and are gender non-conforming in the group "LGBT." The acronym does not capture the rich diversity of experiences and self-identification of youth. Nevertheless, I do use it when discussing the ways in which discrimination and bias within the system based on heterosexism and transphobia affect youth. In other places, I attempt to be more precise in my descriptions. In other places, I also include "queer" and "questioning" youth (LGBTQ).

14. I owe a great debt in my thinking here to many critical race theorists, trans activists, and feminists, including but certainly not limited to Kimberle Crenshaw, *Mapping the Margins: Intersectionality, Identity Politics, and Violence against Women of*

Color, 43 *Stan. L. Rev.* 1241 (1991); and Dean Spade, *Compliance Is Gendered: Struggling for Gender Self-Determination in a Hostile Economy*, in *Transgender Rights* 217–241 (Paisley Currah, Richard A. Juang, & Shannon Price Minter eds. 2006).

15. Robert J. Lukens, *The Impact of Mandatory Reporting Requirements on the Child Welfare System*, 5 *Rutgers J. L. & Pub. Pol'y* 177, 186–196 (2007) ("child welfare system has evolved as the mechanism entrusted to ensure the health and safety of the children in our communities").

16. Children's Bureau, *Child Maltreatment 2008, supra* note 1, at ch. 3.

17. *Id.*

18. Christine Gottlieb, *Reflections on Judging Mothering*, 39 *U. Balt. L. Rev.* 371, 381 (2010).

19. *Id.*

20. Children's Bureau, Admin. for Children & Families, U.S. Dep't of Health & Human Servs., *Child Maltreatment 2006*, http://archive.acf.hhs.gov/programs/cb/pubs/cm06/cm06.pdf (last visited June 23, 2014).

21. Theo Liebmann, *What's Missing from Foster Care Reform? The Need for Comprehensive, Realistic, and Compassionate Removal Standards*, 28 *Hamline J. Pub. L. & Pol'y* 141, 144–145 (2006).

22. Gottlieb, *Reflections on Judging Mothering, supra* note 18, at 379.

23. *Id.* at 381.

24. *Id.* at 385 (comparing *Stanley*, 405 U.S. 645 (holding that a state may not take custody from a parent absent a showing of unfitness), with Adoption and Safe Families Act of 1997 § 302, 42 U.S.C. § 675(5) (2008) (discussing considerations required in case planning once children are in foster care)).

25. Clare Huntington, *Mutual Dependency in Child Welfare*, 82 *Notre Dame L. Rev.* 1485, 1524 (2007) (arguing for state support to be centerpiece of child welfare system, as it would reduce poverty, lead to less child abuse and neglect, and enable individuals to lead productive lives).

26. *See, e.g.*, Troxel v. Granville, 530 U.S. 57, 65–66 (2000) (after surveying the Court's treatment of parental rights, concluding: "In light of this extensive precedent, it cannot now be doubted that the Due Process Clause of the Fourteenth Amendment protects the fundamental right of parents to make decisions concerning the care, custody, and control of their children.").

27. Gottlieb, *Reflections on Judging Mothering, supra* note 18, at 384.

28. *See, e.g.*, Md. Code Ann., Cts. & Jud. Proc. § 3–8a-03 (West 2010); N.C. Gen. Stat. Ann. § 7b-1601 (West 2010).

29. *See, e.g.*, Ga. Code Ann. § 15–11–2(11) (West 2010) (describing status offenses as including truancy, running away from home, incorrigibility, and unruly behavior).

30. Puzzanchera & Kang, *Easy Access to Juvenile Court Statistics: 1985–2008, supra* note 1 (1,653,300 delinquency cases processed in 2008).

31. Sickmund *et al.*, *Easy Access to Juvenile Court Statistics: 1985–2011, supra* note 1 (last visited Oct. 30, 2011).

32. Melissa Sickmund, *Juveniles in Residential Placement, 1997–2009* (Office of Juvenile Justice and Delinquency Prevention 2010), www.ncjrs.gov/pdffiles1/ojjdp/229379.pdf (last visited June 23, 2014).

33. *See generally* Perry L. Moriearty, *Combating the Color-Coded Confinement of Kids: An Equal Protection Remedy*, 32 N.Y.U. Rev. L. & Soc. Change 285 (2008).

34. James Bell & Laura John Ridolfi, *Adoration of the Question* 8 (W. Haywood Burns Institute 2008), http://cjjr.georgetown.edu/pdfs/pre_work/Adoration_of_the_Question_Reflections_on_the_Failure_to_Reduce_Racial__Ethnic_Disparities.pdf (last visited July 21, 2014).

35. *Id.* at 6.

36. Ann Skelton, *From Cook County to Pretoria: A Long Walk to Justice for Children*, 6 NW J. L. & Soc. Pol'y 413, 415 (2011) ("The first annual report of the Juvenile Court of Cook County, from 1900, stated: 'The law, this Court, this idea of a separate court to administer justice like a kind and just parent ought to treat his children has gone beyond the experimental stage and attracted the attention of the entire world.'").

37. Joseph Margulies, *Deviance, Risk, and Law: Reflections on the Demand for the Preventive Detention of Suspected Terrorists*, 101 J. Crim. L. & Criminology 729, 750 (2011).

38. *See* Michael Pinard, *The Logistical and Ethical Difficulties of Informing Juveniles about the Collateral Consequences of Adjudications*, 6 Nev. L.J. 1111, 1114–1115 (2006).

39. *See* A.M. v. Butler, 360 F.3d 787, 790 (7th Cir. 2004). *See also* People v. Nguyen, 209 P.3d 946, 948, 957 (Cal. 2009) (finding that juvenile adjudications fall under the "prior conviction" exception, and later use of that adjudication to enhance adult sentencing was appropriate) (citing Apprendi v. New Jersey, 530 U.S. 466, 490 (2000)).

40. Robert E. Shepherd, Jr., *Collateral Consequences of Juvenile Proceedings: Part I*, Crim. Just., Summer 2000, at 59.

41. Nat'l Council of Juvenile and Family Court Judges, *Juvenile Delinquency Guidelines: Improving Court Practice in Juvenile Delinquency Cases* 21 (2005): "The juvenile delinquency court is focused on identifying the underlying issues causing the delinquent behavior and providing interventions to address these issues. Both courts have a goal of community safety. The juvenile delinquency court, however, accomplishes this goal through individualized responses as opposed to standard sentencing, an important difference."

42. *See, e.g.*, Russell K. Robinson, *Masculinity as Prison: Sexual Identity, Race, and Incarceration*, 99 Cal. L. Rev. 1309, 1356–1357 (2011) (describing homosexuality as a "space of overlapping, contradictory, and conflictual definitional forces") (citing Eve Kosofsky Sedgwick, *Epistemology of the Closet* 45 (1990)).

43. For a discussion of this issue in the context of elder LGBT persons, *see* Nancy J. Knauer, *"Gen Silent": Advocating for LGBT Elders*, 19 Elder L.J. 289, 312–316 (2012) (discussing reasons that elder LGBT persons might remain closeted).

44. Robinson, *Masculinity as Prison*, *supra* note 42, at 1357 (citing *Sedgwick, Epistemology of the Closet*, *supra* note 42, at 85). *See also* Kenneth L. Karst, *Constitutional Equality as a Cultural Form: The Courts and the Meanings of Sex and*

Gender, 38 *Wake Forest L. Rev.* 513, 540 (2003) (quoting James Baldwin, who, speaking in support of the latter view, said: "There's nothing in me that is not in everybody else, and nothing in everybody else that is not in me. We're trapped in language, of course. But homosexual is not a noun" (internal citation omitted)).

45. *See* Linda D. Garnets & Douglas C. Kimmel, *The Meaning of Sexual Orientation*, in *Psychological Perspectives on Lesbian, Gay, and Bisexual Experiences* 23–25 (Linda D. Garnets & Douglas C. Kimmel eds., 2 ed. 2003) (describing essentialist, social constructionist, and interactionist frameworks for understanding sexual orientation).

46. *See, e.g.*, Dean Spade, *Resisting Medicine, Re/Modeling Gender*, 18 *Berkeley Women's L.J.* 15, 24–25 (2003) (discussing the oppressive relationship between medicine and gender transgressive people).

47. Shannon Price Minter, *Do Transsexuals Dream of Gay Rights?* in *Transgender Rights* 147 (Paisley Currah, Richard A. Juang, & Shannon Price Minter eds. 2006) (noting that dominant understanding of what it meant to be gay in working-class urban communities of African Americans and immigrants in early twentieth century and before was based not on same-sex behaviors or desires, like today, but on gender presentation or gender status).

48. Darren Lenard Hutchinson, *Out yet Unseen: A Racial Critique of Gay and Lesbian Legal Theory and Political Discourse*, 29 *Conn. L. Rev.* 561 (1997).

49. *Majd et al., Hidden Injustice, supra* note 5, at 4.

50. *Ritch C. Savin-Williams, The New Gay Teenager* 44–48 (2005).

51. Nearly 9% of adults either self-identify as gay, lesbian, or bisexual or report having had same-sex sexual experiences as an adult. Of them, 1.7% self-identified as gay or lesbian, 1.1% self-identified as bisexual, and 5.8% self-identify as heterosexual but report some same-sex sexual experiences. Gary J. Gates, *Sexual Minorities in the 2008 General Social Survey: Coming Out and Demographic Characteristics* (Williams Institute 2010), http://williamsinstitute.law.ucla.edu/wp-content/uploads/Gates-Sexual-Minorities-2008-GSS-Oct-2010.pdf (last visited June 23, 2014).

52. *Id.*

53. Shannan Wilber, Caitlin Ryan, & Jody Marksamer, *CWLA Best Practice Guidelines: Serving LGBT Youth in Out-of-Home Care* 16 (Child Welfare League of America 2006), www.nclrights.org/wp-content/uploads/2013/07/bestpracticeslgbtyouth.pdf (last visited June 23, 2014). *See also* Ellen C. Perrin, *Sexual Orientation in Child and Adolescent Health Care* 72 (Springer 2002).

54. Heather M. Berberet, *Putting the Pieces Together for Queer Youth: A Model of Integrated Assessment of Need and Program Planning*, 85 *Child Welfare* 361, 363 (2006).

55. *Savin-Williams, The New Gay Teenager, supra* note 50, at 202.

56. *Id.* at 192.

57. For those who use it, "queer" is often meant as an all-encompassing term to describe sexual orientation, gender identity, and personal politics, as an embrace of the notion that sexuality and gender are social constructs instead of biological givens, more fluid than allowed by the binaries of straight/gay and male/female. Many of those who self-identify as queer are drawn to the term because "it's the one that leaves the

most for discovery.... It's not really limiting." Rona Marech, *Nuances of Gay Identities Reflected in New Language: "Homosexual" Is Passé in a "Boi's" Life*, San Francisco Chron., Feb. 8, 2004, www.sfgate.com/news/article/Nuances-of-gay-identities-reflected-in-new-2824367.php (last visited June 23, 2014).

58. * *Caitlin Ryan & Donna Futterman, Lesbian and Gay Youth: Care and Counseling* 10 (1998); *see also* Luke Boso, *Disrupting Sexual Categories of Intimate Preference*, 21 Hastings Women's L.J. 59, 78 (2010) ("No one is 100 percent anything.").

59. *See* Elvia R. Arriola, *The Penalties for Puppy Love: Institutionalized Violence against Lesbian, Gay, Bisexual and Transgendered Youth*, 1 J. Gender, Race & Just. 429, 458–468 (1998); Sonia Renee Martin, Note, *A Child's Right to Be Gay: Addressing the Emotional Maltreatment of Queer Youth*, 48 Hastings L.J. 167, 174 (1996). California enacted a ban on reparative therapy, which was enjoined by a federal district court judge. Welch v. Brown,—F.Supp.2d——, 2012 WL 6020122 E.D.Cal., 2012. The case is presently on appeal before the Ninth Circuit Court of Appeals.

60. Jason Ciancietto & Sean Cahill, *Youth in the Crosshairs: The Third Wave of Ex-Gay Activism* 64–66 (Nat'l Gay & Lesbian Task Force 2006), http://thetaskforce.org/downloads/reports/reports/YouthInTheCrosshairs.pdf (last visited June 23, 2014).

61. American Psychological Association, *Just the Facts about Sexual Orientation and Youth: A Primer for Principals, Educators & School Personnel*, 6 (2008) http://www.apa.org/pi/lgbt/resources/just-the-facts.pdf (quoting statements by the American Academy of Pediatrics, the American Counseling Association, the American Psychiatric Association, the American Psychological Association, and the National Association of Social Workers critical of the tenets of reparative therapy) (last visited Aug. 7, 2014).

62. The American Psychiatric Association (APA) notes that sexuality researchers have begun to distinguish between "sexual orientation," referring to an individual's sexual arousal or desire patterns, and "sexual orientation identity," referring to acknowledgment and internalization of sexual orientation. Am. Psychiatric Ass'n, *Therapies Focused on Attempts to Change Sexual Orientation (Reparative or Conversion Therapies)*, COPP Position Statement, APA Document Reference no. 200001, 30 (2005), http://media.mlive.com/news/detroit_impact/other/APA_position_conversion%20therapy.pdf (last visited June 23, 2014).

63. *Id.*

64. Franklin Romeo, *Beyond a Medical Model: Advocating for a New Conception of Gender Identity in the Law*, 36 Colum. Hum. Rts. L. Rev. 713, 718 (2005) (describing evolution from biological model to medical model).

65. *Am. Psychiatric Ass'n, Diagnostic and Statistical Manual of Mental Disorders* 576 (4th ed. 2000) (*DSM-IV*).

66. 754 N.Y.S.2d 846 (2003).

67. Id. *See also* Doe v. Yunits, WL 33162199 (Jan. 10, 2003) (holding that a transgender girl considered a boy by her school but with GID diagnosis could proceed with a disability claim against the school in challenging the dress-code policy that prohibited her from wearing "'girls'" clothes).

68. Judith Butler, *Undiagnosing Gender* in *Transgender Rights* 275 (Paisley Currah, Richard A. Juang, & Shannon Price Minter eds. 2006).

69. *See, e.g.*, Lynn Wardle, *Parenthood and the Limits of Adult Autonomy*, 24 *St. Louis. U. Pub. L. Rev.* 169, 189–193 (2005) (arguing against gay-parent adoption).

70. Ruthann Robson, *Our Children: Kids of Queer Parents and Kids Who Are Queer: Looking at Sexual Minority Rights from a Different Perspective*, 64 *Alb. L. Rev.* 915, 924 (2000) ("As a lesbian myself, I am unwilling to engage in an argument that assumes that my sexual desires are pathological.").

71. *See, e.g.*, Eric Ferrero, Joshua Freker, & Travis Foster, 1 *Too High a Price: The Case against Restricting Gay and Lesbian Parenting* (ACLU Lesbian and Gay Rights Project 2004), www.buddybuddy.com/adoption.html (noting studies that prove that children of gay and lesbian-headed households are no more likely to be gay or lesbian than children of other households) (last visited June 23, 2014).

72. *Zack Wahls on Gay Marriage*, video available on YouTube, www.youtube.com/watch?v=VI4dROR3BsM&feature=related (clip starts at 0:40) (last visited Mar. 21, 2012); *also at YouTube—Zach Wahls Presents What Should Be Obvious (Mirror)*, www.youtube.com/watch?v=jK9Lvf4-jCQ&feature=related (last visited Mar. 21, 2012).

73. Ashley Harness, *I Was Zach Wahls Once Too—Let's Move On*, *Velvetpark* (Dec. 7, 2011, 4:52 p.m.), http://velvetparkmedia.com/blogs/i-was-zach-wahls-once-too—let's-move ("This is the ethical itch of the Zach Wahls phenomenon. It circles the drain of the lowest common denominator of political rhetoric: sameness. And the lure of sameness creates new closets made by our own movement. I built my own, once upon a time. And today, nobody is talking about Zach's sister, Zebby, who suffice it to say, bears a striking resemblance to Justin Bieber") (last visited June 23, 2014).

74. *See, e.g.*, Cook v. Cook, 965 So.2d 630, 633–34 (La. Ct. App.) (2007) (in custody action, mother procured expert witness who testified that there was no reliable evidence that children raised by lesbian couples were more likely to be lesbian to rebut father's claim that their daughters would have distorted view of female role models and suffer greatly if raised in environment with lesbian mother).

75. *See, e.g.*, Richard Posner, *Sex and Reason* (1992) ("[I]f [a] hypothetical cure for homosexuality were something that could be administered—costlessly, risklessly, without side effects—before a child had become aware of his homosexual propensity, you can be sure that the child's parents would administer it to him, believing, probably correctly, that he would be better off, not yet having assumed a homosexual identity").

76. National Conference of State Legislators, *Defining Marriage: State Defense of Marriage Laws and Same-Sex Marriage*, www.ncsl.org/default.aspx?tabid=16430 (last visited Aug. 7, 2014).

77. Liz Halloran, *With Repeal of "Don't Ask, Don't Tell," an Era Ends* (NPR, Sept. 20, 2011), www.npr.org/2011/09/20/140605121/with-repeal-of-dont-ask-dont-tell-an-era-ends (last visited June 23, 2014).

78. American Psychological Ass'n, *Practice Guidelines for LGB Clients*, www.apa.org/pi/lgbt/resources/guidelines.aspx (last visited June 23, 2014).

79. GLSEN, *States with Safe Schools Laws*, http://glsen.org/node/2922 (last visited Aug. 7, 2014).

80. Ariz. Rev. Stat. Ann. § 15–716(c)(1) to (3) (West 2000) (prohibiting any course of study that (1) "promotes a homosexual life-style," (2) "portrays homosexuality as a positive alternative life-style," or (3) "[s]uggests that some methods of sex are safe methods of homosexual sex"); La. Rev. Stat. Ann. § 17:281(A)(3) (West 2001) (prohibiting "sexually explicit materials depicting male or female homosexual activity"); S.C. Code Ann. § 59–32–30(A)(5) (Law. Co-op. 1976) (forbidding health education programs from discussing "alternate sexual lifestyles from heterosexual relationships" except in the context of sexually transmitted disease instruction).

81. SIECUS (Sexuality Information and Education Council of the United States), *SIECUS Fact Sheet: Lesbian, Gay, Bisexual, Transgender and Questioning Youth* (2010), www.siecus.org/index.cfm?fuseaction=Page.ViewPage&PageID=1196#_ednref1 (last visited June 23, 2014).

82. *See, e.g.*, Ala. Code § 16–40A-2(c)(8) (1995) (requiring sex education materials to emphasize "in a factual manner and from a public health perspective, that homosexuality is not a lifestyle acceptable to the general public and that homosexual conduct is a criminal offense under the laws of the state"); Tex. Health & Safety Code Ann. §85.007 (requiring education programs for those eighteen and younger to state "that homosexual conduct is not an acceptable lifestyle and is a criminal offense" notwithstanding the fact that the state's laws criminalizing homosexual sex were found unconstitutional by Lawrence v. Texas).

83. *Washington Blade, National LGBT Community Reeling from 4th Teen Suicide in a Month*, Oct. 1, 2010, www.washingtonblade.com/2010/10/01/national-lgbt-community-reeling-from-4th-teen-suicide-in-a-month (last visited June 23, 2014). One study estimates that LGBT youth are up to four times more likely to attempt suicide than their heterosexual peers. Paul Gibson, *Report of the Secretary's Task Force on Youth Suicide: Prevention and Interventions in Youth Suicide*, U.S. Dep't of Health & Human Servs. (1989).

84. *See, e.g.*, Ga. Stat. Ann. §15–11–2(11) (West 2010) (describing status offenses as including truancy, running away from home, incorrigibility, and unruly behavior).

85. *See, e.g.*, Mass. Gen. Laws. Ann. Ch. 119 §39 (2003).

86. *See, e.g.*, Majd et al., *Hidden Injustice, supra* note 5, at 71 (quoting defense attorney, who notes, "I somewhat blame the judicial system in that they're [telling youth], 'You're not obeying your parents.' But if your parents order you not to be gay, how do you do that? If they tell you how to be and you refuse to be who you're not, they charge you with being beyond control.")

87. Wesley Ware, *Locked Up and Out: Lesbian, Gay, Bisexual and Transgender Youth in Louisiana's Juvenile Justice System* 16 (Juvenile Justice Project of Louisiana 2010), http://jjpl.org/site/wp-content/uploads/2011/07/locked-up-and-out.pdf (last visited June 24, 2014).

88. *See, e.g.*, Wisconsin v. Yoder, 406 U.S. 205 (1972) (in holding that an Amish father may withdraw his fifteen-year-old daughter from school notwithstanding the state's

compulsory education law, the Court relied on Yoder's religious liberty as well as the primary role of the parents in raising children, which the Court found to be an indisputable part of tradition); Pierce v. Soc'y of Sisters, 268 U.S. 510 (1925) (striking down Oregon statute requiring children to attend public schools).

89. Angela Irvine, *We've Had Three of Them: Addressing the Invisibility of Lesbian, Gay, Bisexual and Gender Non-conforming Youths in the Juvenile Justice System*, 19 Colum. J. Gender & L. 675, 690 (2010) (citing studies).

90. *Id.*

91. *See generally* Nicholas Ray, *Lesbian, Gay, Bisexual and Transgender Youth: An Epidemic of Homelessness* (Nat'l Gay & Lesbian Task Force Policy Inst. 2006), www.thetaskforce.org/downloads/reports/reports/HomelessYouth.pdf (last visited June 24, 2014); Bryan N. Cochran *et al.*, *Challenges Faced by Homeless Sexual Minorities: Comparison of Gay, Lesbian, Bisexual, and Transgender Homeless Adolescents with Their Heterosexual Counterparts*, 92 Am. J. Pub. Health 773 (2002).

92. Majd et al., *Hidden Injustice, supra* note 5, at 72.

93. *Id.*

94. Amnesty Int'l, *USA: Stonewalled: Police Abuse and Misconduct against Lesbian, Gay, Bisexual and Transgender People in the U.S.* 3 (2005), http://www.amnesty.org/en/library/info/AMR51/122/2005 (last visited Aug. 7, 2014).

95. Michael Kent Curtis & Shannon Gilreath, *Transforming Teenagers into Oral Sex Felons: The Persistence of the Crime against Nature after* Lawrence v. Texas, 43 Wake Forest L. Rev. 155, 156 (2008); *see also* M. Blake Huffman, *North Carolina Courts: Legislating Compulsory Heterosexuality by Creating New Crimes under the Crime against Nature Statute Post-*Lawrence v. Texas, 20 Law & Sexuality 1 (2011) (noting heterosexist underpinnings of the decisions by the North Carolina and Georgia legislatures to enact statutory schemes in which vaginal intercourse between minors is considered a significantly less serious offense than other forms of sex).

96. *Lawrence*, 539 U.S. at 578 ("The present case does not involve minors. . . . [It] does involve two adults who, with full and mutual consent from each other, engaged in sexual practices common to a homosexual lifestyle.").

97. William N. Eskridge, Jr., *Dishonorable Passions: Sodomy Laws in America, 1861–2003* 297 (2008). *See also* Huffman, *North Carolina Courts, supra* note 95, at 27 (Legislative history of the North Carolina law makes plain the connection between maintenance of crimes against nature laws and animus against gay people; in a 1999 Senate hearing on a bill to decriminalize sodomy, a notoriously anti-gay Republican senator wondered aloud whether the bill, if passed, would "legalize homosexuality").

98. Majd et al., *Hidden Injustice, supra* note 5, at 62–63.

99. Kate Sutherland, *From Jailbird to Jailbait: Age of Consent Laws and the Construction of Teenage Sexualities*, 9 Wm. & Mary J. Women & L. 313, 314–315 (2003).

100. Michael J. Higdon, *Queer Teens and Legislative Bullies: The Cruel and Invidious Discrimination behind Heterosexist Statutory Rape Laws*, 42 U.C. Davis L. Rev. 195 (2008).

101. *See, e.g.*, Alan Guttmacher Institute, *Facts on American Teens' Sexual and Reproductive Health* (Aug. 2011) (noting 2010 study that found that seven in ten teens of both sexes have had intercourse by their nineteenth birthday); Bonnie L. Halpern-Feisher et al., *Oral versus Vaginal Sex among Adolescents: Perceptions, Attitudes and Behavior*, 15 Pediatrics 845, 845 (2005) (noting that approximately 20% of surveyed adolescents near the age of fourteen had already had oral sex, and over 30% indicated an intention to have oral sex within the next six months).

102. Higdon, *Queer Teens and Legislative Bullies, supra* note 100, at 225.

103. Tex. Penal Code Ann. § 21.11(b)(1) (It is an affirmative defense to prosecution under this section [defining indecency with a child] that the actor: (1) was not more than three years older than the victim and of the opposite sex.).

104. Ala. Code 1975 § 13A-6-62 and Ala. Code 1975 § 13A-6-63. Higdon, *Queer Teens and Legislative Bullies, supra* note 100, at 228 (describing that Alabama law provides an affirmative defense for the crime of rape in the second degree, providing that a defendant is not guilty unless "the actor is at least two years older than the member of the opposite sex" and noting that no such exception exists for the statute governing sodomy in the second degree).

105. *Franklin E. Zimring, American Travesty: Legal Responses to Adolescent Sexual Offending* 52–54 (2004); *see also* Suzanne Meiners-Levy, *Challenging the Prosecution of Young "Sex Offenders": How Developmental Psychology and the Lessons of Roper Should Inform Daily Practice*, 79 Temp. L. Rev. 499, 506 (2006) (describing legal arguments that can be made to challenge prosecutions of youth for sexual activity when they themselves are under the age of consent);

106. In two Massachusetts cases, lawyers for youth charged in these situations alleged selective prosecution, moving for discovery from the state as to whether it was prosecuting girls at the same rate as boys in opposite-sex statutory rape scenarios and straight youth at the same rate as gay youth. *See* Commonwealth v. Bernardo B., 453 Mass. 158, 900 N.E.2d 834 (2009); Commonwealth v. Washington, 928 N.E.2d 910 (2010).

107. Kay L. Levine, *No Penis, No Problem*, 33 Fordham Urb. L.J. 357, 358 (2006) (describing "gendered assumptions" that males are perpetrators and females victims in statutory rape scenarios).

108. Anthony Petrosino et. al., *Formal System Processing of Juveniles: Effects on Delinquency*, 1 Campbell Systematic Reviews (2010), doi 10.4073/csr.2010.1.

109. Dorothy E. Roberts, *Prison, Foster Care, and the Systemic Punishment of Black Mothers*, 59 UCLA L. Rev. 1474, 1486–87 (2012); Dorothy E. Roberts, *Child Welfare and Civil Rights*, 2003 U. Ill. L. Rev. 171, 172–73 (2003); Dorothy E. Roberts, *Punishing Drug Addicts Who Have Babies: Women of Color, Equality, and the Right of Privacy*, 104 Harv. L. Rev. 1419, 1440–42 (1991).

110. In Utah, for example, unmarried, cohabiting individuals in sexual relationships may not be foster parents. Utah Code. Ann. § 512–302–10 (1) (West 2010). Arkansas has a similar ban. Ark. Admin. Code 016.15.3–5 (2010).

111. Ala. Admin. Code § 660–5–29–02 (4) (a).

112. *See* Libby Adler, *The Gay Agenda*, 16 Mich. J. Gender & L. 147, 202 (2009).

113. Rudy Estrada & Jody Marksamer, *Lesbian, Gay, Bisexual, and Transgender Young People in State Custody: Making the Child Welfare and Juvenile Justice Systems Safe for All Youth through Litigation, Advocacy, and Education*, 79 Temp. L. Rev. 415, 423–424 (2006).

114. Sarah Valentine, *Traditional Advocacy for Non-traditional Youth: Rethinking Best Interest for the Queer Child*, 2008 Mich. St. L. Rev. 1053, 1060 (2008) (citing article in Oct. 18, 1996, *Dayton Daily News* regarding case).

115. *See* Eve Kosofsky Sedgwick, *How to Bring Your Kids Up Gay: The War on Effeminate Boys*, in *Tendencies* 161 (Duke Univ. Press 1993) ("[A]dvice on how to help your kids turn out gay, not to mention your students, your parishioners, your therapy clients, or your military subordinates, is less ubiquitous than you might think. On the other hand, the scope of the institutions whose programmatic undertaking is to prevent the development of gay people is unimaginably large.").

116. Barbara Fedders, *Coming Out for Kids: Recognizing, Respecting, and Representing LGBTQ Youth*, 6 Nev. L.J. 774, 797 (2006).

117. Ware, *Locked Up and Out*, *supra* note 87.

118. Bur. of Justice Statistics, *Sexual Victimization in Juvenile Facilities Reported by Youth, 2008–2009* (Jan. 2010), at 1.

119. *See, e.g.*, Christopher D. Man & John P. Cronan, *Forecasting Sexual Abuse in Prison: The Prison Subculture of Masculinity as a Backdrop for "Deliberate Indifference,"* 92 J. Crim. L. & Criminology 127, 166 (2002) ("an inmate who is openly gay or who is a transvestite or a pre-operational transsexual . . . is a clear target of sexual aggression").

120. *See generally* Robinson, *Masculinity as Prison*, *supra* note 42.

121. *Id. See also* Sharon Dolovich, *Strategic Segregation in the Modern Prison*, 48 Am. Crim. L. Rev. 1 (2010) (discussing wing within Los Angeles County Jail, into which gay and transgender inmates are sent for their own protection from violence).

122. Dolovich, *Strategic Segregation in the Modern Prison, supra* note 121.

123. *See generally* Jody Marksamer, *A Place of Respect* (2011), www.nclrights.org/wp-content/uploads/2013/07/A_Place_Of_Respect.pdf (last visited Aug. 11, 2014).

124. *Id.*

125. *See, e.g.*, Ware, *Locked Up and Out*, *supra* note 87; Randi Feinstein *et al.*, *Justice for All? A Report on Lesbian, Gay, Bisexual and Transgendered Youth in the NY Juvenile Justice System* 15, 18 (Urban Justice Ctr. 2001), http://njjn.org/uploads/digital-library/resource_239.pdf (last visited Aug. 11, 2014); Majd et al., *Hidden Injustice, supra* note 5; Marksamer, *A Place of Respect*, *supra* note 123; and Wilber *et al.*, *CWLA Best Practice Guidelines*, *supra* note 53. *See also* Barbara Fedders, *LGBT Youth in the Child Welfare and Juvenile Justice Systems: Charting a Way Forward*, 23 Temp. Pol. & Civ. Rts. L. Rev. (forthcoming 2015).

126. Wilber *et al.*, *CWLA Best Practice Guidelines*, *supra* note 53, at 42.

127. Foster Care Non-Discrimination Act, www.leginfo.ca.gov/pub/03–04/bill/asm/ab_0451–0500/ab_458_cfa_20030814_120849_asm_floor.html.

128. Memorandum from Jess McDonald, Director, Ill. Dep't of Children & Family Servs., to Rules & Procedures Bookholders, Child Prot. & Child Welfare Staff, Purchase of Serv. Agency Staff, www.state.il.us/dcfs/docs/policyGuides/Policy_Guide_2003.02 (last visited July 21, 2014).

129. Lambda Legal, *Rodriguez v. Johnson et al.*, www.lambdalegal.org/in-court/cases/rodriguez-v-johnson-et-al (last visited June 23, 2014).

130. Office of Children & Family Services, New York State, *OCFS Policy & Procedures Manual: Lesbian, Gay, Bisexual, Transgender, and Questioning Youth (PPM 3442.00)*, www.nycourts.gov/ip/judicialinstitute/transgender/220U.pdf (last visited June 23, 2014).

131. Maria Luisa Tucker, *The State Adopts New Rules for LGBT Youths in Juvenile Detention*, Village Voice, June 3, 2008, www.villagevoice.com/news/0823,doing-right-keeping-quiet,457815,2.html (last visited June 23, 2014).

132. R.G. v. Koller, 415 F. Supp. 2d 1129, 1157 (D. Haw. 2006).

133. Marksamer, *A Place of Respect, supra* note 123.

134. For an excellent summary of case law in this area, *see* Estrada & Marksamer, *Lesbian, Gay, Bisexual, and Transgender Young People in State Custody, supra* note 113, at 201.

135. *Id.*

136. *Id.*

137. American Psychiatric Association, *Therapies Focused on Attempts to Change Sexual Orientation (Reparative or Conversion Therapies), supra* note 62, at 34.

138. *Majd et al., Hidden Injustice, supra* note 5, at 6.

139. Caitlin M. Cullitan, *Please Don't Tell My Mom! A Minor's Right to Informational Privacy*, 40 J.L. & Educ. 417 (2011); Holning Lau, *Pluralism: A Principle for Children's Rights*, 42 Harv. C.R.-C.L. L. Rev. 317 (2007) (citing *Bloch v. Ribar*, 156 F.3d 673, 685 (6th Cir. 1998), publicly revealing information concerning an individual's sexuality and choices about sex infringes upon an aspect of our lives that are personal and private).

140. *Majd et al., Hidden Injustice, supra* note 5, at 108.

141. *Id. See also* Barbara Fedders, *Building on Advocacy for Girls and LGBT Youth to Promote Liberatory Laws, Policies and Services for All Youth in the Juvenile Justice System*, in *A New Juvenile Justice: Total Reform for a Broken System* (NYU Press, forthcoming 2015).

142. *Majd et al., Hidden Injustice, supra* note 5, at 44.

143. Eric Rofes, *Making Our Schools Safe for Sissies*, 77 High Sch. J. 37 (1993–1994), www.jstor.org/stable/40364629?seq=2 (last visited June 23, 2014).

144. Natalie Loder Clark, Parens Patriae *and a Modest Proposal for the Twenty-First Century: Legal Philosophy and a New Look at Children's Welfare*, 6 Mich. J. Gender & L. 381, 443 (2000) ("The child welfare system needs to shrink, to intervene in fewer families, to close cases more quickly, to recognize the damage done by its very attempts to help children as well as by its authoritarian meddling and bureaucratic self-preservation. It needs, in far more cases than it does now, to do nothing.")

ABOUT THE CONTRIBUTORS

Annaka Abramson—Annaka Abramson is a second-year student at University of California, Berkeley Law. She has published work on issues relevant to sexual consent among the severely mentally ill.

Paul R. Abramson—Professor Abramson is a Professor of Psychology at UCLA and has conducted extensive research on human sexuality. He is the author or co-author of *Sarah: A Sexual Biography, With Pleasure: Thoughts on the Nature of Human Sexuality, Sexual Nature/Sexual Culture, A House Divided: Suspicions of Mother-Daughter Incest, Sexual Rights in America* (NYU Press), *Romance in the Ivory Tower: The Rights and Liberty of Conscience*, and *Sex Appeal: Six Ethical Principles for the Twenty-First Century*. Professor Abramson has also served as an expert witness for over three decades in criminal and civil litigation involving sexual crimes. He teaches the very popular undergraduate class on "Sex and the Law" at UCLA as well.

Hazel G. Beh—Professor Beh teaches Contacts, Advanced Torts and Insurance Law, and legal writing at the William S. Richardson School of Law, where she currently serves as co-director of the Health Law Policy Center at the Law School. She has a J.D., a Ph.D. in American studies, and a master of social work. She has written extensively on children and sex, including articles on the developmental effects of sex education and the recognition of the sexual rights of minors in the abstinence-only sex education debate.

Piotr Bobkowski—Professor Bobkowski joined the faculty at the William Allen White School of Journalism and Mass Communications at the University of Kansas in 2011 after a one-year research assistantship at the Carolina Population Center. His research explores adolescents' and emerging adults' motivations to consume and produce social media content and how new and traditional media affect them. He also teaches information management, reporting, and ethics to undergraduate students in the school's news and information and strategic communications tracks.

Sacha M. Coupet—Professor Coupet has a Ph.D. in clinical psychology from the University of Michigan and a J.D. from the University of Pennsylvania. She is an Associate Professor of Law at Loyola University Chicago School of Law, where she also serves as the Director of Research for the Civitas ChildLaw Center. She is also a fellow with the Center for Children, Law, & Policy at the University of Houston Law Center and former chair of the Association of American Law Schools Section on Children and the Law. Her teaching and research focus on children and families. She continues to publish and present nationally on many topics related to children and families.

Jennifer Ann Drobac—Tenured at the Indiana University–Robert H. McKinney School of Law, Professor Drobac holds her doctoral (J.S.D.) and J.D. degrees from Stanford Law School. Her scholarly work has been published in a variety of law reviews and journals. In 2005, she finished her first textbook, *Sexual Harassment Law: History, Cases and Theory*. In 2009, she was a profiled expert for *Now* newsmagazine on PBS for the story "Is Your Daughter Safe at Work?" concerning the sexual harassment of working teenagers. Professor Drobac's upcoming book, *Worldly but Not Yet Wise*, explores why the scientific facts concerning adolescent neurological and psychosocial development are incongruent with civil law designed to protect teenagers from sexual predation. She is a member of the American Law Institute.

Barbara Fedders—Professor Fedders is a Clinical Associate Professor of Law at the University of North Carolina School of Law. Before joining the UNC faculty in 2008, Professor Fedders was a clinical instructor at the Harvard Law School Criminal Justice Institute for four years. Her areas of expertise include criminal procedure and juvenile delinquency, and she teaches courses in criminal lawyering and juvenile justice. Prior to law teaching, she worked for the Massachusetts Committee for Public Counsel Service as a public defender and Soros Justice Fellow. She continues to publish and present on topics related to children in conflict with the law, criminal procedure, and LGBT youth.

Seth F. Kreimer—Professor Kreimer has taught at the University of Pennsylvania since 1981. He is currently the Kenneth W. Gemmill Professor of Law. He is a nationally known expert and scholar in the area of constitutional law, particularly in the areas of the First Amendment and individual rights. He is a member of the American Law Institute, a board member of the American Civil Liberties Union, Philadelphia Chapter, and he has served as co-counsel in numerous cases that raise constitutional issues. Professor Kreimer has published and presented extensively on privacy, censorship, and free expression.

Ellen Marrus—Professor Marrus is the George Butler Research Professor of Law and Director of the Center for Children, Law & Policy at the University of Houston Law Center. Starting at the University of Houston Law Center in 1995, Professor Marrus was the director of clinical legal education and developed several clinics that related to representation of children and families. She is also an advisory board member of the National Juvenile Defender Center and co-director for the Southwest Regional Juvenile Defender Center. She was also the founder and first chair of the Association of American Law Schools' Section on Children and the Law. Her scholarship and teaching concentrate on children, and she takes a holistic approach to her discussion of issues facing children in the legal system. Professor Marrus has published the casebook *Children and Juvenile Justice*, has written many articles about children and the law, and has presented nationally on this topic.

Autumn Shafer—Professor Shafer teaches at Texas Tech University, College of Media and Communication. Her research spans the health communication spectrum, from the design and evaluation of strategic health campaigns, to examining the effects of mass media on health-related attitudes and behaviors, to investigating how individuals process persuasive health messages. She approaches research questions from an interdisciplinary perspective that draws from communication, public health, psychology, and consumer behavior. Much of Professor Shafer's research is focused on adolescents and sexual health. Her experimental research explores the psychological mechanisms that underlie the processing and persuasive effects of narratives.

Franklin E. Zimring—Professor Zimring is the William G. Simon Professor of Law and Wolfen Distinguished Scholar at the University of California, Berkeley. Professor Zimring's primary areas of research are criminal justice and family law, with an emphasis on empirical research to inform legal policy. He is also the author or co-author of many books, including topics such as the changing legal world of adolescence, the scale of imprisonment, deterrence, and drug control.

INDEX

Acting out, girls, 88
Acquiesce, 40; lay definition, 32
Adam Walsh Child Protection and Safety Act, 76, 82
Addams, Jane, 227
Adolescent consent, 43–48. *See also* Consent
Adolescent neurological, cognitive, and psychological development, 48–55
Adolescent sexual danger, 76
Age of consent: generally, 50, 59–60; laws, 235–236
Amie's Law, 72, 82
Amygdala, 49
Ashcroft v. Free Speech Coalition, 140
Assent: lay definition, 31; legal assent, 61–63; medical assent, 34

Barnes v. Barnes, 45
Beam, Chris, 194
Benes, Francis, 50
Boys Don't Cry, 195
Brown v. Entertainment Merchants Association, 146–147
Bunge, Silvia, 56–57
Burke, Phyllis, 192

California Penal Code § 261.5, 36, 37–40, 44
California Safe Schools Coalition, 210
Capacity, juvenile, 34, 45; adolescent and physical appearance, 55–56
Catcher in the Rye, 18
Cauffman, Elizabeth, 52–53, 54, 55

Cell phones, 143
Chancellor v. Pottsgrove Sch. Dist., 46, 47
Child Online Protection Act (COPA), 139–140
Child pornography, 15, 134, 135, 138, 141, 143, 144; prosecution of, 137, 140, 142, 147
Child welfare system, 225–226
Childhood sexual development, 7
Childhood sexual rights, 7
Childhood sexuality, 6–7
Clark v. Roccanova, 150
Code of Federal Rules, 34
Cognitive development, 50–52
Consent, 12–16, 30, 149; capacity to consent, 32; contractual consent, 32–33, consent under tort law, 33; impaired consent, 149; juvenile consent, 34, 39, 41; lay definition, 31; legal definition, 32; legal consent, 60; legal consent, civil, 35, 40, 45, 58–63; legal consent, criminal, 35, 37
Continuity within juvenile justice, 103–104
Contraceptives, 21–22
Counterarguing, 115–116
Crazy, Stupid, Love, 14–15, 18, 21
Crossover youth, 94, 98, 99
Cultivation theory, 119
Cyberbullying 146

Data limitations on childhood sexuality, 10–12
Declaration of Independence, 24

259

Defense attorneys and female offenders, 103
Delinquency, of girls, 88, 95
Delinquent youth, 89, 94; definition, 94; profile of, 89
Dependency, 93
Detention alternatives for girls, 104–105
Digital images, 139, 148
Diminished capacity, 34; developing capacity, 34; incapacitated, 33; psychosocial immaturity, 34
Disparate treatment of girls, 88; by families, 88; by juvenile justice system, 88, 102
Doe v. Bell, 232
Doe v. Oberweis Dairy, 40–43, 42, 43, 47
Doe v. Peterson, 151–152
Doe v. Starbucks, 30, 35, 36–37, 40, 43, 45, 46
Doe v. Willits Unified School District, 46
Doe v. Yunits, 212
Donaldson v. Department of Real Estate, 38–40, 42, 47
Doshay, Lewis, J., 77

Egalia Preschool, 188
Escobar, Jonathan, 212
Ewert, Marcus, 194

Facebook, 124
Fanny Hill, 18
Faragher v. City of Boca Raton, 35
Finland, 22
First Amendment, 20, 137, 139, 146
Fischer, Kurt, 51, 54
Fourteenth Amendment, 18
Free speech, 137

Garnett v. State, 12, 28n27
Gates, Gary, 229
Gault, Gerald, 16–17
Gender atypicality, 196
Gender awareness, 189

Gender bias awareness, 103
Gender Dysphoria, 200–201
Gender identity: clinics, 192; rights for children, 215–216
Gender Identity Disorder (GID), 189, 190–193, 198–200, 231–232
Gender Management Service Clinic, 197
Giedd, Jay, 48, 49
Girls' behavior, 87–88; exploring sexuality, 88; promiscuous, 88, 93, 96; and sexual abuse, 97
Graham v. Florida, 57–58
Green, Jamison, 192; 207–208
Guttman scale, 15

Happiness, 23–25
House of refuge, 90–91

I am J, 194
Immoral female behavior, 92–93; 96
In re Alex, 201–202
In re Gault, 16–18
Increase of girls in delinquency, 98–99
Indiana Rape Shield Statute, 45
Industrial School for Girls (Massachusetts), 91
Informed consent, 16
Institutional review boards (IRB), 34
Internet, 141

Jefferson, Thomas, 24
Juvenile courts, 91–94, 95–98, 99–103, 226–227; adjudicatory hearing, 101; detention hearing, 100–101; disposition, 101–103; informal handling, 100; intake, 99–100; juvenile court proceedings, 99–103; petition, 100; types of cases, 93
Juvenile sex offenders, danger and, 83–85

Kiernan-Johnson, Eileen, 195
Kilodavis, Cheryl, 194

King County (Washington State) Adult-Juvenile Detention Policies, 214
Kramer, Donald, 55

Lawrence v. Texas, 235
LGBT youth: defined, 228–232; discrimination, 239; in the juvenile justice system, 238–239; sex education, 176; sexual health, 167; sexually assaulted, 238; vulnerability to prosecution, 235
Locke, John, 24
Louie, Louie, 18
Luna, 194

M. v. North Lawrence Community Sch. Corp., 46, 47
Ma Vie en Rose, 195
MacArthur Juvenile Adjudicative Competence Study, 51
Magazines, gender oriented, 112, 118
Maine Human Rights Commission, 210–211
Maines, Nicole, 211
Masturbation, 6, 7, 9, 13
Mathis, Coy, 211
Meagan's Law, 82
Media, effects of, 118–119; theories, 118–120
Media characters, 115, 118
Media engagement, 113
Media multitasking, 114
Media practice model, 109–111; application of, 120–121
Media processing, 113–116; arousal, 114; narratives in, 114–116. See also Counterarguing
Media production, by youth, 123, 124
Media selection, 111–113; personal characteristics of, 111
Meritor Savings Bank v. Vinson, 40
Miller v. California, 21, 137
Miller v. Skumanick, 133–137
Mummy Laid An Egg, 19

My Princess Boy, 194
Myelin, 50

National Adolescent Perpetrator Network, 82, 83
National Task Force on Juvenile Sexual Offending, 81
Neurological development, 48–50
New York v. Ferber, 138
Nude pictures, 144, 145, 148
Nudity, 134, 136, 138

Obscene, 127, 139
Obscene phone call, 16–17
Oregon Equality Act, 209–210
Oregon Safe Schools Act, 210
Osborne v. Oho, 138
"Out-of-control" girls, 88

Parens patriae, 213
Parrotfish, 194
Pathways into juvenile court, girls', 95–98; assaultive behavior, 98; girls' sexuality, 96; mental health disorders, 97; prostitution, 98; runaways, 96, 97, 98; sexual abuse, 97; source of referral, boys, 95, source of referral, girls, 95; status offender, 98–99
People v. Tobias, 37–38, 39, 43, 47
Perspective, 54
Peters, Julie Anne, 194
Placements for girls, 105
Planned Parenthood, 21
Phonication, 21
Pre-juvenile courts, 89–91; treatment of girls, 89–91; treated like adults, 90
Primary sources of information theory, 118
Programs for girls, 89, 101–103; decreasing recidivism, 105; detention, 104–105; improving outcomes, 103–106; improving programming 105–106; placements, 105; reformatories, 101–102; resources for girls, 106

Psychosocial development, 52–53
Puberty, 166

R. G. v. Koller, 240
Referral to juvenile justice, 89
Reparative therapy, 230
Responsibility, development of, 53–54
Restatement (Second) of Contracts §15, 56–57
Restatement (Second) of Torts §892A cmt. 2(b), 56–57
Roe v. Orangeburg County School District, 45
Roland Humphrey Is Wearing a What?, 195
Roper v. Simmons, 57
"Rule of sevens," 56

Sex and the City, 14
Sex and the media, 14–15
Sex education, 19–23, 163, 164–166, 233; abstinence only, 163, 165, 169–171, 174, 175, 178; comprehensive, 163, 165, 169–170, 178; international human rights, 177; values education, 169, 171
Sex information, child's right, 172–173
Sex offender registry, 76
Sex offending: juveniles, 72; patterns, 72–76
Sexting, 21, 133, 141, 142, 143, 144
Sexual development, 166
Sexual harassment, 30, 44. See also *Doe v. Oberweis Dairy*; *Doe v. Starbucks*
Sexual health, 167; of adolescents, 168; of minority youth, 167; of sexual minorities, 167–168
Sexual identity, 122, 123
Sexual literacy, 16, 19–23
Sexual media, 108–109, 111, 114; exposure to 121. See also Social networking
Sexual media diets, 117, 118
Sexual norms, 110
Sexual orientation, 20
Sexual pleasure, 7–10, 19
Sexual predators, 79
Sexual Rights, 7

Sexual scripts, 110, 112–113
Sexual themes: advertisements with, 17; movies, 118; music videos, 117; television, 117–118
Sexually transmitted disease (STD), 167
"Shake, Rattle & Roll," 18
Simon, Jonathan, 77
Social networking, 139
Soper, Jennifer, 55
Sowell, Elizabeth, 49
Specialized placement for LGBT youth, 242–243
Status offender, 88, 93, 98
Statutory rape, 12–14, 41
Steinberg, Laurence, 51, 52–53, 54, 55
Stocker, Storm, 188

Teenage sexuality, 11–12
Temperance, 54
10,000 Dresses, 194
Third-party distribution, 151
Title VII Civil Rights Act of 1964, 35, 42, 46
Transgender children: defined, 186–188; in the child welfare system, 213; in the juvenile justice system, 214–215, 239; in the media, 193–196; perceptions and treatment of, 196–202; in schools, 208–212; social stigma, 197–198
Transgender Children's Bill of Human Rights, 215
Transgenderism: and homosexuality, 191; prevalence, 190
Transitioning: medical and surgical, 204–206; social, 203–204
Treatment clinicians, 80; for juvenile sex offenders, 80–86
Treatment programs, 89, 101–103, 102

Ulysses, 18
United Nations Convention on the Rights of the Child (UNCRC), 216
United States Supreme Court, and adolescent development, 57–58

United States v. Windsor, 233
Uses and gratification theory, 119

Videos, 141

Wilson, James, 24
Wittlinger, Ellen, 194

Woodhouse, Barbara Bennett, 172
World Professional Association for
    Transgender Health standards of care
    (WPATH-SOC), 204–206

Yogyakarta Principles, 215
YouTube, 122, 124

Sacha M. Coupet is Associate Professor of Law and Director of Research of the Civitas ChildLaw Center at Loyola University Chicago School of Law.

Ellen Marrus is George Butler Research Professor of Law and Director of the Center for Children, Law & Policy at the University of Houston Law Center.

In the
FAMILIES, LAW, AND SOCIETY
Series

About the cover: Design by Adam B. Bohannon